THE WHOLE WORLD
STAMP
CATALOG

For Raymond

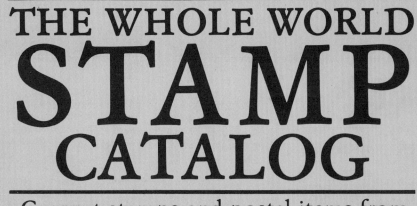

THE WHOLE WORLD STAMP CATALOG

Current stamps and postal items from
over 200 countries and where to buy them

Researched and written by Richard West

Compiled by Robin Ellis

CRESCENT BOOKS

New York

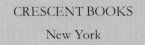

Acknowledgements

Editor Jackie Fortey
Editorial Assistant Tish Francis
Designers Reg Boorer, Pete Saag, Clive Sutherland
Design Assistants Mark Pearson, Dave Rhodes
Maps Ingrid Jacob, Bob Burns

This book would not have been possible without the many postal authorities, philatelic organizations and individuals who contributed so much of their time and made available to us the material reproduced here. The authors would particularly like to thank Jan Lanigan for her patience and support, and for her encouragement in the early stages of the project; Frank Spencer for his invaluable expertise in checking the information contained in the book; V. K. Midha for his advice on postal stationery; and G. M. Haworth for all his assistance with locating material. Thanks go to Lynn C. Franklin, Mark Lewerenz, Diane Huntzicker, Joseph B. Franklin, Lucinda Vardey and Sophia Yurkevich. Also to Chantal Desmazières and Manuela Caballero of Scorpio Agency, Paris, Stephen G. Edelstein of the Inter-Governmental Philatelic Corporation, Sanders Fowler III of the United States Post Office, Connie Buckmaster of the British Post Office, Miss G. Grunewald of the United Nations Postal Administration (New York), Monsieur A. Varga of Théodore Champion S.A., Paris, Monsieur C. Cataneo of Agence des Timbres-Post d'Outre Mer, Paris, The Macao Tourist Office, Wang Yongsheng of The China National Stamp Corporation, Norio Irie of the Japan Uni Agency, M. A. Siala of the Libyan Philatelic Association, Bishnu Lal Shresta, Senõra Monica de Armitage, Lucy Czerniecka, Jurek Gostkowski, Elizabéth Waters, Mr. J. G. Miletic, Jacqueline Ellis, Simon Ellis, Ann Bond and Valerie Russell.

We would like to express our gratitude for the overwhelming response we received from the post offices and philatelic bureaux all over the world, who sent us philatelic material and information. Special thanks go to the British Post Office, the United States Post Office, the United Nations Postal Administration, the Crown Agents, the Inter-Governmental Philatelic Corporation, the Universal Postal Union, Berne, and the Arab Postal Union.

The following philatelic agencies also kindly assisted us: Albimpeks (Albania), Artia (Czechoslovakia), Ars Polana (Poland), FTO Hemus (Bulgaria), Ilexim (Rumania), Intersapa (South Africa, South West Africa, Bophuthatswana, Venda, Transkei), Mezhdunarodnaya Kniga (USSR), Philatelia Hungarica (Hungary and Mongolia), The Korean Stamp Corporation and Philimex, Paris, (North Korea), The China National Stamp Corporation (People's Republic of China) and Xunhasaba (Vietnam).

We are very grateful for the help given by M. & N. Haworth, Lowfield House, Clitheroe, Lancs., and D. M. Aerogrammes International Ltd., 94 Hilton Rd., Lanesfield, Wolverhampton; also to Stanley Gibbons Ltd., David Field Ltd., the Harry Allen New Issue Service, Urch Harris Ltd., A. Denny & Sons, Stephen Mayer International Ltd., Michael Bale Ltd., John Lister Ltd., Cameo Stamps, Lake & Brooks Ltd., James Davis & Sons, and H. D. Kelly. Finally, we would like to thank all the embassies in London who helped to verify information.

First published in Great Britain in 1981 by Pan Books Ltd, London

Created, designed and produced by Ventura Publishing Ltd, 44 Uxbridge Street, London W8 7TG

All correspondence concerned with the contents of this book should be addressed to Ventura Publishing Ltd, 44 Uxbridge Street, London W8 7TG

a   b   c   d   e   f   g   h
Library of Congress Cataloging in Publication Data:
The Whole World Stamp Catalog.
1. Postage-stamps – Catalogs. I. West, Richard, 1930-
HE6224.W46   769.56   80-29172
ISBN 0-517-31397-9

Typesetting by Servis Filmsetting Ltd, Manchester and Inline Graphics, London

Color origination by Amilcare Pizzi s.p.a., Cinisello Balsamo, Italy and D.S. Colour International Ltd, London
Printed and bound in Italy by Amilcare Pizzi s.p.a., Cinisello Balsamo.

The stamps and other philatelic items in this book are reproduced two-thirds actual size.

Contents

Introduction

The Whole World Stamp Catalog has been compiled with the direct assistance of postal authorities everywhere and with the support of many knowledgeable collectors. Much of the information given has never before been consolidated into a single full-colour book. It sets out to provide much more than general background information and lists of stamps. Whet your collecting appetite by looking through these pages at the vast range of stamp material available! All the countries in the world which produce stamps valid for internal and international mails are included (local private issues have deliberately been omitted). Full colour illustrations show typical definitives, commemoratives, postal stationery and other items. The text gives details of how to obtain them from post offices, which can be done by a personal visit or, more usually, by writing to the addresses given. We hope that you expand your collection successfully with our help.

It is important to use the guidelines and hints given and to remember that post offices vary greatly in the services they offer to stamp enthusiasts. Do not expect equally high standards of service and understanding of your requirements. Great care should be taken with currencies and order forms. Stamps do sometimes sell out at post offices and may be unavailable by the time your request reaches its destination. In compiling this volume, we have greatly enlarged our own experience and understanding and you will do the same. Even so, we must state that although currencies, addresses and descriptions of items available were correct at the time of going to press, subsequent alterations must be expected. Maps and texts have purely philatelic purposes and are of no political significance.

How to use the book

This book is divided into seven geographical sections, **Europe and Scandinavia, North America and the Caribbean, Central and South America, Middle East, Asia, North Africa and Africa, and Australasia and the Pacific Islands.** Each section is introduced by its own philatelic map, showing the stamp-issuing countries and the town in which each country's main philatelic bureau is located. (This is usually, but not always, the capital city.) Every stamp-issuing country has an entry in the book, accompanied by a small map to pin-point its position on the globe. A short introduction, giving brief geographical, historical and philatelic details, is followed by the address of the philatelic bureau. A description of the country's currency is provided, with an approximate indication of its present exchange rate with the pound sterling and the US dollar.

The page illustrated here will give some idea of what can be found throughout the book, although the range of material varies considerably from one country to another. Generally, each page includes three major categories as follows:
1. **Definitives**
2. **Commemoratives**
3. **Postal stationery and other items**
This last category covers a variety of postal items, in addition to postal stationery, including stamp booklets, postage due labels and adhesive 'instructional' labels. The **Glossary** on page 8 describes the types of stamps and other items included in the book and explains basic philatelic terms.

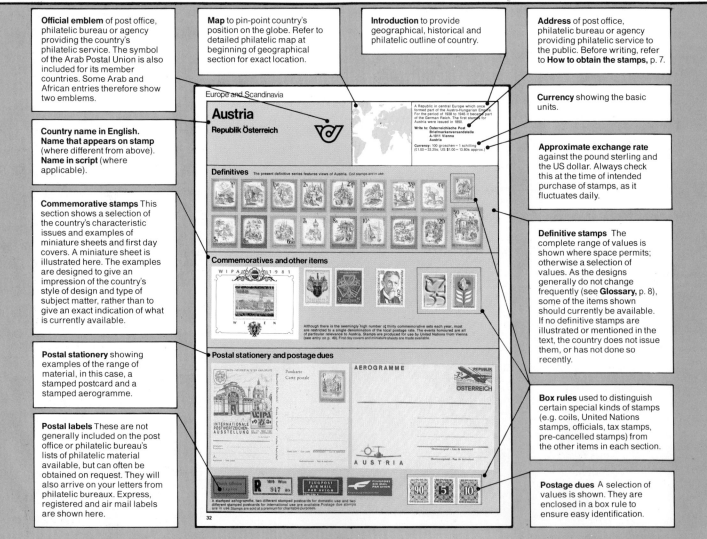

Official emblem of post office, philatelic bureau or agency providing the country's philatelic service. The symbol of the Arab Postal Union is also included for its member countries. Some Arab and African entries therefore show two emblems.

Country name in English. Name that appears on stamp (where different from above). **Name in script** (where applicable).

Commemorative stamps This section shows a selection of the country's characteristic issues and examples of miniature sheets and first day covers. A miniature sheet is illustrated here. The examples are designed to give an impression of the country's style of design and type of subject matter, rather than to give an exact indication of what is currently available.

Postal stationery showing examples of the range of material, in this case, a stamped postcard and a stamped aerogramme.

Postal labels These are not generally included on the post office or philatelic bureau's lists of philatelic material available, but can often be obtained on request. They will also arrive on your letters from philatelic bureaux. Express, registered and air mail labels are shown here.

Map to pin-point country's position on the globe. Refer to detailed philatelic map at beginning of geographical section for exact location.

Introduction to provide geographical, historical and philatelic outline of country.

Address of post office, philatelic bureau or agency providing philatelic service to the public. Before writing, refer to **How to obtain the stamps**, p. 7.

Currency showing the basic units.

Approximate exchange rate against the pound sterling and the US dollar. Always check this at the time of intended purchase of stamps, as it fluctuates daily.

Definitive stamps The complete range of values is shown where space permits; otherwise a selection of values. As the designs generally do not change frequently (see **Glossary**, p. 8), some of the items shown should currently be available. If no definitive stamps are illustrated or mentioned in the text, the country does not issue them, or has not done so recently.

Box rules used to distinguish certain special kinds of stamps (e.g. coils, United Nations stamps, officials, tax stamps, pre-cancelled stamps) from the other items in each section.

Postage dues A selection of values is shown. They are enclosed in a box rule to ensure easy identification.

How to obtain the stamps

Most countries today realize the value of sales of stamps to the philatelic public, and offer a facility by which, at the very least, information is provided. From experience it has been found that there are very, very few countries which will not respond to a request for details about new stamp issues. Often this information is sent in envelopes neatly adorned with some stamps from the country concerned, and almost without exception, no charge is made for this service. The nature of this information varies and can be quite lavish, comprising bulletins sent out regularly to those who request that they be included on a mailing list.

However, it is possible to go one stage further than just receiving information. More and more countries are prepared to supply the collector direct with his or her stamp requirements. Before you decide to buy stamps direct from an overseas post office, there are a few points you should remember:

1. Naturally only the stamps currently in use will be offered for sale. Stamps which have become obsolete will generally not be available. Care should be taken in cases of long sets of stamps where one or two values may already be obsolete. The post office may supply you with the stamps still in stock, but you will be left with an incomplete set: it may be very difficult to obtain the missing stamps separately from a stamp dealer.

2. Always write in the first place to check on the conditions that the post office imposes. Some, for example, while freely offering information, do not sell single stamps to collectors. Others want each order to be worth a specified minimum sum of money. A few add handling, postage and packing charges to each order.

3. If the post office offers a 'deposit' scheme, whereby, provided you maintain an account which is kept in credit, you will automatically receive all new issues from the country, do so. If you are collecting on a country-by-country basis, this is a certain way of ensuring you do not miss any issue – provided of course you keep your account in credit.

4. Check very carefully any currency and trading restrictions that may be in force. Can you send money to another country; can you receive stamps from another country? Sending currency overseas can be an expensive procedure which you should check carefully before starting. Also be aware of any Customs formalities and charges that may be necessary for importing stamps.

If, after consideration, you decide to buy your new issues direct from the issuing post office, your collection will soon start taking shape. When you do write to an overseas post office, please mention that you obtained the address from this book and always print your name and address clearly. Never forget the important role played by the stamp dealer. The post office will only be able to supply you with stamps it still has in stock: other issues you will need to obtain from dealers. You may also decide that you do not wish to collect on a 'country' basis. As you look through the stamps illustrated here, you will quickly realize why more and more collectors are turning to 'thematic', or 'topical', collecting. This type of collecting pays more attention to the *design* of the stamp than the country of origin. There are many themes or topics suitable for collecting: animals, birds, cars, famous people – the list could go on.

If you decide to build a 'thematic' or 'topical' collection, it would be pointless opening a standing order to receive all new issues from an overseas post office. Equally you might find it inconvenient to keep ordering separately any set that fits into your theme (although of course it will be useful to receive information about new issues, so that you can decide which stamps you need for your collection). Once again, it is the stamp dealer who can come to your rescue, supplying the various stamps you need for your collection.

Glossary

Philatelic terms that occur throughout the book are explained below, followed by some additional definitions which may be useful.

Aerogrammes

Specially-designed blue sheets of paper sold by many postal administrations for use as letters to be sent by air mail: the sheet is folded and sealed, not requiring an envelope. Sometimes an aerogramme has the 'stamp' already printed on the sheet; sometimes the aerogramme is unstamped, requiring a postage stamp to be affixed.

Airmail stamps

Stamps produced for use on items to be sent by air. Their designs often include the words 'Air Mail' or 'Aereo', with a pictorial reference to air travel.

Booklets

Small books containing stamps, often in a combination of denominations to satisfy basic postal rates. A page of stamps in a booklet is usually referred to as a 'pane' and is attached by the adhesive edging, stitching or stapling. A sachet booklet is a booklet containing stamps loose inside the cover. Occasionally booklets of commemorative stamps are produced

Coil stamps

Coil stamps are produced in a long strips or rolls, usually intended for sale from vending machines. With a very few exceptions, definitive stamps are generally used for this purpose.

Commemorative stamps

Commemoratives may be used to celebrate the anniversary of an important event, to record some major current happening, to honour a famous individual, to act as a vehicle for propaganda, or simply to give publicity to a project. Increasingly, commemorative stamps are being used to 'mirror' some aspect of life in a country: its flora and fauna, its ships and aircraft, its local customs or industries.

Definitive stamps

Other names for definitive stamps are 'the permanent issue' or 'regular' stamps. They are stamps brought into use for a fairly lengthy period of time and are intended for day-to-day postal requirements. They may show portraits of rulers, Coats-of-Arms, maps, landscapes or similar designs which will not 'date'. The average 'working life' of a definitive is five years, but different countries vary considerably in changing their designs. Australia, for example, changes the design of the most commonly used stamps every year, while Great Britain has not changed the design of her definitives for nearly fifteen years. Most definitives are issued in the form of sheets, although some are issued in rolls or 'coils', (see **Coil stamps),** and they are also frequently made available in booklets. Some countries do not issue definitive stamps, having decided that the commemorative stamps they issue are sufficient to cover all their postal needs.

Discount stamps

Occasionally post offices sell stamps at 'discount' rates, enabling those who post a vast number of items to enjoy a somewhat reduced postage rate. The United States Post Office issues definitive stamps in unusual denominations for this very reason. Sweden has experimented with the idea of offering ordinary customers the chance of buying a booklet of stamps at a discount.

First day covers

Envelopes to which are affixed a set of new stamps, the stamps being postmarked on their first day of issue. Many post offices prepare their own first day covers, but in some cases the preparation of covers is left to local collectors or dealers and they are not sold through the post office. In this book the former are described as being 'made available', the latter are described as being 'prepared'.

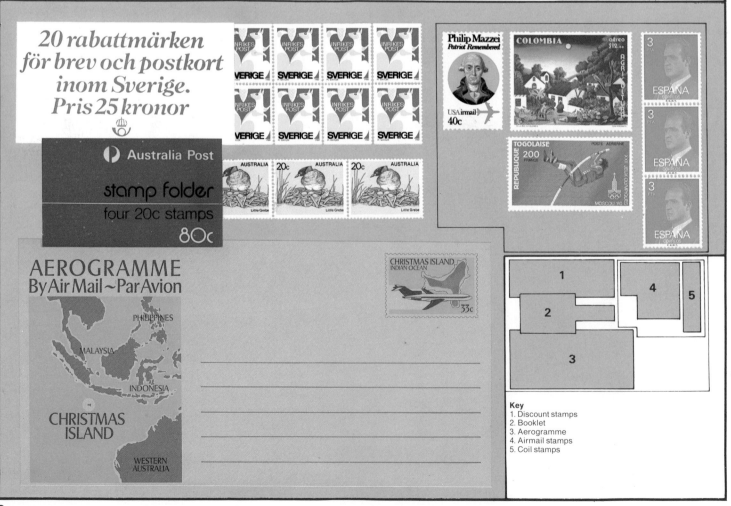

Key
1. Discount stamps
2. Booklet
3. Aerogramme
4. Airmail stamps
5. Coil stamps

Labels

A variety of adhesive instructional labels are available from many post offices at no cost, including 'Air Mail', 'Express', 'Special Delivery', 'Parcel Post' labels and so on. Some countries also produce seals for use at Christmas and Easter, intended to raise money for charity.

Maximum cards

Several post offices are now producing postcards which reproduce on one side, in enlarged form, the designs on stamps. The card, appropriate stamp and postmark are collectively called a 'maximum card' by collectors.

Miniature or souvenir sheet

A small sheet of stamps with a highly decorated border. Often such a sheet will combine the various values, normally of a commemorative set. On other occasions miniature sheets contain just one or two stamps which are additional to the stamps in a commemorative set.

Official stamps

The name given to stamps intended for use by government departments.

Postage due or 'To pay' labels

Stamps which indicate that additional postal charges need to be paid on an item of mail.

Postal stationery

This term refers to such items as postcards, envelopes, letter cards and aerogrammes. They are often available already printed with a stamp 'device' to show that the postal charges have been paid.

Postcards

Simple cards, normally intended to take a message on one side, and the name and address to which they are to be sent on the other. Some post offices sell postcards with a stamp already printed. Pictorial postcards are also sometimes available. At one time double or 'reply' postcards were popular: one half was used for an outgoing message, while the second half could then be used for a reply. (See also **Maximum cards**).

Pre-cancelled stamps

Stamps which already have been obliterated. They are used for bulk postings, so that the post office does not need to postmark each individual item.

Premium/Charity stamps

Sometimes stamps are put on sale at a price higher than the postage value of the stamp; the difference is used as a donation to a specific cause. For example, the annual 'Health' stamps issued in New Zealand are sold at a premium to help Children's Health Camps. The cost of the stamp and the premium itself are frequently both shown on the stamp. These stamps are also known as 'Semi-postals', and charity stamps.

Presentation packs

Many post offices are now offering stamps in decorative folders, which frequently give information about the stamps concerned. 'Souvenir packs' are similar, but tend to be of a more luxurious nature. The new issues of one year are often gathered together as a year pack.

Registered envelope

A special envelope intended for mail which has to be accounted for at all stages of its journey from sender to destination. Also sometimes called 'certified' mail.

Specimen stamps

Some countries distribute free of charge, samples of forthcoming stamps overprinted 'specimen' for publicity purposes. Such stamps are normally only sent to regular purchasers of stamps from the country concerned.

Tax stamps

These do not pay any postal charges, but have to be affixed to all items of mail. The revenue raised from their sale is donated to some specific cause.

Vending machine stamps

A recent trend has been to issue 'blank' (no denomination) stamps from machines, the denomination as required being printed on at the time of purchase.

Key
1. Postage due and 'To pay' labels
2. Specimen stamp
3. Vending machine stamp
4. Premium/charity stamps
5. Official stamps
6. Tax stamp
7. Pre-cancelled stamps
8. Maximum card
9. Postcard

Other terms

Block

A number of stamps joined together. Collectors referring to 'a block of four stamps' mean four stamps joined together, usually in a regular shape (i.e. two rows of two stamps rather than four stamps in a strip). In Germany a 'bloc' refers to a miniature sheet.

Error

The name given to a major fault on a stamp, such as colour missing or the perforation holes not being present when they should be. A small variation to a stamp design, as seen by comparing one stamp in a sheet to the next, is called a 'variety'.

Express post and special delivery stamps

Some post offices issue stamps designed for items that require immediate delivery.

Gutter pairs

Today, many stamps are printed in sheets which comprise two or more blocks of stamps (i.e. a sheet of 50 may comprise two blocks of 25) separated by a margin, known as a 'gutter'. Pairs of stamps on either side of, or attached to, a gutter are known as 'gutter pairs'.

Overprint

A legend printed onto an existing stamp. This might be of a commemorative nature, when there is insufficient time to produce a proper commemorative stamp. Overprinting can also be the result of a country's change of name, a change in political status, or currency changes. It can take place to make up a shortage of a certain value of stamp with a stamp of a different denomination. The overprint which changes the face value of a stamp is known as a 'surcharge'.

Perforation

The name given to the tiny holes between stamps which ensure that the stamps can be separated from each other with ease. The size of the holes (and equally the teeth) varies, so collectors have devised a way of measuring perforations by referring to the number of holes (or teeth) in 2cm. There are special gauges available for measuring perforations. Two methods of perforating a sheet of stamps are recognized. 'Comb' perforated sheets result in stamps with neat, even corners. Sheets which are 'line' perforated often produce stamps with ragged corners. Perforated stamps normally have holes, but there are exceptions, the most usual being slits, referred to as rouletting. The first stamps were without perforations and are referred to as 'imperforate'. On rare occasions today, some stamps are deliberately issued imperforate. A stamp, intended to be perforated, which accidentally fails to receive its perforations, is regarded as an error. However, stamps from booklets and coils are often without perforation holes on the outer edges as a matter of course, not error.

Sheet and sheetlet

Most stamps are produced in the form of sheets (say containing any number from about 25 stamps upwards). Smaller sheets, say of about ten stamps, are referred to as 'sheetlets'.

Se-tenant

Two, or more, stamps differing from each other in some way – colour, design, value – which are issued joined together are said to be 'se-tenant'.

Tab

The name given to the decorative margins of sheets of stamps, particularly from Israel. Although these labels have no postal value they have a connection with the stamps. Therefore it is popular to collect a stamp attached to its 'tab'.

Used and unused

A stamp which has been on an item of mail through the postal system and has thus received a cancellation (postmark) is said to be 'used'. A stamp which on the front is as issued by the post office (in other words with no postmark) is said to be 'unused'. An unused stamp which still has all its original gum on the back unmarked in any way is said to be 'mint'. Sometimes stamps, issued mainly for postage, are nevertheless used for revenue purposes. Such stamps will then often be 'cancelled' by means of a signature or similar device, but not with a postmark. Generally speaking one should try to avoid including stamps used for revenue purposes in a postage stamp collection.

Hints for the collector

There are many superb books that have been written on the subject of building up a stamp collection. A local stamp dealer, bookshop or library should be able to help you. You will be able to find out about the range of stamp albums and stock books for storing your stamps that are available; how to mount and present your stamps in the most attractive way; what 'tools' you will need. While stamp collecting is a hobby you can enjoy on your own, you can considerably increase your pleasure by sharing your hobby with others: there is probably a society for stamp collectors in your area. Your local library or information office should be able to provide you with a contact address. Go along to a meeting – you are certain to enjoy yourself in the company of others who also enjoy stamps. Reading books will provide you with much information, but never forget that there are magazines published for stamp collectors. Ask your local newsagent for details of those that are available: give each a try, then take out a regular subscription to those you enjoy most. Stamp magazines not only provide you with a wealth of fascinating articles and information, but also carry pages of advertisements from stamp dealers, which will help you build up your collection.

The more you learn, the more you will enjoy your hobby. Therefore never miss an opportunity to see stamps on display. Many museums have collections of stamps, while several post offices have their own Postal Museums. Stamp exhibitions are held regularly, at which you will have a chance to see both stamps on display to admire, and stamps for sale from the dealers present at the exhibition.

The world is vast: the world of stamp collecting is just as vast – and diverse. One of the joys of the hobby is that it can be adapted to suit any tastes – and all demands and pockets. Find out more for yourself – and enjoy yourself.

Philatelic Society addresses

United Kingdom
The British Philatelic Federation
1 Whitehall Place
London SW1A 2HE

The Royal Philatelic Society
London
41 Devonshire Place
London W1N 1PE

The National Philatelic Society
1 Whitehall Place
London SW1A 2HE

United States of America
The American Philatelic Society
336 South Frazer Street
State College, PA 16801

Society of Philatelic Americans
PO Box 9401
Wilmington, DE 19809

The Collectors' Club
22 East 35th Street
New York, NY 10016

The American Topical
Association
3306 North 50th Street
Milwaukee, WI 53216

Australia
Royal Philatelic Society of
Victoria
Box 2071S
Melbourne 3000

Philatelic Society of New
South Wales
Box 601
GPO Sydney 2001

Philatelic Society of South
Australia
Box 1937
GPO Adelaide 5001

Philatelic Society of Western
Australia
PO Box 62
North Perth 6006

Canada
Royal Philatelic Society of
Canada
PO Box 1054
Station A
Toronto M5W 1GS

New Zealand
Federation of New Zealand
Philatelic Societies Inc.
PO Box 435
New Plymouth

Royal Philatelic Society of New
Zealand Inc.
PO Box 1269
Wellington, CI

South Africa
The Philatelic Federation of
Southern Africa
PO Box 375
Johannesburg 2000

Royal Philatelic Society of
Cape Town
PO Box 1973
Cape Town 8000

Philatelic Society of
Johannesburg
PO Box 4967
Johannesburg 2000

Philatelic Society of Natal
20 Garvock
14 Umbilo Road
Durban 4001

Europe · Scandinavia

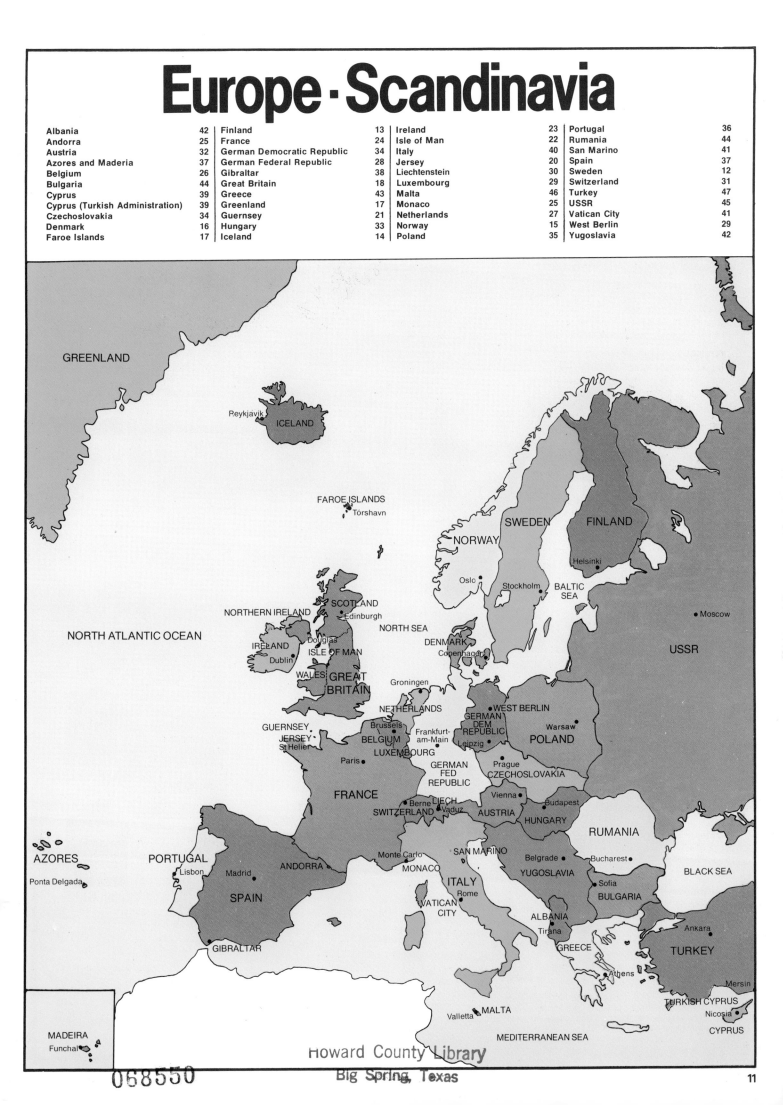

11

Sweden

Sverige

A Kingdom in Europe and the largest of the Scandinavian countries. The postal service was established in 1636, the first stamps being issued in 1855. Sweden is unusual in that the stamps are not issued in large sheets, but only in booklets and rolls. About once a year an issue is prepared in the form of a miniature sheet.

Write to: PFA The Swedish Post Office
Stamps and Philatelic Service
S-105 02 Stockholm
Sweden

Currency: 100 öre = 1 krona
(£1.00 = 10.50Skr; US $1.00 = 4.40Skr approx.)

Definitives

The main criterion regarding definitive stamps is that they are on sale for some considerable time. While certain values feature the portrait of the King, others are more thematic in design, being issued as postage rates require.

Commemoratives

About twenty commemorative stamps are issued each year, although at times sets may consist of more than one of these stamps (sometimes there may be up to six stamps in a set). Themes vary, but all have significance to Sweden. Annual issues promote tourism, honour past Nobel Prize winners, and celebrate Christmas.

Postal stationery and other items

Stamped stationery is available, including aerogrammes, envelopes and postcards. A recent innovation has been the issue of 'discount' stamps, showing no face value, but valid up to a specified postage rate, being in fact sold at a discount off that rate. First day covers are available for all stamp issues, both definitive and commemorative.

Finland

Suomi

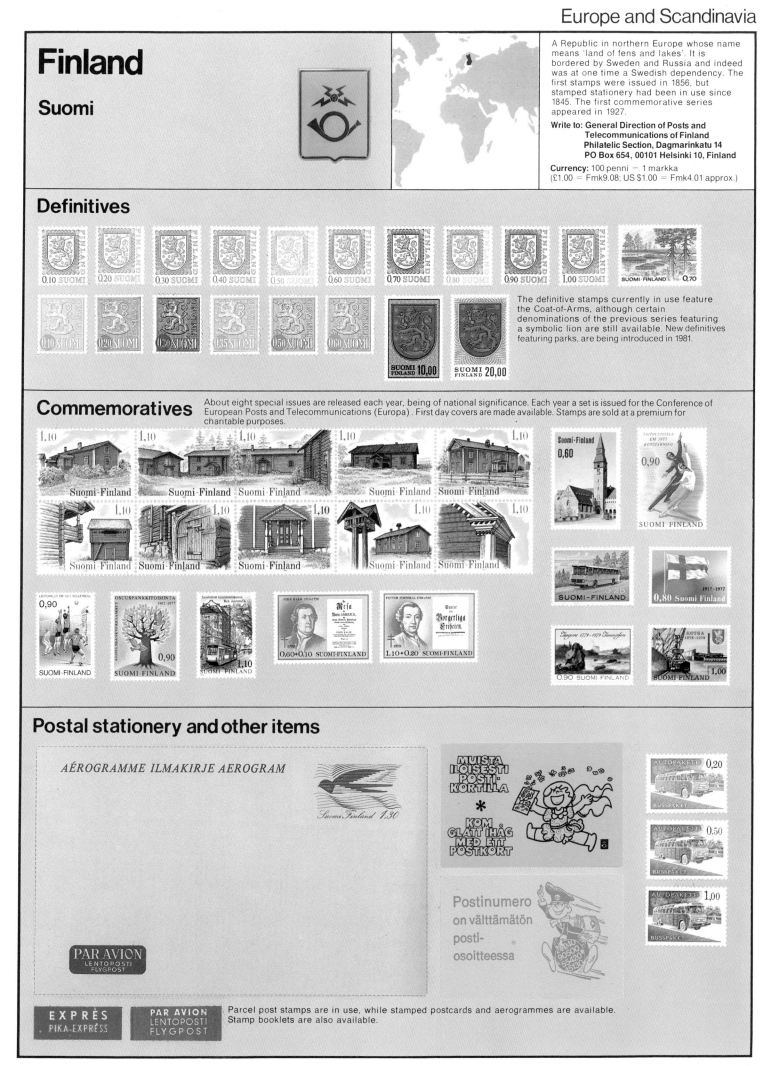

A Republic in northern Europe whose name means 'land of fens and lakes'. It is bordered by Sweden and Russia and indeed was at one time a Swedish dependency. The first stamps were issued in 1856, but stamped stationery had been in use since 1845. The first commemorative series appeared in 1927.

Write to: General Direction of Posts and Telecommunications of Finland Philatelic Section, Dagmarinkatu 14 PO Box 654, 00101 Helsinki 10, Finland

Currency: 100 penni = 1 markka (£1.00 = Fmk9.08; US $1.00 = Fmk4.01 approx.)

Definitives

The definitive stamps currently in use feature the Coat-of-Arms, although certain denominations of the previous series featuring a symbolic lion are still available. New definitives featuring parks, are being introduced in 1981.

Commemoratives

About eight special issues are released each year, being of national significance. Each year a set is issued for the Conference of European Posts and Telecommunications (Europa). First day covers are made available. Stamps are sold at a premium for charitable purposes.

Postal stationery and other items

AÉROGRAMME ILMAKIRJE AEROGRAM

Parcel post stamps are in use, while stamped postcards and aerogrammes are available. Stamp booklets are also available.

Iceland

Ísland

This independent Republic is an island to the south east of Greenland, which can boast the oldest democratic assembly in Europe, the parliament having been established in 930 AD. It was once under Danish rule, and indeed Danish stamps were used from 1870. In 1873 distinctive stamps for Iceland were issued.

Write to: Philatelic Sales Department
Frimerkjasalan
PO Box 1445, 121 Reykjavik
Iceland

Currency: 100 aurar = 1 new krona
(£1.00 = 14.64Kr ; US $1.00 = 6.48Kr approx.)

Commemoratives and other items

The average of six commemorative sets each year are relevant to Iceland. A set for the Conference of European Posts and Telecommunications (Europa) appears each year. Year Packs are produced containing the stamps of a twelve-month period. There are no definitives at present in use. An aerogramme, without a printed stamp, is available.

Norway

Norge

Noreg

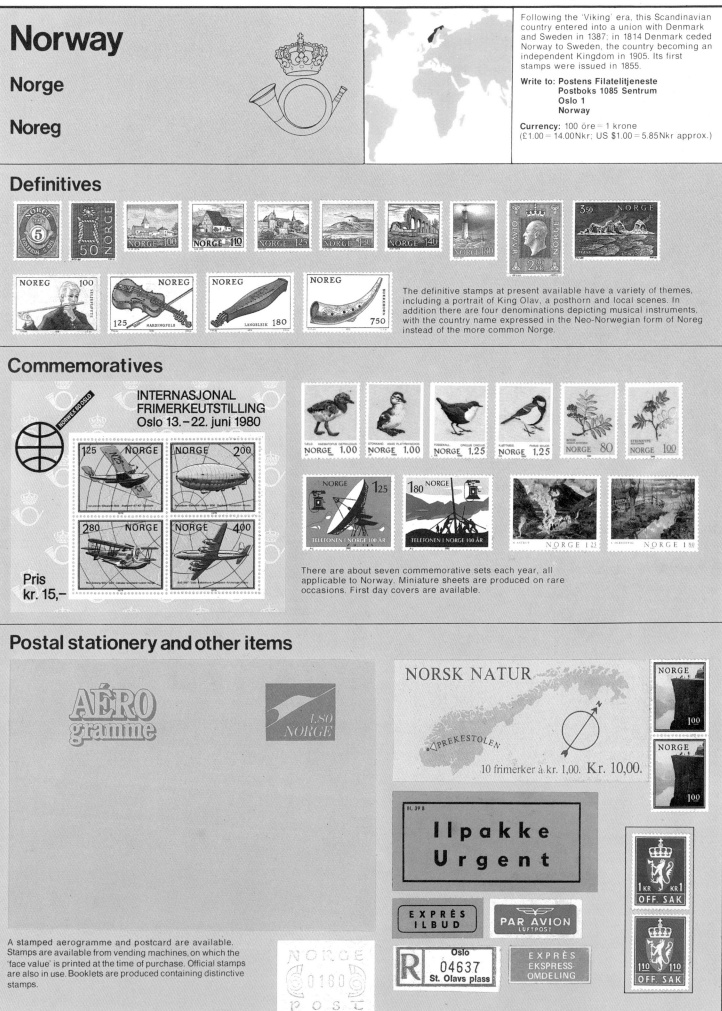

Following the 'Viking' era, this Scandinavian country entered into a union with Denmark and Sweden in 1387; in 1814 Denmark ceded Norway to Sweden, the country becoming an independent Kingdom in 1905. Its first stamps were issued in 1855.

Write to: Postens Filatelitjeneste
Postboks 1085 Sentrum
Oslo 1
Norway

Currency: 100 öre = 1 krone
(£1.00 = 14.00 Nkr; US $1.00 = 5.85 Nkr approx.)

Definitives

The definitive stamps at present available have a variety of themes, including a portrait of King Olav, a posthorn and local scenes. In addition there are four denominations depicting musical instruments, with the country name expressed in the Neo-Norwegian form of Noreg instead of the more common Norge.

Commemoratives

INTERNASJONAL FRIMERKEUTSTILLING
Oslo 13.–22. juni 1980

Pris kr. 15,–

There are about seven commemorative sets each year, all applicable to Norway. Miniature sheets are produced on rare occasions. First day covers are available.

Postal stationery and other items

A stamped aerogramme and postcard are available. Stamps are available from vending machines, on which the 'face value' is printed at the time of purchase. Official stamps are also in use. Booklets are produced containing distinctive stamps.

Denmark

Danmark

Denmark, a Kingdom and the smallest of the Scandinavian countries, was the first to issue stamps, in 1851. The first records of the existence of Denmark stem from reports of raids by the Vikings in the ninth century.

Write to: Postens Filateli
Radhuspladsen 59
DK-1550 Copenhagen V
Denmark
Currency: 100 öre = 1 krone
(£1.00 = 14.80Dkr; US $1.00 = 6.50Dkr approx.)

Definitives

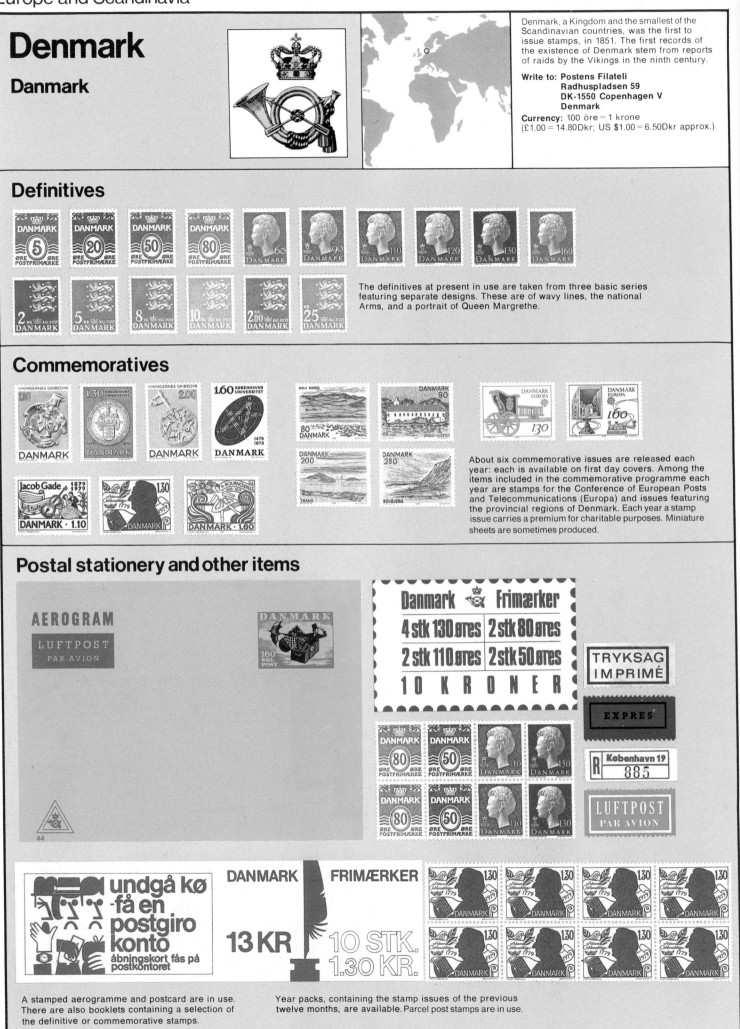

The definitives at present in use are taken from three basic series featuring separate designs. These are of wavy lines, the national Arms, and a portrait of Queen Margrethe.

Commemoratives

About six commemorative issues are released each year: each is available on first day covers. Among the items included in the commemorative programme each year are stamps for the Conference of European Posts and Telecommunications (Europa) and issues featuring the provincial regions of Denmark. Each year a stamp issue carries a premium for charitable purposes. Miniature sheets are sometimes produced.

Postal stationery and other items

A stamped aerogramme and postcard are in use. There are also booklets containing a selection of the definitive or commemorative stamps.

Year packs, containing the stamp issues of the previous twelve months, are available. Parcel post stamps are in use.

Greenland

Kalaallit Nunaat

Grønland

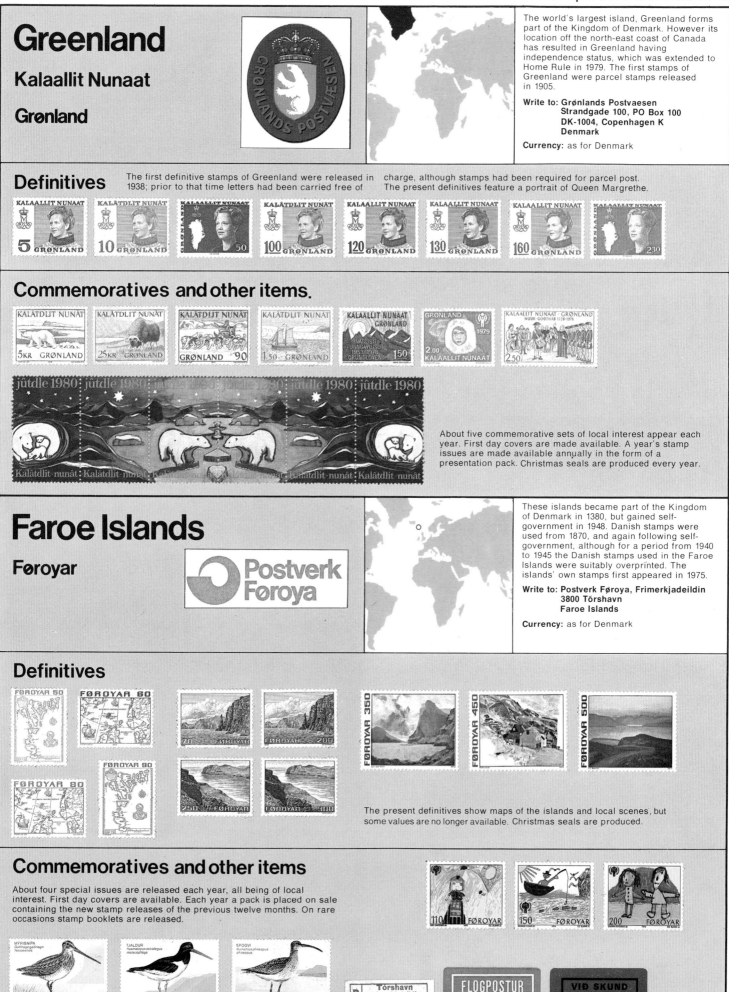

The world's largest island, Greenland forms part of the Kingdom of Denmark. However its location off the north-east coast of Canada has resulted in Greenland having independence status, which was extended to Home Rule in 1979. The first stamps of Greenland were parcel stamps released in 1905.

Write to: Grønlands Postvaesen
Strandgade 100, PO Box 100
DK-1004, Copenhagen K
Denmark

Currency: as for Denmark

Definitives

The first definitive stamps of Greenland were released in 1938; prior to that time letters had been carried free of charge, although stamps had been required for parcel post. The present definitives feature a portrait of Queen Margrethe.

Commemoratives and other items.

About five commemorative sets of local interest appear each year. First day covers are made available. A year's stamp issues are made available annually in the form of a presentation pack. Christmas seals are produced every year.

Faroe Islands

Føroyar

These islands became part of the Kingdom of Denmark in 1380, but gained self-government in 1948. Danish stamps were used from 1870, and again following self-government, although for a period from 1940 to 1945 the Danish stamps used in the Faroe Islands were suitably overprinted. The islands' own stamps first appeared in 1975.

Write to: Postverk Føroya, Frimerkjadeildin
3800 Tórshavn
Faroe Islands

Currency: as for Denmark

Definitives

The present definitives show maps of the islands and local scenes, but some values are no longer available. Christmas seals are produced.

Commemoratives and other items

About four special issues are released each year, all being of local interest. First day covers are available. Each year a pack is placed on sale containing the new stamp releases of the previous twelve months. On rare occasions stamp booklets are released.

Great Britain

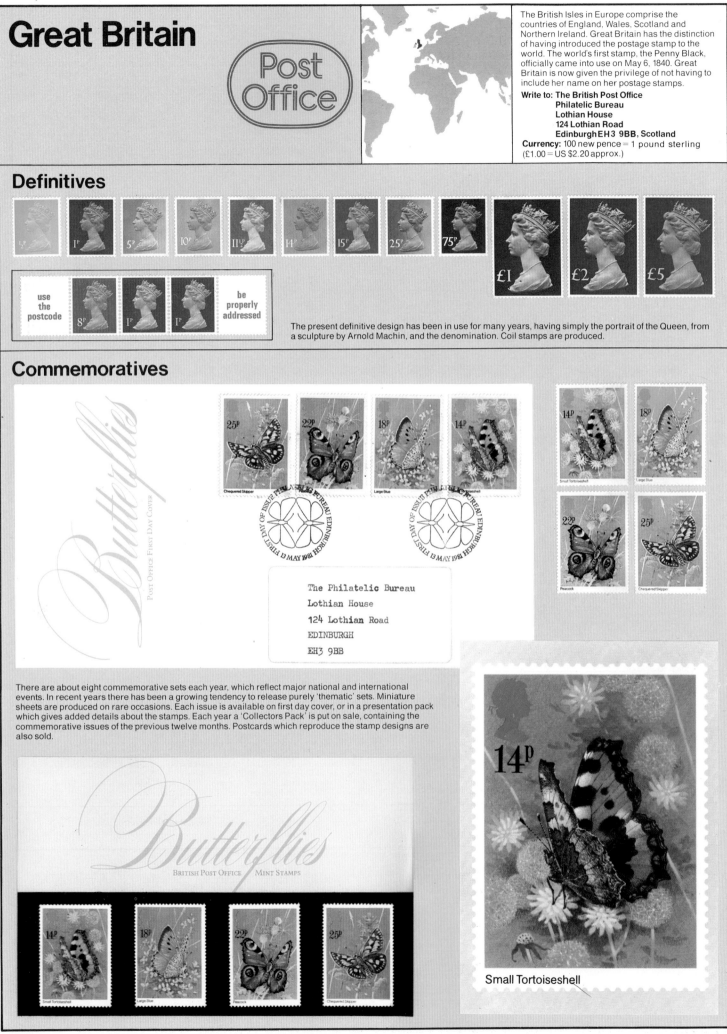

Post Office

The British Isles in Europe comprise the countries of England, Wales, Scotland and Northern Ireland. Great Britain has the distinction of having introduced the postage stamp to the world. The world's first stamp, the Penny Black, officially came into use on May 6, 1840. Great Britain is now given the privilege of not having to include her name on her postage stamps.

Write to: The British Post Office
Philatelic Bureau
Lothian House
124 Lothian Road
Edinburgh EH3 9BB, Scotland
Currency: 100 new pence = 1 pound sterling (£1.00 = US $2.20 approx.)

Definitives

use the postcode

be properly addressed

The present definitive design has been in use for many years, having simply the portrait of the Queen, from a sculpture by Arnold Machin, and the denomination. Coil stamps are produced.

Commemoratives

There are about eight commemorative sets each year, which reflect major national and international events. In recent years there has been a growing tendency to release purely 'thematic' sets. Miniature sheets are produced on rare occasions. Each issue is available on first day cover, or in a presentation pack which gives added details about the stamps. Each year a 'Collectors Pack' is put on sale, containing the commemorative issues of the previous twelve months. Postcards which reproduce the stamp designs are also sold.

The Philatelic Bureau
Lothian House
124 Lothian Road
EDINBURGH
EH3 9BB

Butterflies

Butterflies
POST OFFICE FIRST DAY COVER

Butterflies
BRITISH POST OFFICE / MINT STAMPS

Small Tortoiseshell

Country Stamps

Northern Ireland

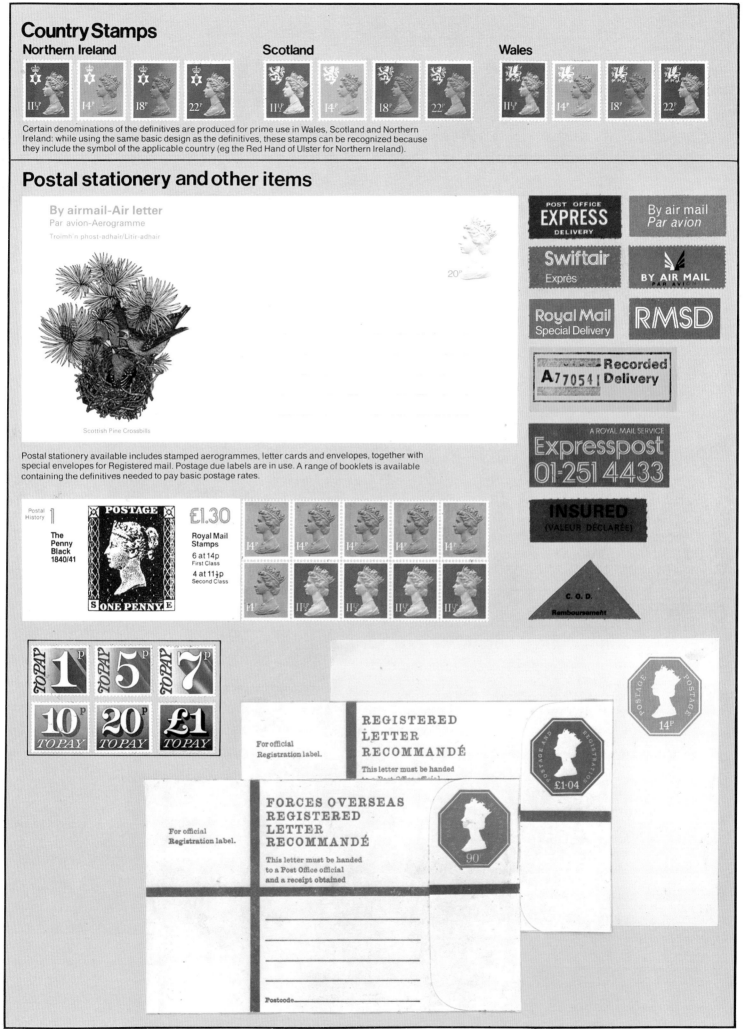

Scotland

Wales

Certain denominations of the definitives are produced for prime use in Wales, Scotland and Northern Ireland: while using the same basic design as the definitives, these stamps can be recognized because they include the symbol of the applicable country (eg the Red Hand of Ulster for Northern Ireland).

Postal stationery and other items

By airmail-Air letter
Par avion-Aerogramme
Troimh'n phost-adhair/Litir-adhair

20ᵖ

Scottish Pine Crossbills

Postal stationery available includes stamped aerogrammes, letter cards and envelopes, together with special envelopes for Registered mail. Postage due labels are in use. A range of booklets is available containing the definitives needed to pay basic postage rates.

Postal History 1

POSTAGE
ONE PENNY

The Penny Black 1840/41

£1.30

Royal Mail Stamps

6 at 14p
First Class

4 at 11½p
Second Class

POST OFFICE EXPRESS DELIVERY

By air mail Par avion

Swiftair Exprès

BY AIR MAIL PAR AVION

Royal Mail Special Delivery

RMSD

A770541 Recorded Delivery

A ROYAL MAIL SERVICE
Expresspost
01-251 4433

INSURED
(VALEUR DÉCLARÉE)

C. O. D.
Remboursement

TO PAY 1ᵖ
TO PAY 5ᵖ
TO PAY 7ᵖ
10ᵖ TO PAY
20ᵖ TO PAY
£1 TO PAY

REGISTERED LETTER RECOMMANDÉ

This letter must be handed to a Post Office official

For official Registration label.

FORCES OVERSEAS REGISTERED LETTER RECOMMANDÉ

This letter must be handed to a Post Office official and a receipt obtained

For official Registration label.

Postcode

POSTAGE POSTAGE 14ᵖ

POSTAGE AND REGISTRATION £1·04

90ᵖ

Jersey

Jersey, the largest of the Channel Islands, used the stamps of Great Britain from 1840 until 1969. Separate issues appeared between 1941 and 1944 for the period of German Occupation, while in 1948 (Third Anniversary of Liberation), and from 1958, stamps were produced in designs for Jersey, but valid throughout the UK.

Write to: Jersey Philatelic Bureau
PO Box 304, St Helier
Jersey, Channel Islands
via Great Britain

Currency: 100 pence = 1 pound sterling
(US $1.00 = £0.45 approx.)

Definitives

Following postal independence in 1969, distinctive definitive stamps were issued. New smaller definitives are being introduced from 1981 showing the Coats-of-Arms of famous Jersey families. The previous definitives featured the Coats-of-Arms of the Parishes of Jersey.

Commemoratives

These appear about four times a year, normally confined to local events, and are always accompanied by a first day cover and presentation pack. Very rarely a miniature sheet is also released.

Postal stationery and other items

Postal stationery consists of stamped aerogrammes, and registered envelopes on which the 'postage stamp' is handstamped. Booklets containing the current definitives are sold, there being two types: one for sale from vending machines, and a second for 'over the counter' sales. Postage due labels are in use.

DE BAGOT **JERSEY POSTAGE STAMPS £1.32**
12 at 1p • 6 at 3p
CONTENTS: 6 at 7p • 6 at 10p

Guernsey

Bailiwick of Guernsey

Guernsey Post Office

One of the Channel Islands, the Bailiwick of Guernsey includes Alderney, Herm, Jethou and Sark. Although self-governing, Guernsey has belonged to the British Crown since 1066. British stamps were in use from 1840 to 1969: at times Great Britain issued stamps primarily for use in the Channel Islands but also valid throughout the United Kingdom.

**Write to: Philatelic Bureau
Postal Headquarters
Guernsey, Channel Islands
via Great Britain**

Currency: 100 pence = 1 pound sterling
(US $1.00 = £0.45 approx.)

Definitives

Basic British stamps were in use from 1840 but, starting in 1958, and up to 1969, certain denominations were prepared in designs applicable solely to Guernsey. These stamps were valid for postage throughout the United Kingdom. During the German Occupation in the Second World War, separate stamp issues were prepared inscribed Guernsey. When Guernsey became postally independent in 1969, stamp issues inscribed Guernsey were again released. The current definitives show Guernsey's coinage over the years, but a new £5 Arms defintiive is to be added. Presentation packs and first day covers are prepared for the definitives.

Commemoratives

The first commemorative set might be considered that issued in 1948 for the Third Anniversary of Liberation, being mainly put on sale in Guernsey and Jersey, and at a few selected post offices in Great Britain. Commemorative sets now appear about four times a year, mostly of a local nature. Each is accompanied by a presentation pack and first day cover. Very occasionally miniature sheets are released.

Postal stationery and other items

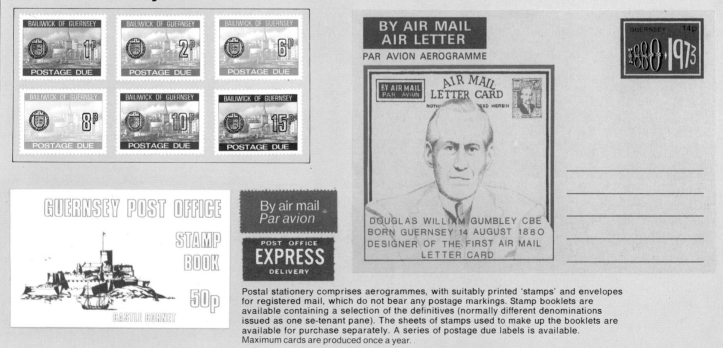

Postal stationery comprises aerogrammes, with suitably printed 'stamps' and envelopes for registered mail, which do not bear any postage markings. Stamp booklets are available containing a selection of the definitives (normally different denominations issued as one se-tenant pane). The sheets of stamps used to make up the booklets are available for purchase separately. A series of postage due labels is available. Maximum cards are produced once a year.

Isle of Man

This island off the coast of Great Britain for many years used British stamps, although, given the opportunity to control its own postal affairs, it assumed the responsibility in 1973. Earlier, the British Post Office had issued stamps for prime use in the Isle of Man but valid throughout the United Kingdom. Its own stamps appeared in 1973.

Write to: Philatelic Bureau
PO Box 10.M
Douglas, Isle of Man
via Great Britain

Currency: 100 pence = 1 pound sterling
(US $1.00 = £0.45 approx.)

Definitives

The current definitive series is divided into two sections: the lower denominations feature local scenes, while the higher values show a fuchsia, Manx cat, chough and Viking warrior. They are available in presentation packs and on first day covers.

Commemoratives

Five commemorative issues are released on average each year, referring to local events, mainly historical. Miniature sheets are occasionally also produced. Each issue is accompanied by a first day cover and presentation pack.

Postal stationery and other items

Booklets containing specially designed stamps are produced. Stamped aerogrammes and registered envelopes are also in use.
Postage due labels are available.

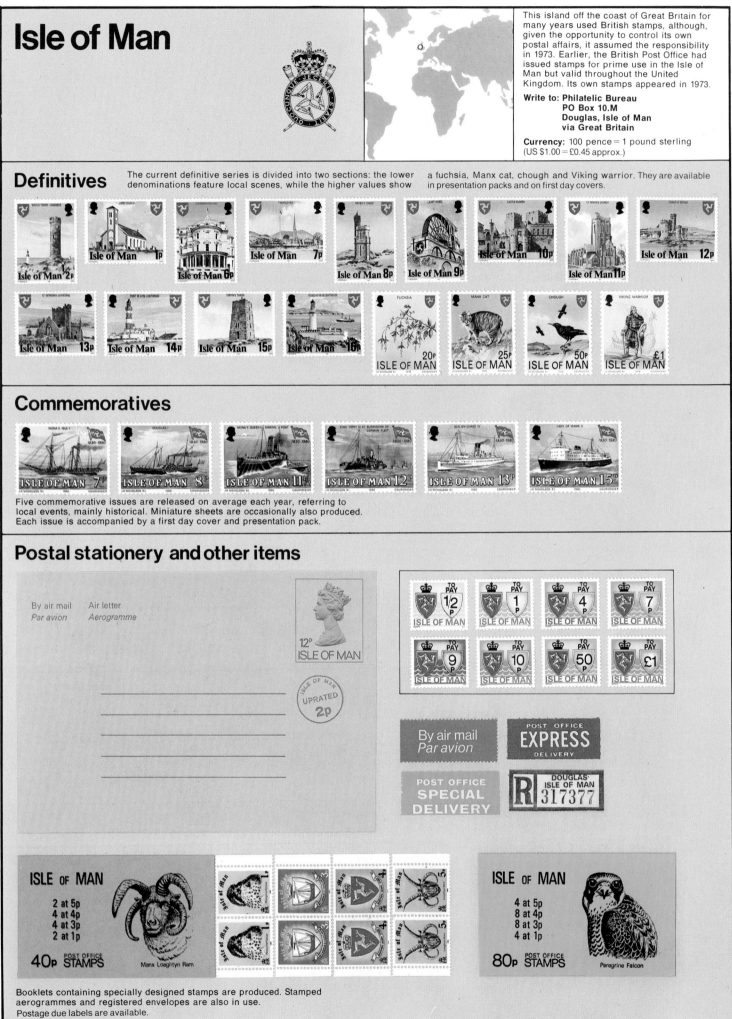

Ireland

Éire

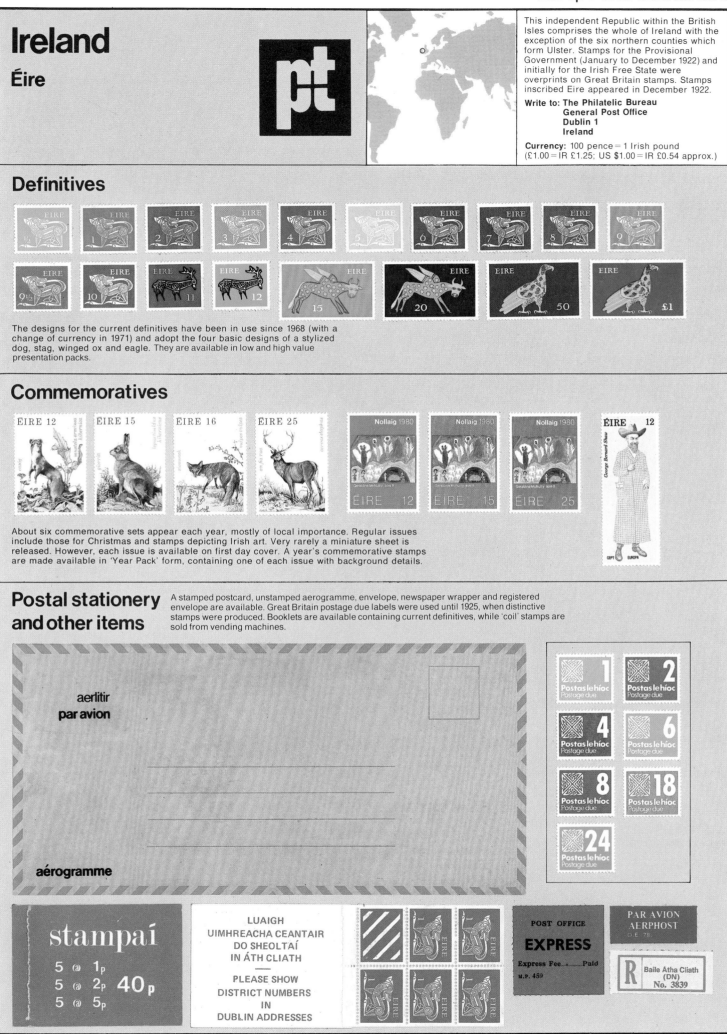

This independent Republic within the British Isles comprises the whole of Ireland with the exception of the six northern counties which form Ulster. Stamps for the Provisional Government (January to December 1922) and initially for the Irish Free State were overprints on Great Britain stamps. Stamps inscribed Eire appeared in December 1922.

Write to: The Philatelic Bureau
General Post Office
Dublin 1
Ireland

Currency: 100 pence = 1 Irish pound
(£1.00 = IR £1.25; US $1.00 = IR £0.54 approx.)

Definitives

The designs for the current definitives have been in use since 1968 (with a change of currency in 1971) and adopt the four basic designs of a stylized dog, stag, winged ox and eagle. They are available in low and high value presentation packs.

Commemoratives

About six commemorative sets appear each year, mostly of local importance. Regular issues include those for Christmas and stamps depicting Irish art. Very rarely a miniature sheet is released. However, each issue is available on first day cover. A year's commemorative stamps are made available in 'Year Pack' form, containing one of each issue with background details.

Postal stationery and other items

A stamped postcard, unstamped aerogramme, envelope, newspaper wrapper and registered envelope are available. Great Britain postage due labels were used until 1925, when distinctive stamps were produced. Booklets are available containing current definitives, while 'coil' stamps are sold from vending machines.

aerlitir
par avion

aérogramme

stampaí
5 @ 1p
5 @ 2p   40p
5 @ 5p

LUAIGH
UIMHREACHA CEANTAIR
DO SHEOLTAÍ
IN ÁTH CLIATH
—
PLEASE SHOW
DISTRICT NUMBERS
IN
DUBLIN ADDRESSES

POST OFFICE
EXPRESS
Express Fee .... Paid
M.P. 459

PAR AVION
AERPHOST
D.E. 76

R Baile Atha Cliath
(DN)
No. 3839

France

This Republic in Europe sees its postal system date back to the reign of Louis XI, although in those days the post was confined to the Court. It was not until 1589 that the privilege was extended to the general public. The first stamps for France appeared in 1849.

Write to: Service Philatélique des PTT
61–63 rue de Douai
F-75436 Paris Cedex 09
France

Currency: 100 centimes = 1 French franc
(£1.00 = 11.06F; US $1.00 = 4.87F approx.)

Definitives
The present definitive series depicts Sabine. Pre-cancelled stamps and coil stamps are available.

Commemoratives

Commemorative issues appear on about thirty occasions each year, reflecting events and people of national importance. Most of the issues comprise just a single stamp. Popular in recent years have been the stamps which depict French Art. First day covers are available. Stamps are issued for the Council of Europe and Unesco. Red Cross stamps, with a surcharge, are issued and are also made available in booklets.

Postal stationery and other items

A stamped aerogramme is in use. Booklets are available containing values from the current definitive series. A set of postage due labels depicting flowers is produced.

Monaco

Monaco achieved independence in 1861, the sovereignty of the country having been recognized by the French in 1512. It was annexed by the French during the French Revolution and placed under Sardinian protection in 1815. Following periods of use of Sardinian and French, Monaco's own stamps were released in 1885.

**Write to: La Direction de l'office des Emissions de Timbres-Poste
2 Avenue St. Michel
Monte Carlo, Monaco**

Currency: 100 centimes = 1 French franc
(£1.00 = 11.06F; US $1.00 = 4.87F approx.)

Definitives, commemoratives and other items

The definitives at present in use depict either Prince Rainier III or local scenes, particularly buildings such as the Palace of Monaco. Air stamps have also been produced featuring Prince Rainier with Princess Grace. There are about fifteen commemorative stamp issues each year, which tend to be either local or thematic in their design. The policy is to release the commemorative sets in batches, so that there may be only three of four actual release dates in the year. Miniature sheets are occasionally produced. First day covers are available. Pre-cancelled stamps, a stamped aerogramme and postcard are in use. There is also a set of postage due labels available.

Andorra

Principat d'Andorra

A state in the Pyrenees which is under the joint control of France and Spain and, even today, has both French and Spanish stamp issues. The first Spanish stamps were introduced in 1928, while three years later there were suitable overprints on the stamps of France, these being replaced in 1932 by stamps inscribed Andorra.

**Write to: Service Philatélique
Postes Françaises d'Andorra-la-Vieille
Principat d'Andorra (via France)**
Write to: address as for Spain, (page 37)

Currency: French and Spanish currency are in use.

Definitives, commemoratives and other items

The present definitives for the French administration depict the Coat-of-Arms. There are no definitives at present in use for the Spanish administration. There are about four commemorative sets issued each year, under Spanish authority (see above): these include sets for the Europa theme and Christmas. The 'French' administration (see right) provides about eight sets a year, again including one for Europa. A series of postage due labels for French Andorra is in use. A postcard for Spanish Andorra is also available.

Belgium

Belgique · België

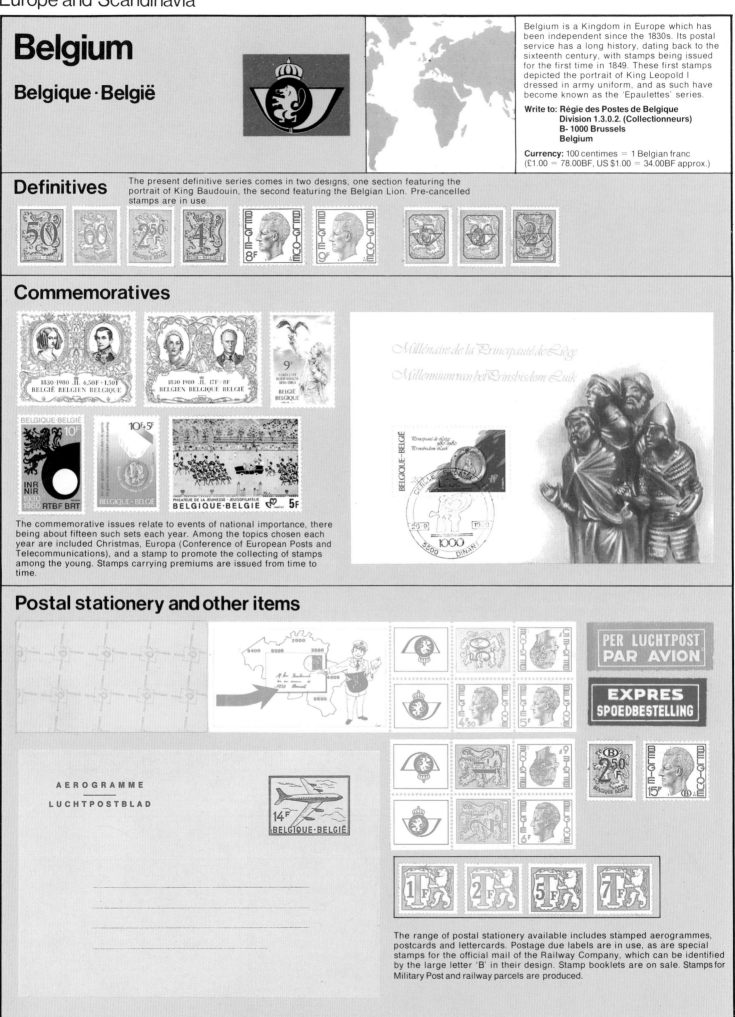

Belgium is a Kingdom in Europe which has been independent since the 1830s. Its postal service has a long history, dating back to the sixteenth century, with stamps being issued for the first time in 1849. These first stamps depicted the portrait of King Leopold I dressed in army uniform, and as such have become known as the 'Epaulettes' series.

Write to: Régie des Postes de Belgique
Division 1.3.0.2. (Collectionneurs)
B- 1000 Brussels
Belgium

Currency: 100 centimes = 1 Belgian franc
(£1.00 = 78.00BF, US $1.00 = 34.00BF approx.)

Definitives

The present definitive series comes in two designs, one section featuring the portrait of King Baudouin, the second featuring the Belgian Lion. Pre-cancelled stamps are in use.

Commemoratives

The commemorative issues relate to events of national importance, there being about fifteen such sets each year. Among the topics chosen each year are included Christmas, Europa (Conference of European Posts and Telecommunications), and a stamp to promote the collecting of stamps among the young. Stamps carrying premiums are issued from time to time.

Postal stationery and other items

AEROGRAMME

LUCHTPOSTBLAD

PER LUCHTPOST
PAR AVION

EXPRES
SPOEDBESTELLING

The range of postal stationery available includes stamped aerogrammes, postcards and lettercards. Postage due labels are in use, as are special stamps for the official mail of the Railway Company, which can be identified by the large letter 'B' in their design. Stamp booklets are on sale. Stamps for Military Post and railway parcels are produced.

Netherlands

Nederland

PTT

A Kingdom in Europe, bordering on the North Sea, which is often incorrectly referred to as Holland. Its first stamps were issued in 1852, these showing a portrait of King William III

Write to: Netherlands Post Office Philatelic Service
Postbus 30051
9700 RN Groningen
The Netherlands

Currency: 100 cents = 1 guilder
(£1.00 = Dfl 5.20; US $1.00 = Dfl 1.80 approx.)

Definitives

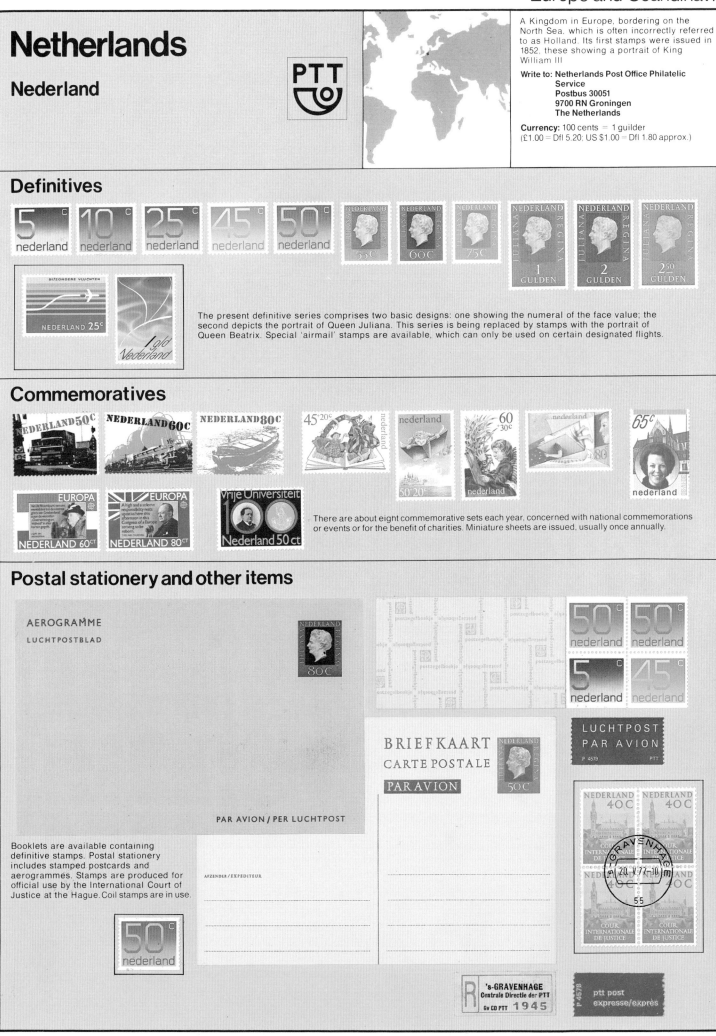

The present definitive series comprises two basic designs: one showing the numeral of the face value; the second depicts the portrait of Queen Juliana. This series is being replaced by stamps with the portrait of Queen Beatrix. Special 'airmail' stamps are available, which can only be used on certain designated flights.

Commemoratives

There are about eight commemorative sets each year, concerned with national commemorations or events or for the benefit of charities. Miniature sheets are issued, usually once annually.

Postal stationery and other items

AEROGRAMME
LUCHTPOSTBLAD

PAR AVION / PER LUCHTPOST

BRIEFKAART
CARTE POSTALE
PAR AVION

LUCHTPOST
PAR AVION

Booklets are available containing definitive stamps. Postal stationery includes stamped postcards and aerogrammes. Stamps are produced for official use by the International Court of Justice at the Hague. Coil stamps are in use.

AFZENDER/EXPEDITEUR

R 's-GRAVENHAGE
Centrale Directie der PTT
Gv CD PTT 1945

ptt post
expresse/exprès

German Federal Republic

Deutsche Bundespost

The German Federal Republic was established in 1949, being frequently referred to today as West Germany. The first stamps as such appeared in 1949, with the first definitive being issued two years later. Germany itself was a federation of the states once ruled by the Austrian Habsburgs – its first stamps were issued in 1872.

Write to: Versandstelle für Postwertzeichen
Postfach 20 00
D-6000 Frankfurt am Main 1
Federal Republic of Germany

Currency: 100 pfennige = 1 Deutschemark
(£1.00 = DM5.00; US $1.00 = DM2.06 approx.)

Definitives

West Germany has two definitive series currently in use: normal stamps issued in sheets featuring industry and technology; stamps issued in coils depicting castles. (also available in sheets from philatelic sources).

Commemoratives and other items

Commemorative issues appear about twenty times a year, honouring events of West German significance. First day covers are produced; first day cards are available. Occasionally stamps are sold at a premium for charitable purposes.

POSTKARTE

MIT LUFTPOST
PAR AVION

Eilzustellung
Exprès

R 562
6052 Mühlheim
am Main 3

Nr.
Remboursement
Nachnahme

Rückseite : Unterschriftsblätter zum Grundgesetz
Wertaufdruck : Phönix-Relief am Bundeshaus in Bonn

Deutsche Bundespost

Inhalt:
2 Postwertzeichen zu 10 Pf
2 Postwertzeichen zu 30 Pf
2 Postwertzeichen zu 50 Pf
2 Postwertzeichen zu 60 Pf

Abgabepreis 3 DM

DBP ** 60
DEUTSCHE BUNDESPOST

DBP * 150
DEUTSCHE BUNDESPOST

TAG DER BRIEFMARKE 1979

Stamped postcards are in use. Booklets are available containing values from the definitive series.
Special stamps are sold from vending machines on which the 'face value' is printed at the time of purchase.

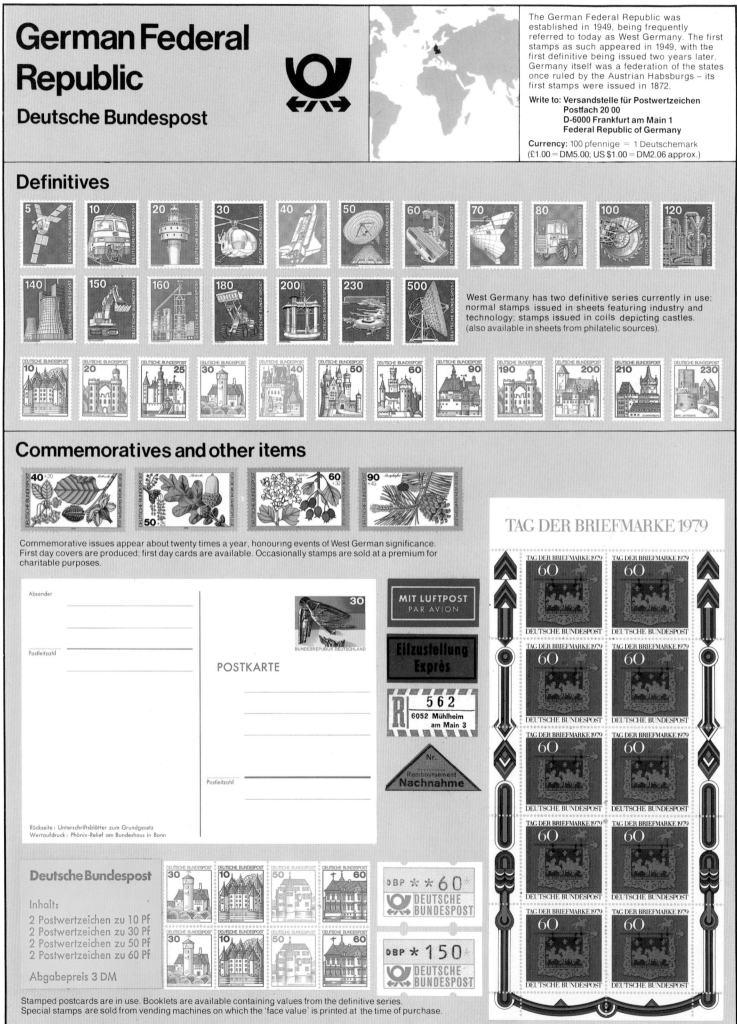

West Berlin

Deutsche Bundespost Berlin

West Berlin has been jointly administered by the United States, France and Great Britain since 1948. It has its own separate stamp issues, which first appeared in 1948.

Write to: Versandstelle für Postwertzeichen
Postfach 12 09 50
D-1000 Berlin 12
Federal Republic of Germany

Currency: 100 pfennige = 1 Deutschemark
(£1.00 = DM5.00; US $1.00 = DM2.06 approx.)

Definitives, commemoratives and other items

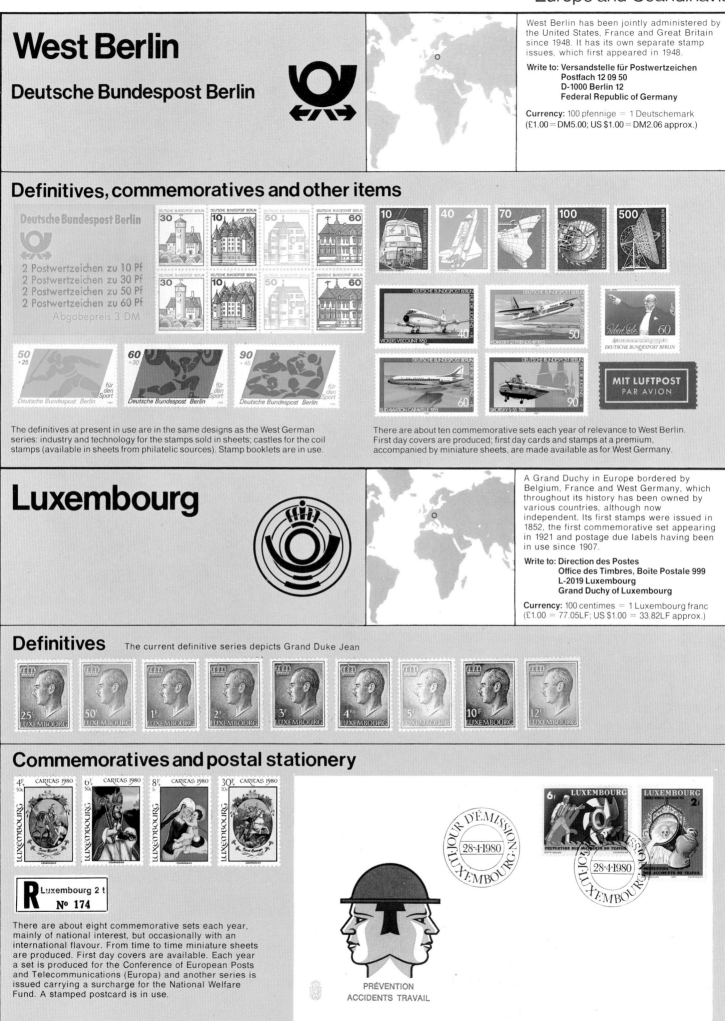

Deutsche Bundespost Berlin

2 Postwertzeichen zu 10 Pf
2 Postwertzeichen zu 30 Pf
2 Postwertzeichen zu 50 Pf
2 Postwertzeichen zu 60 Pf
Abgabepreis 3 DM

The definitives at present in use are in the same designs as the West German series: industry and technology for the stamps sold in sheets; castles for the coil stamps (available in sheets from philatelic sources). Stamp booklets are in use.

There are about ten commemorative sets each year of relevance to West Berlin. First day covers are produced; first day cards and stamps at a premium, accompanied by miniature sheets, are made available as for West Germany.

Luxembourg

A Grand Duchy in Europe bordered by Belgium, France and West Germany, which throughout its history has been owned by various countries, although now independent. Its first stamps were issued in 1852, the first commemorative set appearing in 1921 and postage due labels having been in use since 1907.

Write to: Direction des Postes
Office des Timbres, Boîte Postale 999
L-2019 Luxembourg
Grand Duchy of Luxembourg

Currency: 100 centimes = 1 Luxembourg franc
(£1.00 = 77.05LF; US $1.00 = 33.82LF approx.)

Definitives   The current definitive series depicts Grand Duke Jean

Commemoratives and postal stationery

There are about eight commemorative sets each year, mainly of national interest, but occasionally with an international flavour. From time to time miniature sheets are produced. First day covers are available. Each year a set is produced for the Conference of European Posts and Telecommunications (Europa) and another series is issued carrying a surcharge for the National Welfare Fund. A stamped postcard is in use.

Liechtenstein

Fuerstentum Liechtenstein

Liechtenstein lies sandwiched between Austria and Switzerland. The postal history dates from the sixteenth century and developed because the main post route from Milan to Lindau passed through it. Prior to the issue of Liechtenstein's own stamps in 1912, her postal arrangements were looked after by Austria and Austrian stamps were used.

Write to: Postwertzeichenstelle der Fürstlichen Regierung FL -9490 Vaduz Principality of Liechtenstein

Currency: 100 rappen = 1 Swiss franc
(£1.00 = SFr 4.27; US $1.00 = SFr 1.87 approx.)

Definitives

The first definitives of Liechtenstein featured a portrait of Prince Johann II. The current definitive series was issued in 1978, with designs showing buildings in the country.

Commemoratives

Liechtenstein has always been noted for colourful issues of stamps: many of her commemorative sets over the years have honoured the Royal Family. Each year from 1960, a set has been issued to honour the Conference of European Posts and Telecommunications. Other regular series have appeared for Christmas (from 1957) and with a premium to help charity (from 1928). First day covers are made available.

Postal stationery

Eilsendung Exprès - Espresso

LUFTPOST PAR AVION VIA AEREA

R 9490 Vaduz Postwertzeichenstelle der Fürstl. Regierung 466

Pictorial postcards and maximum cards are in use.

Switzerland

Helvetia

A Republic in Europe which is bounded by France, Germany, Austria and Italy. It consists of a confederation of self-governing cantons, and in fact the first stamps were issued by one such canton, Zurich, in 1843, being quickly followed by Geneva. Stamps for the confederation first appeared in 1850.

Write to: **PTT Philatelic Office**
Parkterrasse 10
CH-3030 Berne
Switzerland

Currency: 100 centimes = 1 Swiss franc
(£1.00 = SFr4.25; US $1.00 = SFr1.77 approx.)

Definitives

The present definitive series in use features famous Swiss architecture. Coil stamps are available, which are also sold as sheets.

Commemoratives and other items

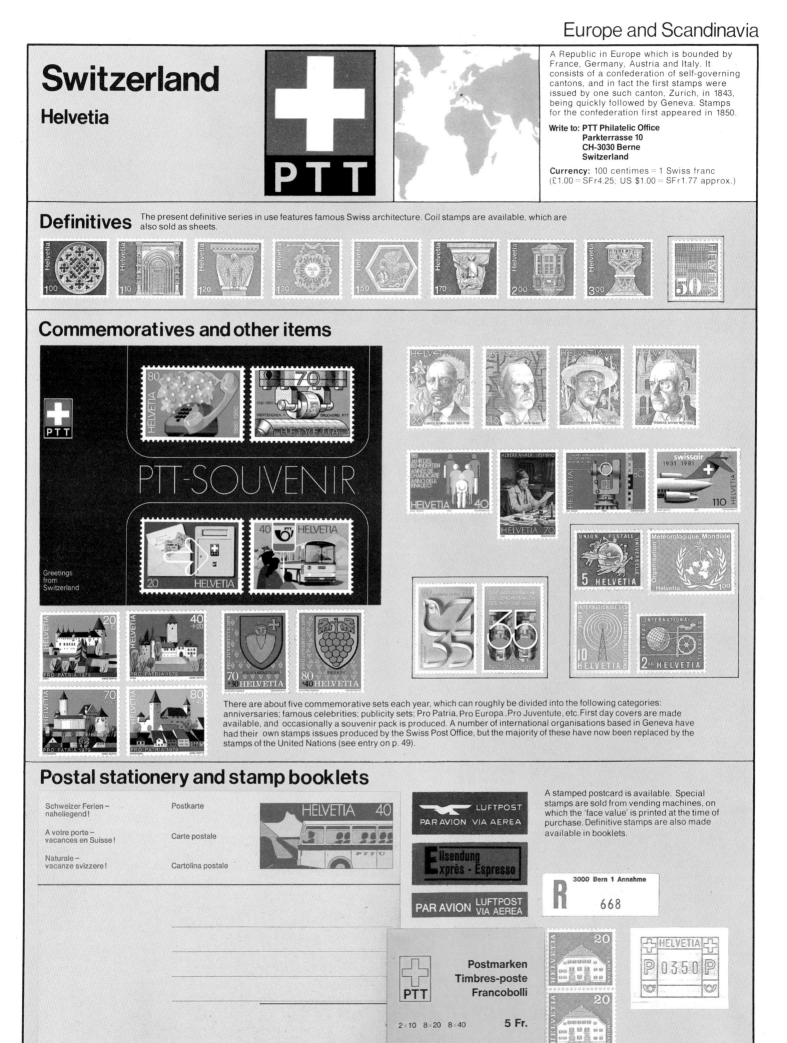

There are about five commemorative sets each year, which can roughly be divided into the following categories: anniversaries; famous celebrities; publicity sets; Pro Patria, Pro Europa, Pro Juventute, etc. First day covers are made available, and occasionally a souvenir pack is produced. A number of international organisations based in Geneva have had their own stamps issues produced by the Swiss Post Office, but the majority of these have now been replaced by the stamps of the United Nations (see entry on p. 49).

Postal stationery and stamp booklets

Schweizer Ferien – naheliegend!

A votre porte – vacances en Suisse!

Naturale – vacanze svizzere!

Postkarte

Carte postale

Cartolina postale

A stamped postcard is available. Special stamps are sold from vending machines, on which the 'face value' is printed at the time of purchase. Definitive stamps are also made available in booklets.

LUFTPOST
PAR AVION VIA AEREA

Eilsendung
Exprès - Espresso

PAR AVION LUFTPOST
VIA AEREA

R 3000 Bern 1 Annahme
668

Postmarken
Timbres-poste
Francobolli

PTT

2×10 8×20 8×40   5 Fr.

Austria

Republik Österreich

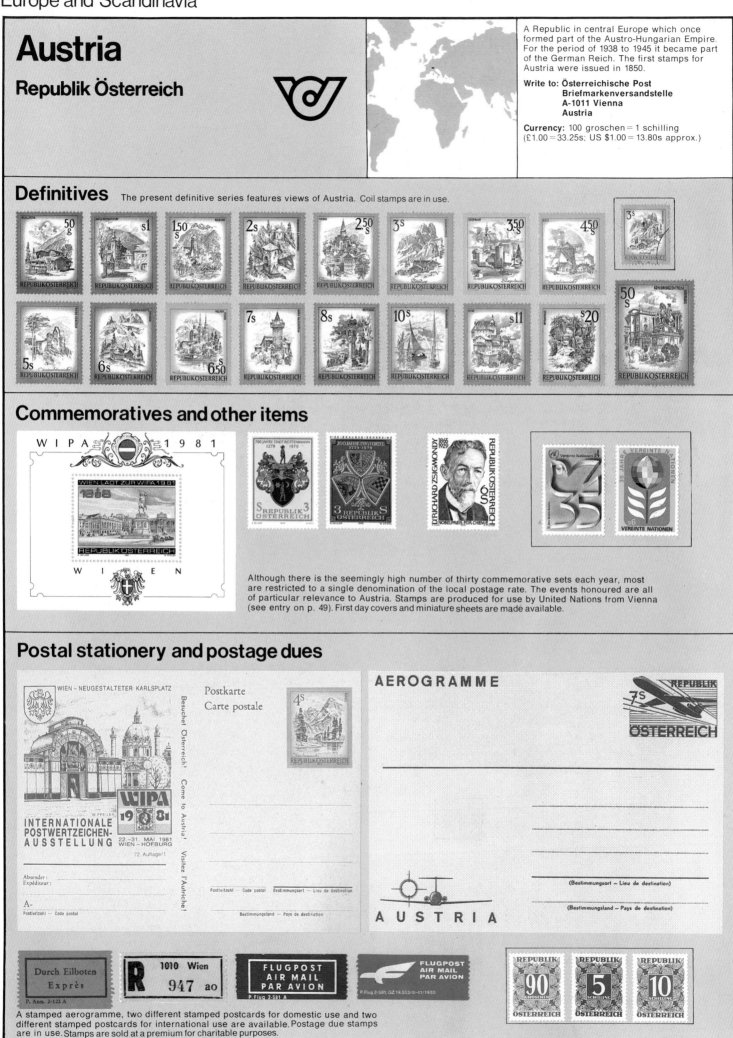

A Republic in central Europe which once formed part of the Austro-Hungarian Empire. For the period of 1938 to 1945 it became part of the German Reich. The first stamps for Austria were issued in 1850.

Write to: Österreichische Post
Briefmarkenversandstelle
A-1011 Vienna
Austria

Currency: 100 groschen = 1 schilling
(£1.00 = 33.25s; US $1.00 = 13.80s approx.)

Definitives

The present definitive series features views of Austria. Coil stamps are in use.

Commemoratives and other items

Although there is the seemingly high number of thirty commemorative sets each year, most are restricted to a single denomination of the local postage rate. The events honoured are all of particular relevance to Austria. Stamps are produced for use by United Nations from Vienna (see entry on p. 49). First day covers and miniature sheets are made available.

Postal stationery and postage dues

A stamped aerogramme, two different stamped postcards for domestic use and two different stamped postcards for international use are available. Postage due stamps are in use. Stamps are sold at a premium for charitable purposes.

Hungary

Magyar Posta

This People's Republic in central Europe was settled by the Magyars in the ninth century. The postal service dates to the seventeenth century, with Austrian stamps being used from 1850, stamps for use in both Austria and Hungary appearing in 1867, and, in 1868, stamps for use in Hungary alone to pay the tax on newspapers. The first postage stamps for Hungary appeared in 1871.

Write to: Philatelia Hungarica
H-1373 Budapest
PO Box 600, Hungary

Currency: 100 filler = 1 forint
(£1.00 = 72.00Ft; US $1.00 = 32.55Ft approx.)

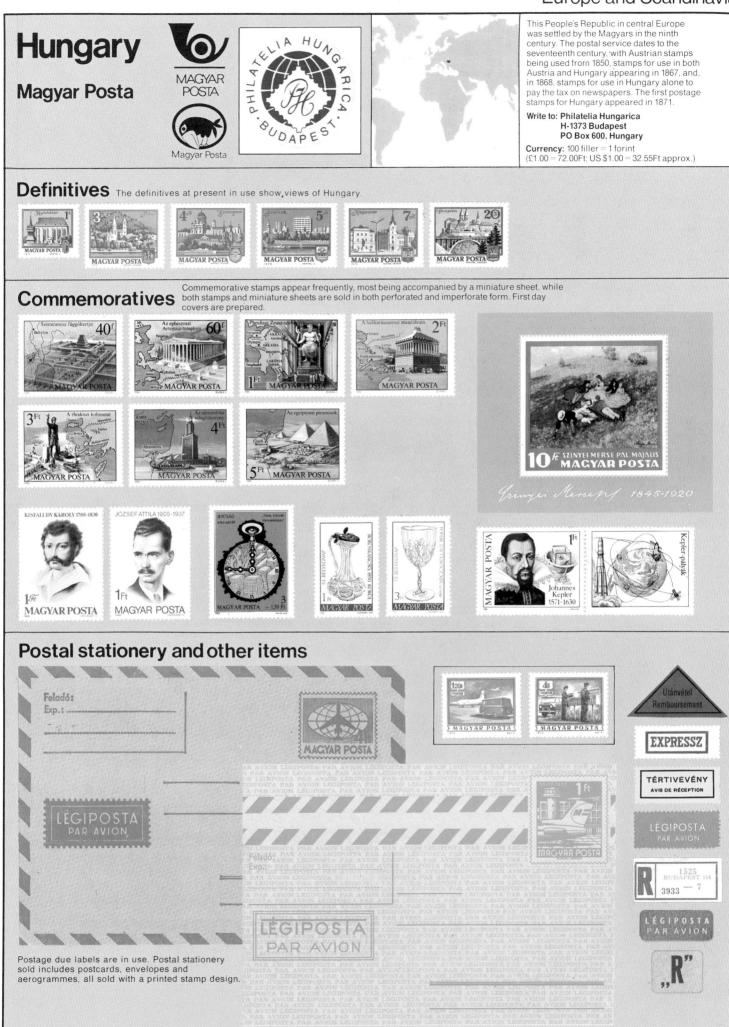

Definitives

The definitives at present in use show views of Hungary.

Commemoratives

Commemorative stamps appear frequently, most being accompanied by a miniature sheet, while both stamps and miniature sheets are sold in both perforated and imperforate form. First day covers are prepared.

Postal stationery and other items

Postage due labels are in use. Postal stationery sold includes postcards, envelopes and aerogrammes, all sold with a printed stamp design.

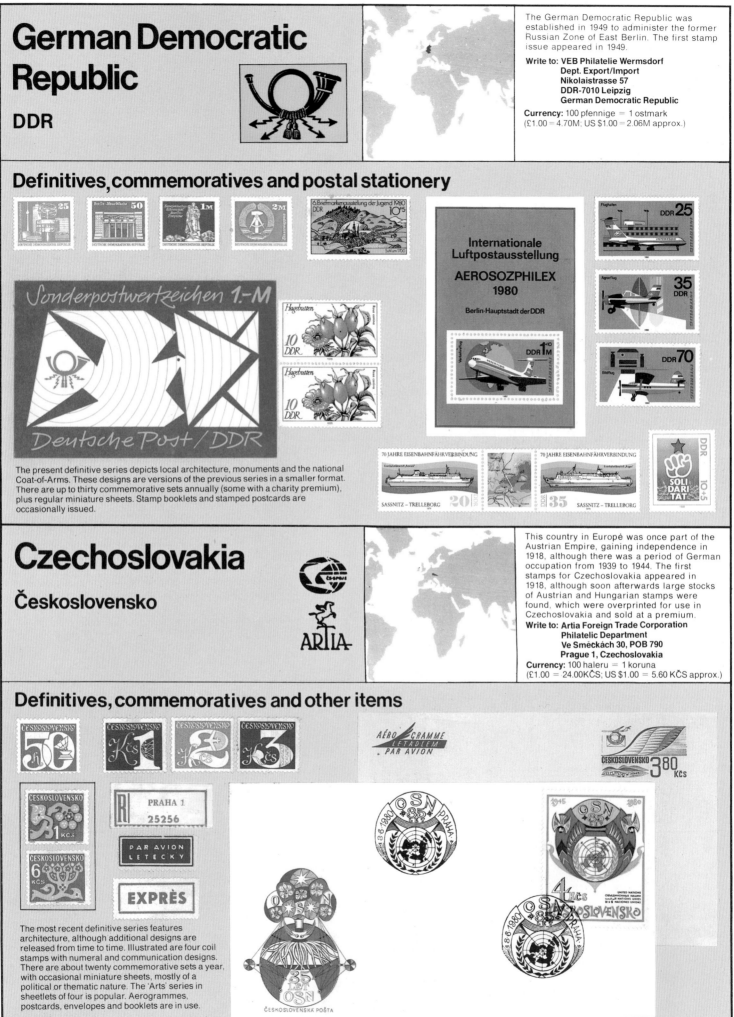

German Democratic Republic

DDR

The German Democratic Republic was established in 1949 to administer the former Russian Zone of East Berlin. The first stamp issue appeared in 1949.

Write to: VEB Philatelie Wermsdorf
Dept. Export/Import
Nikolaistrasse 57
DDR-7010 Leipzig
German Democratic Republic

Currency: 100 pfennige = 1 ostmark
(£1.00 = 4.70M; US $1.00 = 2.06M approx.)

Definitives, commemoratives and postal stationery

The present definitive series depicts local architecture, monuments and the national Coat-of-Arms. These designs are versions of the previous series in a smaller format. There are up to thirty commemorative sets annually (some with a charity premium), plus regular miniature sheets. Stamp booklets and stamped postcards are occasionally issued.

Czechoslovakia

Československo

This country in Europe was once part of the Austrian Empire, gaining independence in 1918, although there was a period of German occupation from 1939 to 1944. The first stamps for Czechoslovakia appeared in 1918, although soon afterwards large stocks of Austrian and Hungarian stamps were found, which were overprinted for use in Czechoslovakia and sold at a premium.

Write to: Artia Foreign Trade Corporation
Philatelic Department
Ve Smečkách 30, POB 790
Prague 1, Czechoslovakia

Currency: 100 haleru = 1 koruna
(£1.00 = 24.00KČS; US $1.00 = 5.60 KČS approx.)

Definitives, commemoratives and other items

The most recent definitive series features architecture, although additional designs are released from time to time. Illustrated are four coil stamps with numeral and communication designs. There are about twenty commemorative sets a year, with occasional miniature sheets, mostly of a political or thematic nature. The 'Arts' series in sheetlets of four is popular. Aerogrammes, postcards, envelopes and booklets are in use.

Poland

Polska

A Communist Republic bordered by Czechoslovakia, East Germany and Russia. Prussian and Austrian stamps were used from 1850, and Russian stamps were introduced in 1856. Poland's own stamps first appeared in 1860.

Write to: Philatelic Department
ARS Polona C.H.Z.
Krak. Przedmieście 7
Skr. Pocztowa 1001
00-950 Warsaw, Poland

Currency: 100 groszy = 1 zloty
(£1.00 = 75zł; US $1.00 = 31zł approx.)

Definitives, commemoratives and other items

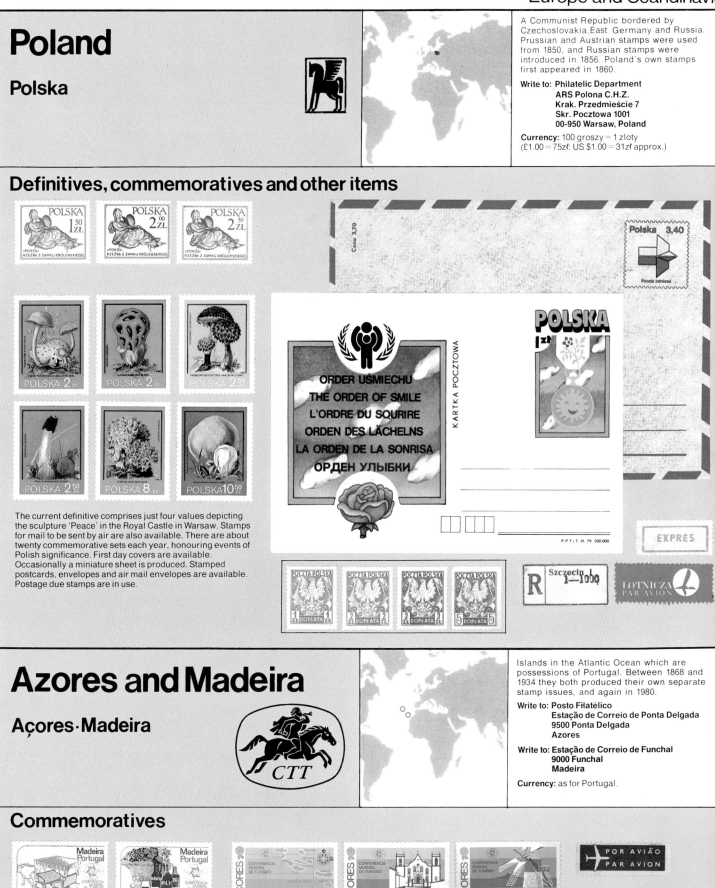

The current definitive comprises just four values depicting the sculpture 'Peace' in the Royal Castle in Warsaw. Stamps for mail to be sent by air are also available. There are about twenty commemorative sets each year, honouring events of Polish significance. First day covers are available. Occasionally a miniature sheet is produced. Stamped postcards, envelopes and air mail envelopes are available. Postage due stamps are in use.

Azores and Madeira

Açores·Madeira

Islands in the Atlantic Ocean which are possessions of Portugal. Between 1868 and 1934 they both produced their own separate stamp issues, and again in 1980.

Write to: Posto Filatélico
Estação de Correio de Ponta Delgada
9500 Ponta Delgada
Azores

Write to: Estação de Correio de Funchal
9000 Funchal
Madeira

Currency: as for Portugal.

Commemoratives

At present only about two commemorative sets a year are planned for each of Azores and Madeira, being of specific reference to the territories. Miniature sheets will from time to time be produced, as will maximum cards reproducing the stamp designs. In general, the definitives of Portugal are in use, although a series depicting native flowers is expected.

Portugal

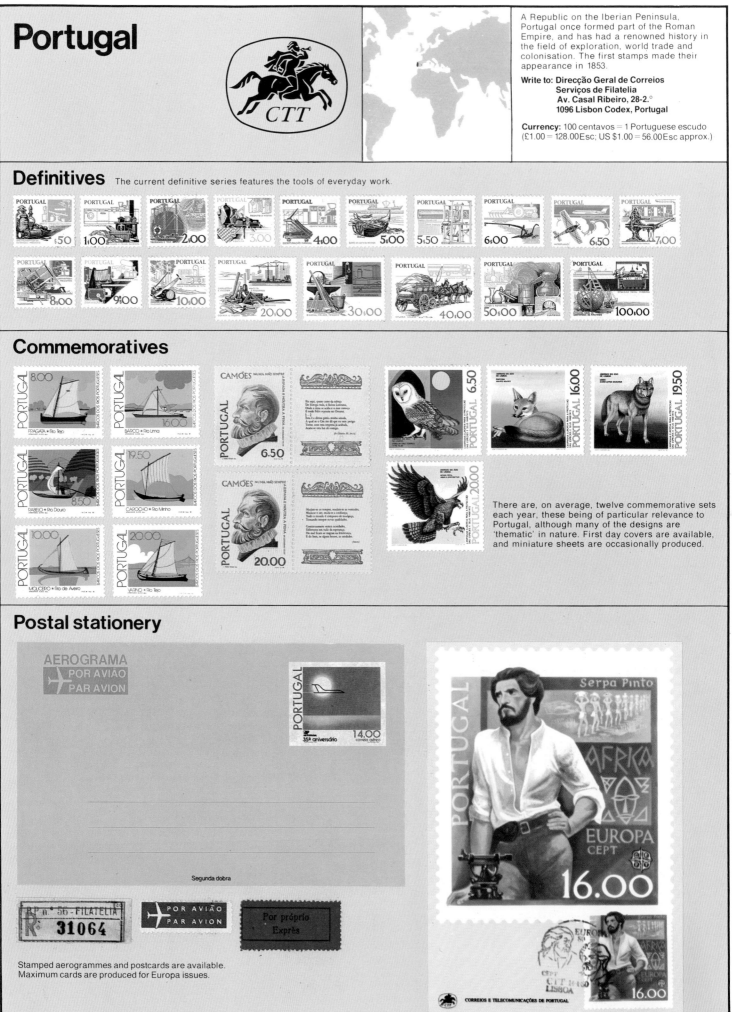

A Republic on the Iberian Peninsula, Portugal once formed part of the Roman Empire, and has had a renowned history in the field of exploration, world trade and colonisation. The first stamps made their appearance in 1853.

Write to: Direcção Geral de Correios
Serviços de Filatelia
Av. Casal Ribeiro, 28-2.°
1096 Lisbon Codex, Portugal

Currency: 100 centavos = 1 Portuguese escudo
(£1.00 = 128.00Esc; US $1.00 = 56.00Esc approx.)

Definitives The current definitive series features the tools of everyday work.

Commemoratives

There are, on average, twelve commemorative sets each year, these being of particular relevance to Portugal, although many of the designs are 'thematic' in nature. First day covers are available, and miniature sheets are occasionally produced.

Postal stationery

Stamped aerogrammes and postcards are available.
Maximum cards are produced for Europa issues.

Spain

España

A Republic in south-west Europe which reached the height of its power in the fifteenth century. The first stamps were issued in 1850, while the first Spanish commemorative set was issued in 1905 to mark the 300th anniversary of the publication of 'Don Quixote' by Cervantes.

Write to: Dirección General de Correos
y Telecomunicación, Philately Section of
the General Post Office
Palacio de Comunicaciones
Madrid, Spain

Currency: 100 centimos = 1 peseta
(£1.00 = 191.00PTA; US $1.00 = 84.00PTA approx.)

Definitives

The current definitives feature a portrait of King Juan Carlos I and are available in normal sheets and coils.

Commemoratives

Commemorative series are issued on frequent occasions, but often consist of just one stamp of low face value. The events commemorated tend to be of national importance. Very rarely is a miniature sheet produced, although first day covers are available.

Other items

A stamped aerogramme is available as are a series of stamped pictorial postcards and maximum cards. Special delivery stamps are produced. Also available is a Valencia 'tax' stamp, but its use is not compulsory.

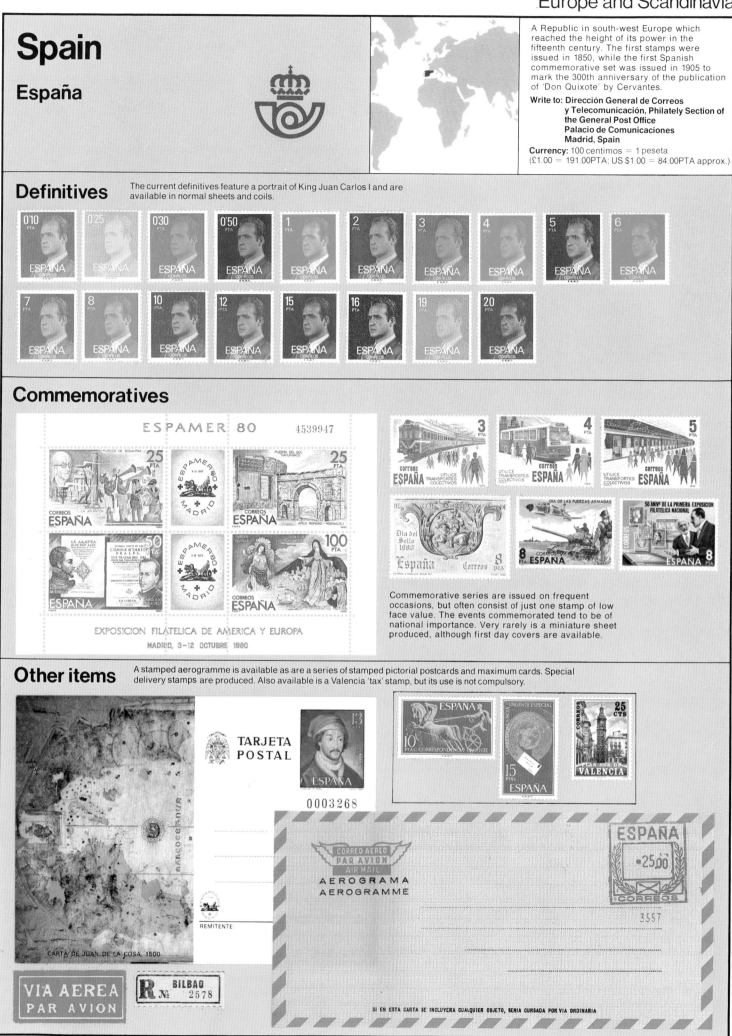

Gibraltar

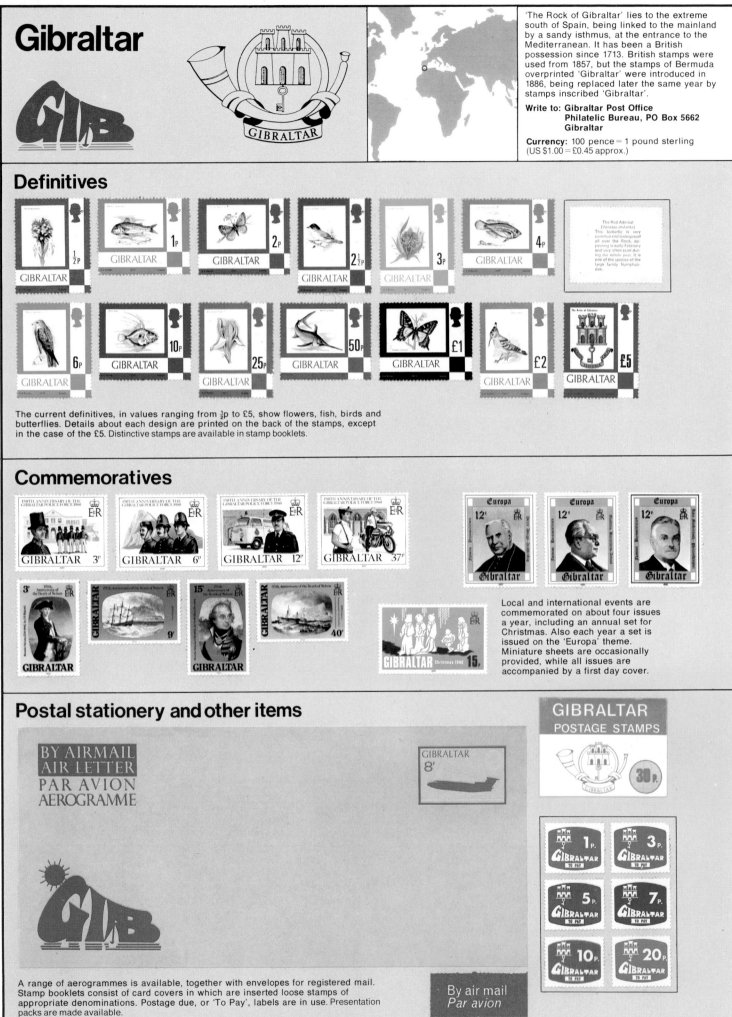

'The Rock of Gibraltar' lies to the extreme south of Spain, being linked to the mainland by a sandy isthmus, at the entrance to the Mediterranean. It has been a British possession since 1713. British stamps were used from 1857, but the stamps of Bermuda overprinted 'Gibraltar' were introduced in 1886, being replaced later the same year by stamps inscribed 'Gibraltar'.

Write to: Gibraltar Post Office
Philatelic Bureau, PO Box 5662
Gibraltar

Currency: 100 pence = 1 pound sterling
(US $1.00 = £0.45 approx.)

Definitives

The current definitives, in values ranging from ½p to £5, show flowers, fish, birds and butterflies. Details about each design are printed on the back of the stamps, except in the case of the £5. Distinctive stamps are available in stamp booklets.

Commemoratives

Local and international events are commemorated on about four issues a year, including an annual set for Christmas. Also each year a set is issued on the 'Europa' theme. Miniature sheets are occasionally provided, while all issues are accompanied by a first day cover.

Postal stationery and other items

A range of aerogrammes is available, together with envelopes for registered mail. Stamp booklets consist of card covers in which are inserted loose stamps of appropriate denominations. Postage due, or 'To Pay', labels are in use. Presentation packs are made available.

Cyprus

Kibris · Cyprus

ΚΥΠΡΟΣ

This island Republic in the Mediterranean has become noted for the rivalry between its Greek and Turkish communities. When Great Britain took over its administration in 1878, British stamps were used. In 1881, British stamps overprinted 'Cyprus' were in use, but were replaced in July of that year by stamps inscribed Cyprus, showing the portrait of Queen Victoria.

Write to: The Philatelic Service
General Post Office
Nicosia, Cyprus

Currency: 1000mils = 1 Cypriot pound
(£1.00 = £C0.87; US $1.00 = £C0.39 approx.)

Definitives

The current definitive series, issued in 1980, shows local archaeological treasures and works of art. As with all the stamps of Cyprus, they are inscribed in English, Turkish and Greek. Booklets on sale from vending machines consist simply of card covers (carrying advertising) into which are stuck stamps of appropriate denominations.

Commemoratives and other items

Commemoratives tend to be of a local nature, honouring Cypriots or commemorating events in the island's history. Very occasionally, an issue is accompanied by a miniature sheet· Each year a series of stamps is issued for Christmas. Issues are available on first day covers. Aerogrammes bearing specially designed 'stamps' and registered envelopes are available, together with postcards and a newspaper wrapper.

Cyprus (Turkish Administration)

Kibris Türk Federe Devleti Postalari

For many years there has been internal conflict in Cyprus between the Greeks and the Turks. In 1964, the Turks established their own postal service, mainly for internal purposes. Stamps have been used to pay such internal postage since 1970, but from 1974 such stamps have replaced the 'Greek' issues of Cyprus for international mail.

Write to: Turkish Federated State of Kibris
Directorate of Postal Department
Philatelic Branch (Lefkoşa)
Mersin 10, Turkey

Currency: as for Turkey

Definitives, commemoratives and postal stationery

New definitives (not illustrated), showing flowers, are expected in 1981. About five commemorative sets appear each year, all of relevance to the Turkish community in Cyprus. An inland postcard is available.

Italy

Italia

A Republic in southern Europe with coastlines on both the Mediterranean and Adriatic Seas. This former Kingdom once comprised smaller Kingdoms and Duchies, which had their own stamps. The stamps of Sardinia were introduced in Italy in 1861, the country having her own stamps two years later.

Write to: Amministrazione delle Poste e delle Telecomunicazioni Ufficio Principale Filatelico 00100 Rome, Italy

Currency: 100 centesimi = 1 Italian lira (£1.00 = L2,342; US $1.00 = L1,007 approx.)

Definitives

The present definitive series, introduced in 1980, depicts castles. Coil stamps are in use.

Commemoratives

There are about fifteen commemorative sets each year, and these refer to local events and personalities. First day covers are made available.

Postal stationery and other items

Stamped aerogrammes and postcards are available. Parcel post stamps are also available, as are Express Letter stamps, postage due labels, Concessional Parcel stamps, and Pneumatic Post stamps.

San Marino

A small independent Republic which is completely surrounded by Italy. It is thought to have been founded in 301 AD by Marinus, a stone-mason. The postal service was started in 1862, at first using Sardinian stamps and later Italian, until the country's own stamps appeared in 1877.

Write to: Ufficio Filatelico
47031 Republic of San Marino

Currency: 100 centesimi = 1 Italian lira
(£1.00 = L2,342; US $1.00 = L1,007 approx.)

Definitives

The present definitive series features the 'Civil Virtues', such as wisdom, love, fortitude.

Commemoratives and other items

There are about ten commemorative sets in any year, which are both local and international in their subject matter, although frequently a 'thematic' approach is used. First day covers are available. A number of items of stamped postal stationery are available, including aerogrammes, postcards and envelopes. Postage due and 'parcel post' stamps have been in use.

Vatican City

Poste Vaticane

A small area within Rome which since 1929 has been under the independent sovereignty of the Pope. The Vatican Palace, the Pope's official residence, is located there. Stamps for Vatican City were first issued in 1929.

Write to: Ufficio Filatelico del Governatorato
Segretaria Generale
001200 Vatican City State

Currency: 100 centesimi = 1 Italian lire
(£1.00 = L2,342; US $1.00 = L1,007 approx.)

Definitives, commemoratives and other items

Definitive stamps are due to be issued in 1981. Air mail stamps are issued in alternate years. Postage dues and aerogrammes are in use. There are about six commemorative sets each year, relating to religious anniversaries or major international events.

Yugoslavia

Jugoslavija

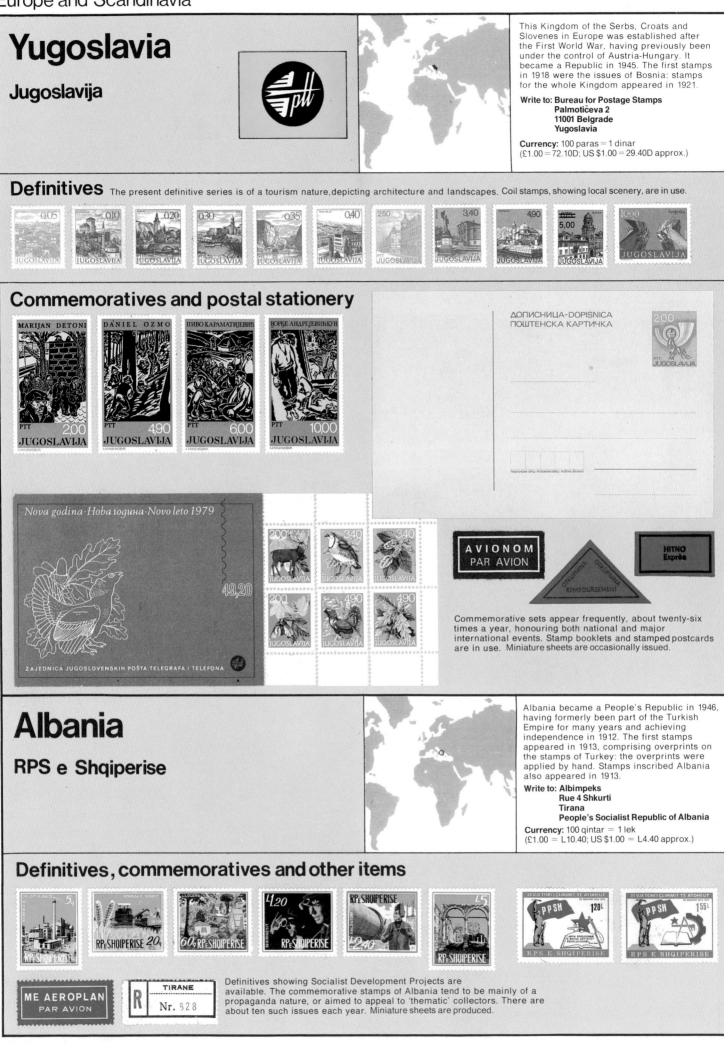

This Kingdom of the Serbs, Croats and Slovenes in Europe was established after the First World War, having previously been under the control of Austria-Hungary. It became a Republic in 1945. The first stamps in 1918 were the issues of Bosnia: stamps for the whole Kingdom appeared in 1921.

Write to: **Bureau for Postage Stamps**
Palmotičeva 2
11001 Belgrade
Yugoslavia

Currency: 100 paras = 1 dinar
(£1.00 = 72.10D; US $1.00 = 29.40D approx.)

Definitives
The present definitive series is of a tourism nature, depicting architecture and landscapes. Coil stamps, showing local scenery, are in use.

Commemoratives and postal stationery

Commemorative sets appear frequently, about twenty-six times a year, honouring both national and major international events. Stamp booklets and stamped postcards are in use. Miniature sheets are occasionally issued.

Albania

RPS e Shqiperise

Albania became a People's Republic in 1946, having formerly been part of the Turkish Empire for many years and achieving independence in 1912. The first stamps appeared in 1913, comprising overprints on the stamps of Turkey: the overprints were applied by hand. Stamps inscribed Albania also appeared in 1913.

Write to: **Albimpeks**
Rue 4 Shkurti
Tirana
People's Socialist Republic of Albania

Currency: 100 qintar = 1 lek
(£1.00 = L10.40; US $1.00 = L4.40 approx.)

Definitives, commemoratives and other items

Definitives showing Socialist Development Projects are available. The commemorative stamps of Albania tend to be mainly of a propaganda nature, or aimed to appeal to 'thematic' collectors. There are about ten such issues each year. Miniature sheets are produced.

Greece

ΕΛΛΑΣ Hellas

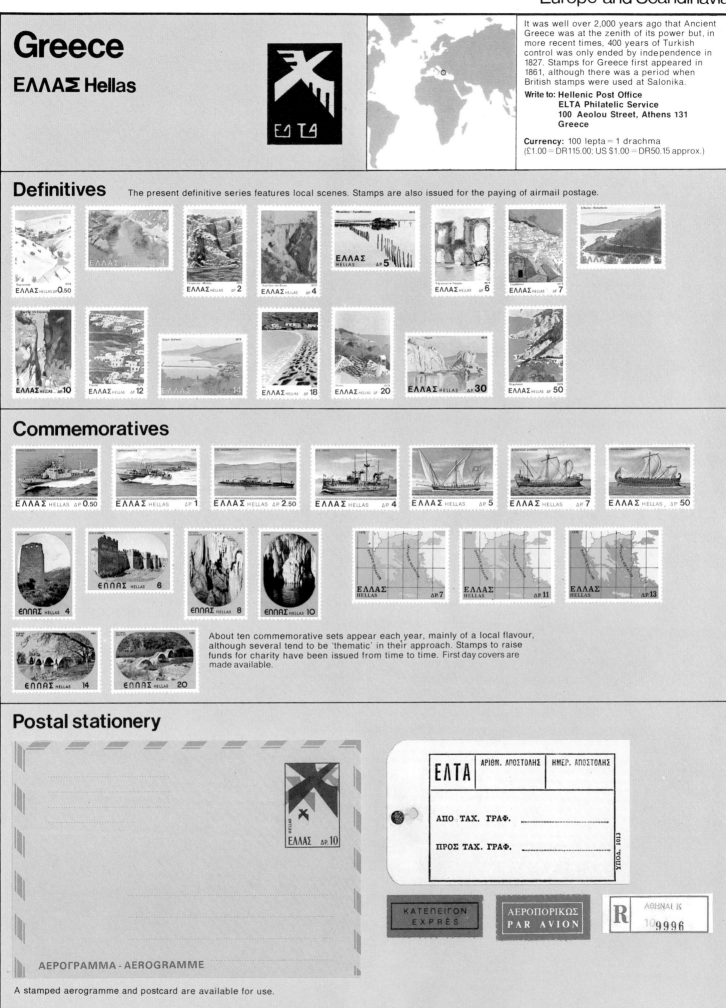

It was well over 2,000 years ago that Ancient Greece was at the zenith of its power but, in more recent times, 400 years of Turkish control was only ended by independence in 1827. Stamps for Greece first appeared in 1861, although there was a period when British stamps were used at Salonika.

Write to: Hellenic Post Office
ELTA Philatelic Service
100 Aeolou Street, Athens 131
Greece

Currency: 100 lepta = 1 drachma
(£1.00 = DR115.00; US $1.00 = DR50.15 approx.)

Definitives

The present definitive series features local scenes. Stamps are also issued for the paying of airmail postage.

Commemoratives

About ten commemorative sets appear each year, mainly of a local flavour, although several tend to be 'thematic' in their approach. Stamps to raise funds for charity have been issued from time to time. First day covers are made available.

Postal stationery

ΑΕΡΟΓΡΑΜΜΑ - AEROGRAMME

A stamped aerogramme and postcard are available for use.

43

Bulgaria

HP БЪЛГАРИЯ.

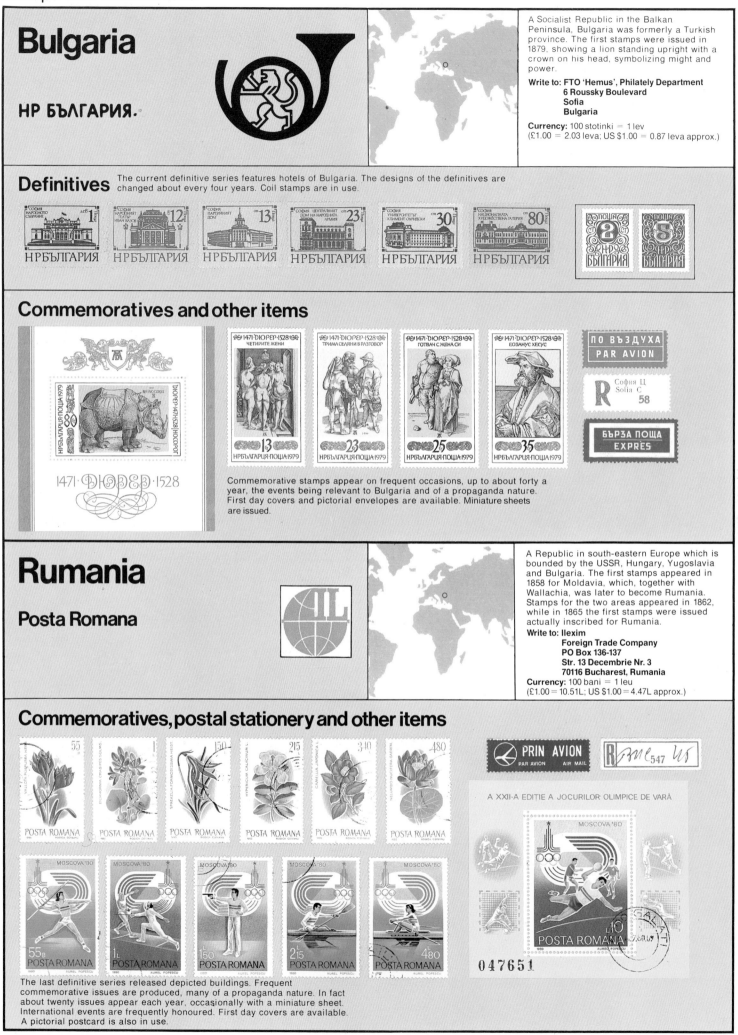

A Socialist Republic in the Balkan Peninsula, Bulgaria was formerly a Turkish province. The first stamps were issued in 1879, showing a lion standing upright with a crown on his head, symbolizing might and power.

Write to: FTO 'Hemus', Philately Department
6 Roussky Boulevard
Sofia
Bulgaria

Currency: 100 stotinki = 1 lev
(£1.00 = 2.03 leva; US $1.00 = 0.87 leva approx.)

Definitives

The current definitive series features hotels of Bulgaria. The designs of the definitives are changed about every four years. Coil stamps are in use.

Commemoratives and other items

Commemorative stamps appear on frequent occasions, up to about forty a year, the events being relevant to Bulgaria and of a propaganda nature. First day covers and pictorial envelopes are available. Miniature sheets are issued.

Rumania

Posta Romana

A Republic in south-eastern Europe which is bounded by the USSR, Hungary, Yugoslavia and Bulgaria. The first stamps appeared in 1858 for Moldavia, which, together with Wallachia, was later to become Rumania. Stamps for the two areas appeared in 1862, while in 1865 the first stamps were issued actually inscribed for Rumania.

Write to: Ilexim
Foreign Trade Company
PO Box 136-137
Str. 13 Decembrie Nr. 3
70116 Bucharest, Rumania

Currency: 100 bani = 1 leu
(£1.00 = 10.51L; US $1.00 = 4.47L approx.)

Commemoratives, postal stationery and other items

The last definitive series released depicted buildings. Frequent commemorative issues are produced, many of a propaganda nature. In fact about twenty issues appear each year, occasionally with a miniature sheet. International events are frequently honoured. First day covers are available. A pictorial postcard is also in use.

USSR
ПОЧТА СССР

The USSR came into being on December 30, 1922, and the first stamps to be inscribed as such first appeared in 1923. These first definitives showed a worker, peasant and soldier. Separate stamp issues for the territories which formed the Union had earlier appeared.

Write to: Mezhdunarodnaya Kniga
Sovinphilatelia
32/34 Smolenskaya Sennaya
121200 Moscow, USSR

Currency: 100 kopecks = 1 rouble
(£1.00 = 1.57R; US $1.00 = 0.73R approx.)

Definitives

There is a definitive series in use, the designs of which are symbolic of Soviet achievement.

Commemoratives and postal stationery

Commemorative stamps appear very frequently, many being of a propaganda nature. However, most issues only comprise a single, low value. Miniature sheets are produced, and first day covers are prepared. The subjects chosen are both national and international, with many designs being thematic in their approach. Up to 400 envelopes and postcards are produced annually, many with specially imprinted stamps.

Malta

A Mediterranean island, the origins of which date back to Stone and Bronze Age, which by the Congress of Vienna became British in 1815 until independence in 1964. British stamps were in use from 1857, but in 1860 a ½d stamp inscribed Malta was released, intended for local use. Further stamps inscribed Malta did not appear until 1885.

**Write to: Philatelic Bureau
General Post Office
Auberge d'Italie
Valletta, Malta**

Currency: 100 mils = 1 cent; 100 cents = 1 pound
(£1.00 = £M0.83; US $1.00 = £M0.38 approx.)

Definitives

The current definitives, released from 1973, show various aspects of local life, ranging from fishing to pottery, fiesta to education. In addition, six stamps have been issued for use on letters being sent by airmail.

Commemoratives

There are about five commemorative sets each year, most of which can be noted for the distinctive, often stylistic, designs. Events commemorated relate directly to Malta. First day covers are available as are presentation packs. Miniature sheets are occasionally produced. Stamps are sold at a premium.

Postal stationery and postage dues

The current series of postage dues was released in 1973. Unstamped aerogrammes and registered envelopes are on sale.

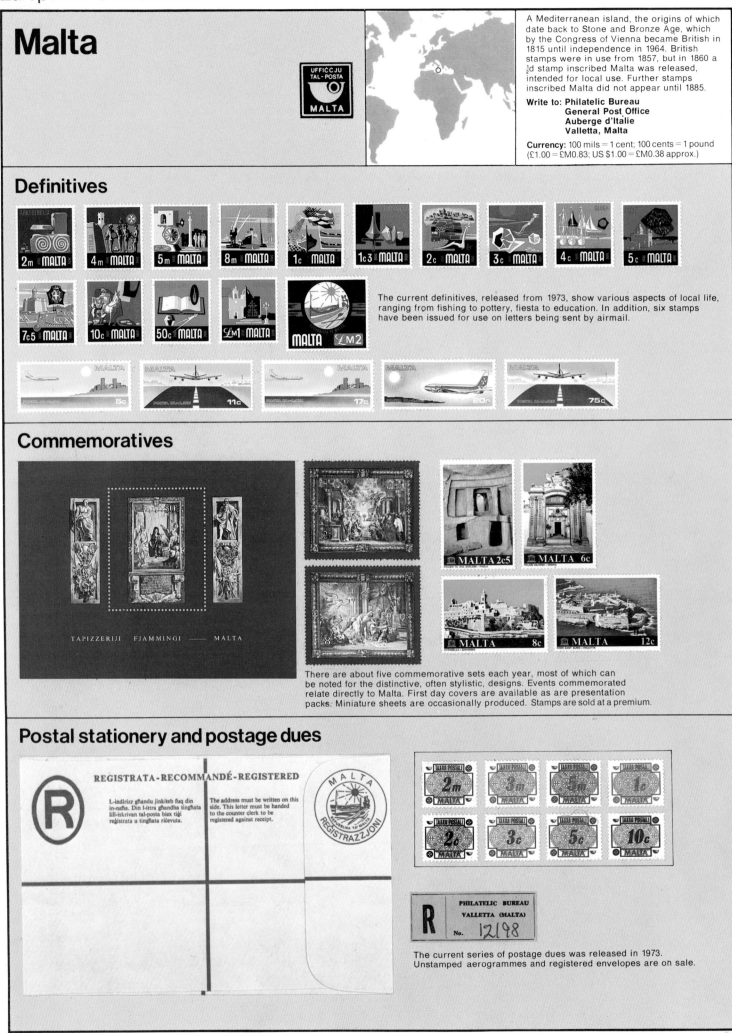

Turkey

Türkiye Cumhuriyeti

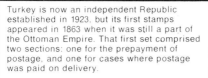

Turkey is now an independent Republic established in 1923, but its first stamps appeared in 1863 when it was still a part of the Ottoman Empire. That first set comprised two sections: one for the prepayment of postage, and one for cases where postage was paid on delivery.

**Write to: Direction Générale des PTT
Départment des Postes
Section de Timbres-Poste
Ankara, Turkey**

Currency: 100 kurus = 1 lira
(£1.00 = 216.00L; US $1.00 = 96.00L approx.)

Definitives

The definitives at present in use comprise two series: one promotes the idea of road safety, while the second features a portrait of Kemal Ataturk, which is changed frequently.

Commemoratives

The commemorative stamps are of Turkish importance, and comprise on average eleven issues a year. The designs are frequently 'thematic Miniature sheets are occasionally issued, usually for local philatelic exhibitions.

Postal stationery and other items

A stamped postcard and aerogrammes are in use, and a stamp booklet is produced from time to time. Official stamps are issued.

North America · Caribbean

Anguilla	62	Cayman Islands	57	Jamaica	63	Turks and Caicos Islands	61
Antigua	59	Cuba	55	Montserrat	61	United Nations (Austria)	49
Bahamas	57	Dominica	56	Netherlands Antilles	68	United Nations (New York)	49
Barbados	58	Dominican Republic	62	Nevis	67	United Nations (Switzerland)	49
Barbuda	59	Grenada	65	St Kitts	65	United States of America	50
Bermuda	54	Grenadines of Grenada	65	St Lucia	56		
British Virgin Islands	66	Grenadines of St Vincent	64	St Vincent	64		
Canada	52	Haiti	55	Trinidad and Tobago	60		

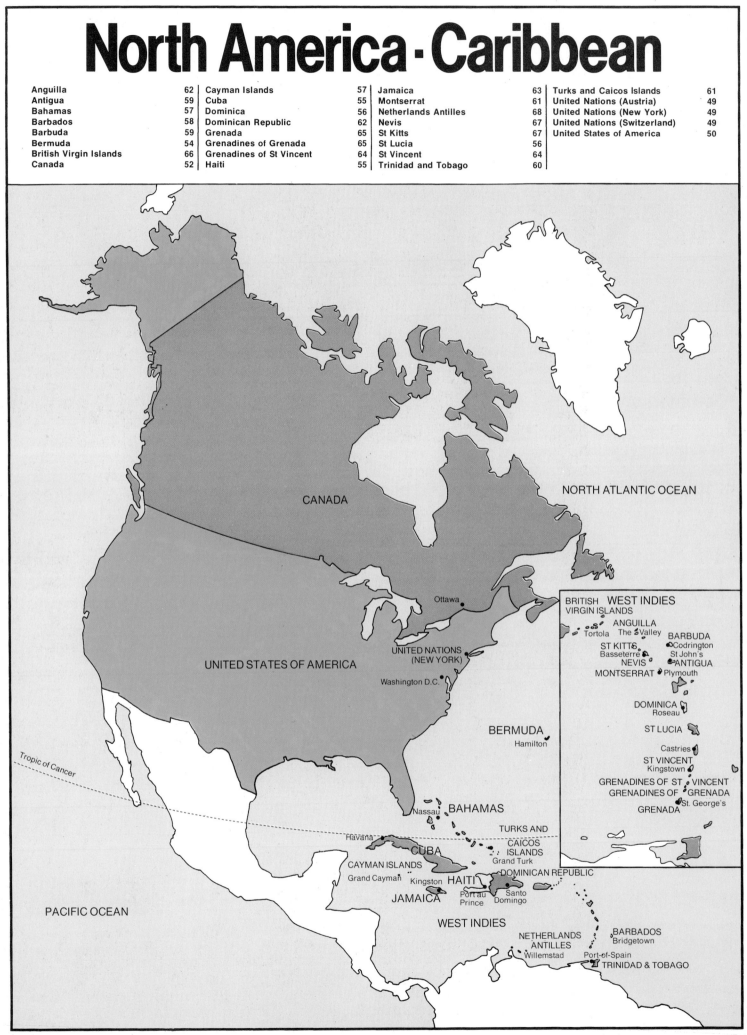

United Nations

New York

The United Nations General Assembly established its own postal administration in 1951 and arrangements were made so that United Nations stamps and postal stationery could be used on mail from the UN Headquarters in New York. Later, similar arrangements were made for United Nations stamps to be used from Geneva and Vienna, such stamps being recorded under Switzerland and Austria.

Write to: United Nations Postal
Administration
PO Box 5900
New York
N.Y. 10017, USA

Currency: as for USA

United Nations Postal
Administration at Vienna
Internationales Zentrum Wien
A-1400 Vienna, Austria

Currency: as for Austria

United Nations Postal
Administration
Palais des Nations
CH-1211 Geneva 10
Switzerland

Currency: as for Switzerland

Definitives
The definitives show symbolic designs, some of which include the United Nations symbol.

Commemoratives
There are, on average seven commemorative sets each year relating to the work of the United Nations. First day covers are available and a miniature sheet is usually issued once every five years.

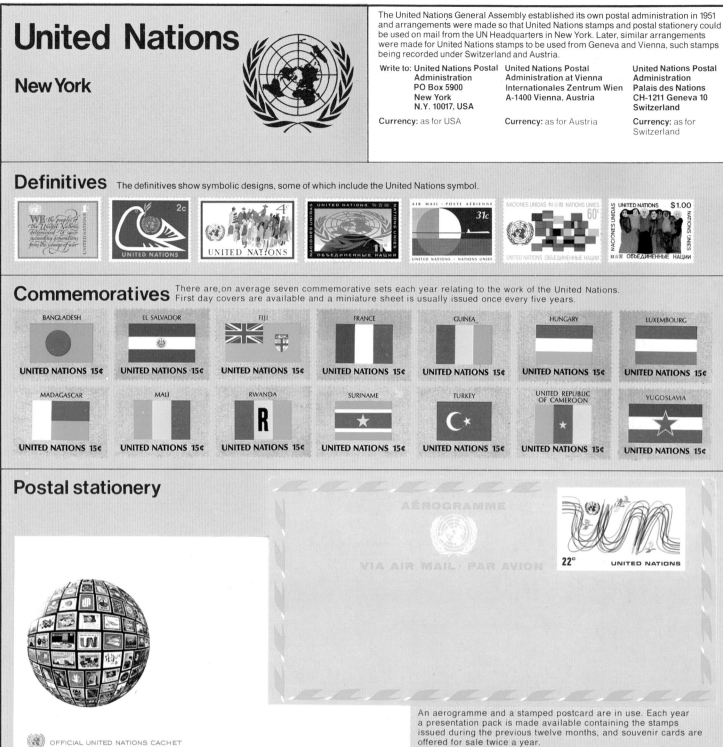

Postal stationery

OFFICIAL UNITED NATIONS CACHET

An aerogramme and a stamped postcard are in use. Each year a presentation pack is made available containing the stamps issued during the previous twelve months, and souvenir cards are offered for sale twice a year.

UN Austria (Vienna) Vereinte Nationen

Stamps were first produced for use at the United Nations Vienna International Centre in 1979. Definitive stamps are in the same designs as the United Nations stamps issued from New York. There are about six commemorative sets each year, relating to major international events. First day covers are available. A postcard is also produced.

UN Switzerland (Geneva) Nations Unies

Stamps were first issued in 1969 for use from United Nations agencies based in Geneva. Previously the Swiss Post Office had provided stamps for these agencies. Definitive stamps are in the same designs as the United Nations stamps issued in New York. There are about six commemorative issues each year reflecting the work of the United Nations. A stamped postcard is available.

United States of America

USA

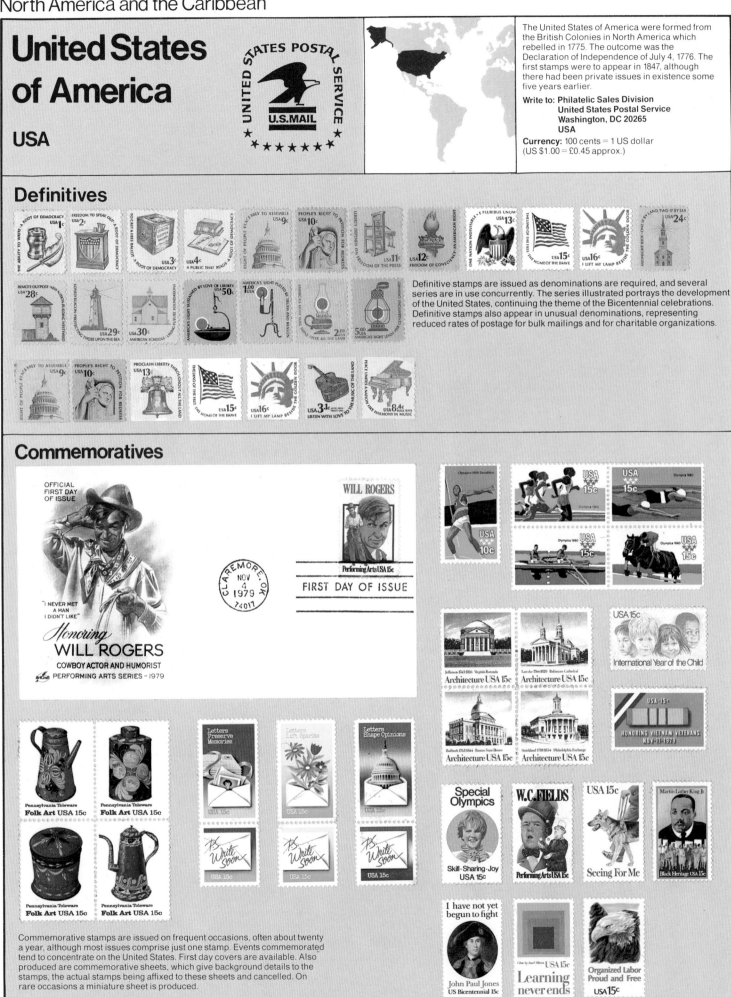

The United States of America were formed from the British Colonies in North America which rebelled in 1775. The outcome was the Declaration of Independence of July 4, 1776. The first stamps were to appear in 1847, although there had been private issues in existence some five years earlier.

Write to: Philatelic Sales Division
United States Postal Service
Washington, DC 20265
USA

Currency: 100 cents = 1 US dollar
(US $1.00 = £0.45 approx.)

Definitives

Definitive stamps are issued as denominations are required, and several series are in use concurrently. The series illustrated portrays the development of the United States, continuing the theme of the Bicentennial celebrations. Definitive stamps also appear in unusual denominations, representing reduced rates of postage for bulk mailings and for charitable organizations.

Commemoratives

Commemorative stamps are issued on frequent occasions, often about twenty a year, although most issues comprise just one stamp. Events commemorated tend to concentrate on the United States. First day covers are available. Also produced are commemorative sheets, which give background details to the stamps, the actual stamps being affixed to these sheets and cancelled. On rare occasions a miniature sheet is produced.

Postal stationery and other items

22c USA

AEROGRAMME VIA AIRMAIL PAR AVION

USAirmail 21c

© USPS 1978

15c STAMPS

by the dawn's early light.

EIGHT STAMPS
Vending Machines Only $1.20

15c Stamps

Sixteen Stamps $2.40

15c Stamps

Twenty Four Stamps $3.60

FIRST, FAST AND RELIABLE
airmail
par avion

EXPRÉS
Special Delivery
PS Label 37

60c
SPECIAL DELIVERY

A range of stationery is produced, including postcards, envelopes and aerogrammes. Frequently the printed 'stamps' on these items are of a commemorative nature. Stamps from the definitive series are made available in booklets and from vending machines. Stamps, booklets and stationery are occasionally released bearing a letter in place of the denomination. These are used at the time of a postage rate increase pending the printing of new stamps inscribed with the required value. Special stamps for airmail postage are in use.

USAirmail 25c

USAirmail 31c

USA 21c
UNITED STATES AIR MAIL

28c
USAirmail
Blanche Stuart Scott
Pioneer Pilot

Glenn Curtiss
Aviation Pioneer
USAirmail 35c

26c
AIRMAIL
Shrine of Democracy
USA

USAirmail 21c

USAirmail 25c

USAirmail 31c

USAirmail 21c

USAirmail 25c

USAirmail 31c

USA 10c
Battle of Kings Mountain, 1780

USA 10c
Landing of Rochambeau, 1780

B
US Postage

B
US Postage

B
US Postage

UNITED STATES POSTAGE DUE
1 CENT

UNITED STATES POSTAGE DUE
5 CENTS

UNITED STATES POSTAGE DUE
10 CENTS

UNITED STATES POSTAGE DUE
50 CENTS

UNITED STATES POSTAGE DUE
1 DOLLAR

UNITED STATES POSTAGE DUE
5 DOLLARS

Canada

Canada Post / Postes Canada

This British Dominion occupies an area in the north of the American Continent almost the size of Europe. The discovery of Canada is credited to John Cabot, a Genoese sailor, in 1497. Stamps inscribed Canada first appeared in 1851: one of the best known Canadian stamps is the 12d black, issued in 1852, showing Queen Victoria.

Write to: Philatelic Service
Canada Post
Ottawa
Canada K1A 0B5

Currency: 100 cents = 1 Canadian dollar (£1.00 = C $2.55; US $1.00 = C $1.20 approx.)

Definitives

The definitive stamps are changed every few years, and tend to take several themes for their design – currently included are flowers, leaves and street scenes. Pre-cancelled and coil stamps are in use.

Commemoratives

Canadian Military Aircraft — Avions militaires canadiens

A number of commemorative series are released each year, although many are confined to the basic inland letter rate. Most of the events commemorated relate solely to Canada. A Christmas issue is released each year: Canada is credited with having issued the first Christmas stamp, a 2c stamp issued in December 1898 which fortuitously was inscribed 'Xmas 1898'. First day covers are made available for new issues. Souvenir packs are occasionally produced.

Postal stationery and other items

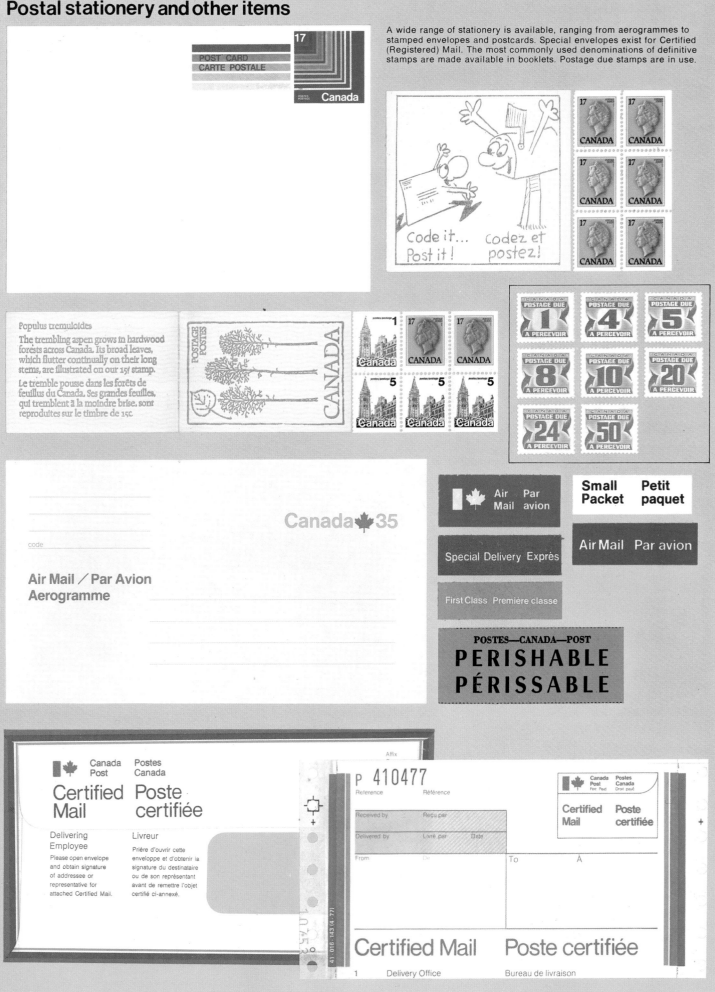

A wide range of stationery is available, ranging from aerogrammes to stamped envelopes and postcards. Special envelopes exist for Certified (Registered) Mail. The most commonly used denominations of definitive stamps are made available in booklets. Postage due stamps are in use.

POST CARD
CARTE POSTALE

17
Canada

Code it... Post it! codez et postez!

Populus tremuloides

The trembling aspen grows in hardwood forests across Canada. Its broad leaves, which flutter continually on their long stems, are illustrated on our 15¢ stamp.

Le tremble pousse dans les forêts de feuillus du Canada. Ses grandes feuilles, qui tremblent à la moindre brise, sont reproduites sur le timbre de 15¢.

Canada 35

code

Air Mail / Par Avion
Aerogramme

Air   Par
Mail avion

Special Delivery   Exprès

First Class   Première classe

Small   Petit
Packet paquet

Air Mail   Par avion

POSTES—CANADA—POST
PERISHABLE
PÉRISSABLE

Canada Post   Postes Canada

Certified Mail   Poste certifiée

Delivering Employee

Please open envelope and obtain signature of addressee or representative for attached Certified Mail.

Livreur

Prière d'ouvrir cette enveloppe et d'obtenir la signature du destinataire ou de son représentant avant de remettre l'objet certifié ci-annexé.

Affix

P 410477

Reference   Référence

Received by   Reçu par

Delivered by   Livré par   Date

From   De   To   À

Canada Post   Postes Canada
Fee Paid   Droit payé

Certified Mail   Poste certifiée

Certified Mail   Poste certifiée

Delivery Office   Bureau de livraison

Bermuda

BERMUDA POST OFFICE

A group of islands in the West Atlantic, known for their idyllic conditions. They were visited by the Spaniard Juan Bermudez in 1515, but were not really inhabited until Sir George Somers was shipwrecked there in 1609. The first stamps appeared in 1848 and were produced by the postmaster of Hamilton, William Perot; they are very rare.

Write to: Philatelic Bureau
General Post Office
Hamilton 5-24
Bermuda

Currency: 100 cents = 1 Bermudan dollar
(£1.00 = B $2.40; US $1.00 = B $1.00 approx.)

Definitives

The current definitives feature the wildlife of Bermuda, ranging from birds to fish.

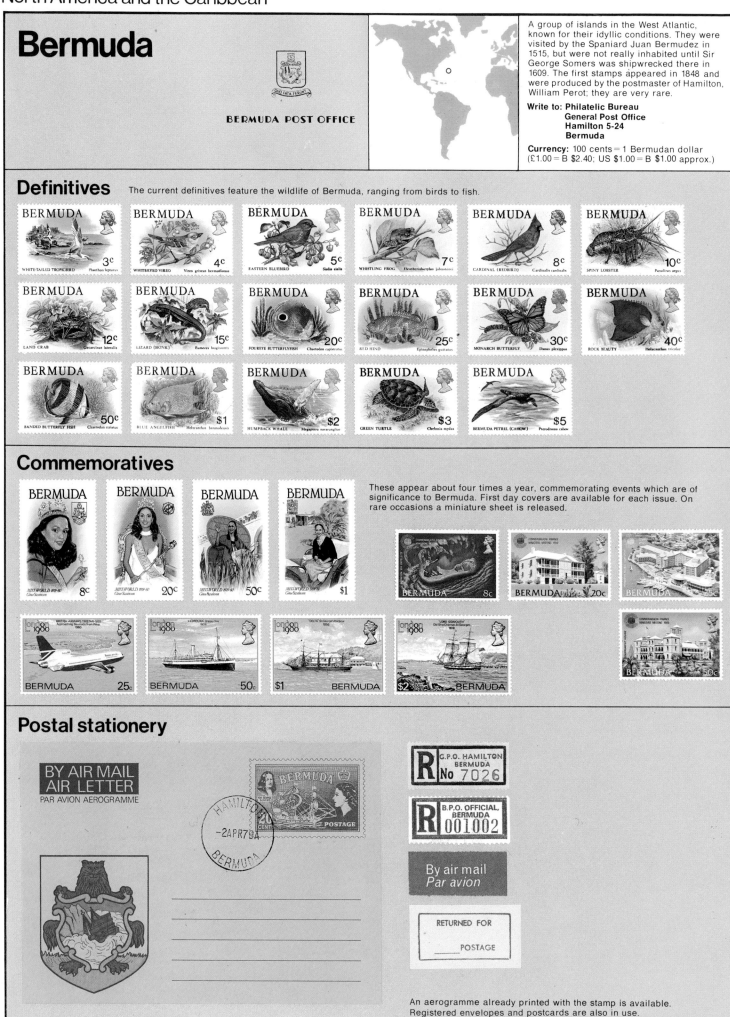

Commemoratives

These appear about four times a year, commemorating events which are of significance to Bermuda. First day covers are available for each issue. On rare occasions a miniature sheet is released.

Postal stationery

An aerogramme already printed with the stamp is available. Registered envelopes and postcards are also in use.

Cuba

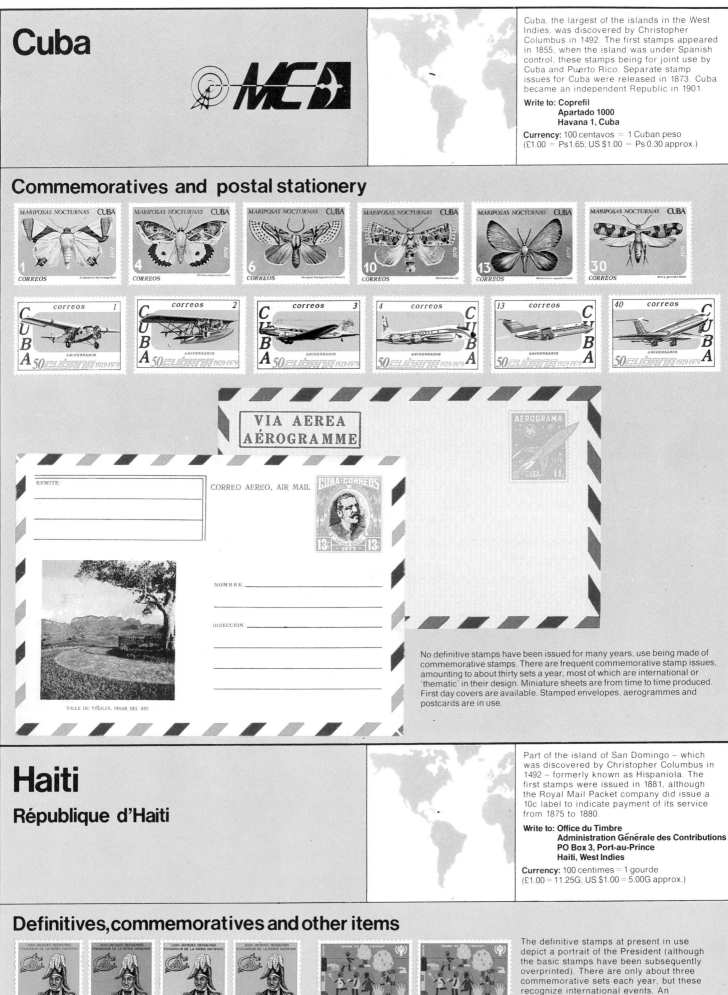

Cuba, the largest of the islands in the West Indies, was discovered by Christopher Columbus in 1492. The first stamps appeared in 1855, when the island was under Spanish control, these stamps being for joint use by Cuba and Puerto Rico. Separate stamp issues for Cuba were released in 1873. Cuba became an independent Republic in 1901.

Write to: Coprefil
Apartado 1000
Havana 1, Cuba

Currency: 100 centavos = 1 Cuban peso
(£1.00 = Ps1.65; US $1.00 = Ps 0.30 approx.)

Commemoratives and postal stationery

No definitive stamps have been issued for many years, use being made of commemorative stamps. There are frequent commemorative stamp issues, amounting to about thirty sets a year, most of which are international or 'thematic' in their design. Miniature sheets are from time to time produced. First day covers are available. Stamped envelopes, aerogrammes and postcards are in use.

VALLE DE VIÑALES, PINAR DEL RIO

Haiti

République d'Haiti

Part of the island of San Domingo – which was discovered by Christopher Columbus in 1492 – formerly known as Hispaniola. The first stamps were issued in 1881, although the Royal Mail Packet company did issue a 10c label to indicate payment of its service from 1875 to 1880.

Write to: Office du Timbre
Administration Générale des Contributions
PO Box 3, Port-au-Prince
Haiti, West Indies

Currency: 100 centimes = 1 gourde
(£1.00 = 11.25G; US $1.00 = 5.00G approx.)

Definitives, commemoratives and other items

The definitive stamps at present in use depict a portrait of the President (although the basic stamps have been subsequently overprinted). There are only about three commemorative sets each year, but these recognize international events. An aerogramme is available.

Dominica

Commonwealth of Dominica

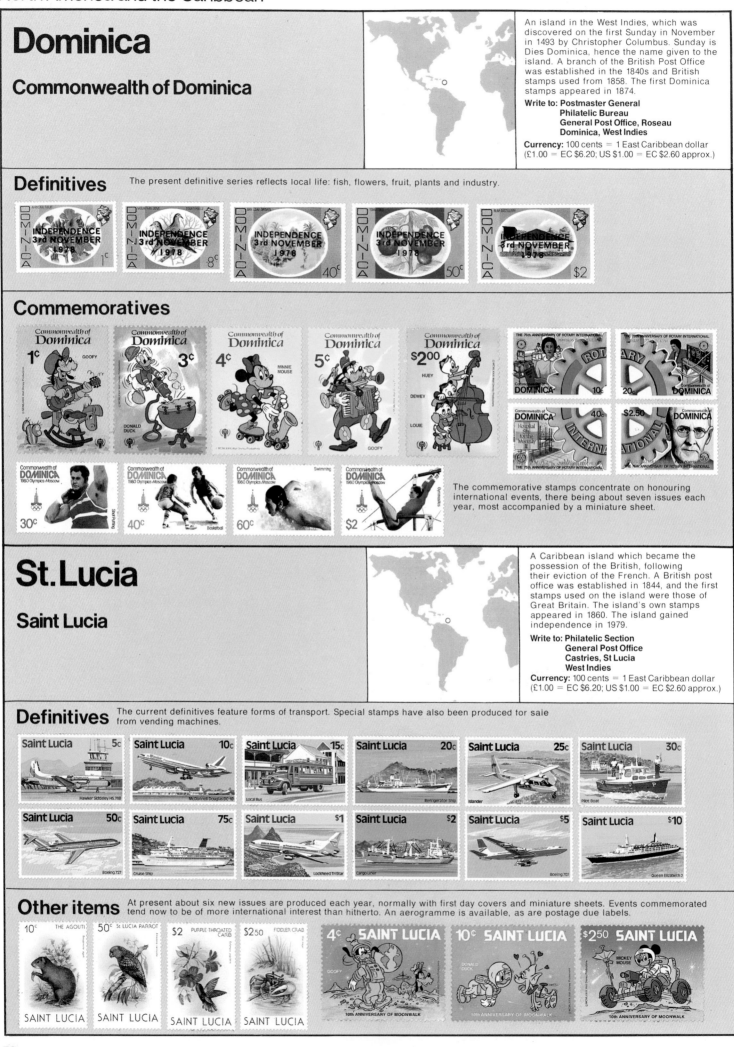

An island in the West Indies, which was discovered on the first Sunday in November in 1493 by Christopher Columbus. Sunday is Dies Dominica, hence the name given to the island. A branch of the British Post Office was established in the 1840s and British stamps used from 1858. The first Dominica stamps appeared in 1874.

Write to: Postmaster General
Philatelic Bureau
General Post Office, Roseau
Dominica, West Indies

Currency: 100 cents = 1 East Caribbean dollar
(£1.00 = EC $6.20; US $1.00 = EC $2.60 approx.)

Definitives

The present definitive series reflects local life: fish, flowers, fruit, plants and industry.

Commemoratives

The commemorative stamps concentrate on honouring international events, there being about seven issues each year, most accompanied by a miniature sheet.

St. Lucia

Saint Lucia

A Caribbean island which became the possession of the British, following their eviction of the French. A British post office was established in 1844, and the first stamps used on the island were those of Great Britain. The island's own stamps appeared in 1860. The island gained independence in 1979.

Write to: Philatelic Section
General Post Office
Castries, St Lucia
West Indies

Currency: 100 cents = 1 East Caribbean dollar
(£1.00 = EC $6.20; US $1.00 = EC $2.60 approx.)

Definitives

The current definitives feature forms of transport. Special stamps have also been produced for sale from vending machines.

Other items

At present about six new issues are produced each year, normally with first day covers and miniature sheets. Events commemorated tend now to be of more international interest than hitherto. An aerogramme is available, as are postage due labels.

Bahamas

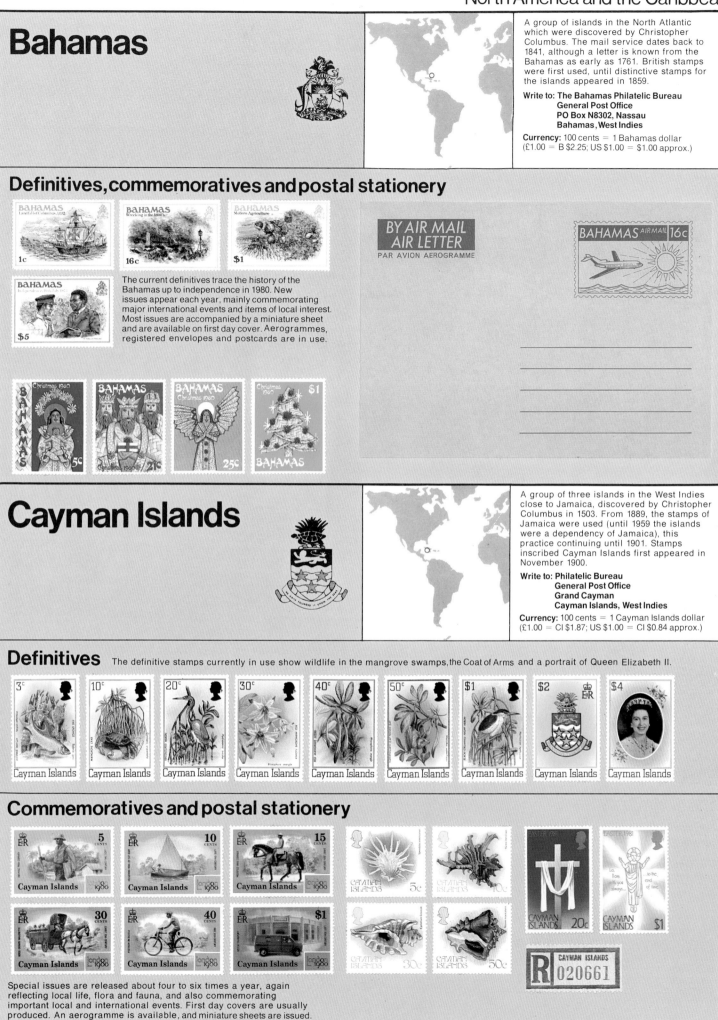

A group of islands in the North Atlantic which were discovered by Christopher Columbus. The mail service dates back to 1841, although a letter is known from the Bahamas as early as 1761. British stamps were first used, until distinctive stamps for the islands appeared in 1859.

Write to: **The Bahamas Philatelic Bureau**
General Post Office
PO Box N8302, Nassau
Bahamas, West Indies

Currency: 100 cents = 1 Bahamas dollar
(£1.00 = B $2.25; US $1.00 = $1.00 approx.)

Definitives, commemoratives and postal stationery

The current definitives trace the history of the Bahamas up to independence in 1980. New issues appear each year, mainly commemorating major international events and items of local interest. Most issues are accompanied by a miniature sheet and are available on first day cover. Aerogrammes, registered envelopes and postcards are in use.

Cayman Islands

A group of three islands in the West Indies close to Jamaica, discovered by Christopher Columbus in 1503. From 1889, the stamps of Jamaica were used (until 1959 the islands were a dependency of Jamaica), this practice continuing until 1901. Stamps inscribed Cayman Islands first appeared in November 1900.

Write to: **Philatelic Bureau**
General Post Office
Grand Cayman
Cayman Islands, West Indies

Currency: 100 cents = 1 Cayman Islands dollar
(£1.00 = CI $1.87; US $1.00 = CI $0.84 approx.)

Definitives

The definitive stamps currently in use show wildlife in the mangrove swamps, the Coat of Arms and a portrait of Queen Elizabeth II.

Commemoratives and postal stationery

Special issues are released about four to six times a year, again reflecting local life, flora and fauna, and also commemorating important local and international events. First day covers are usually produced. An aerogramme is available, and miniature sheets are issued.

Barbados

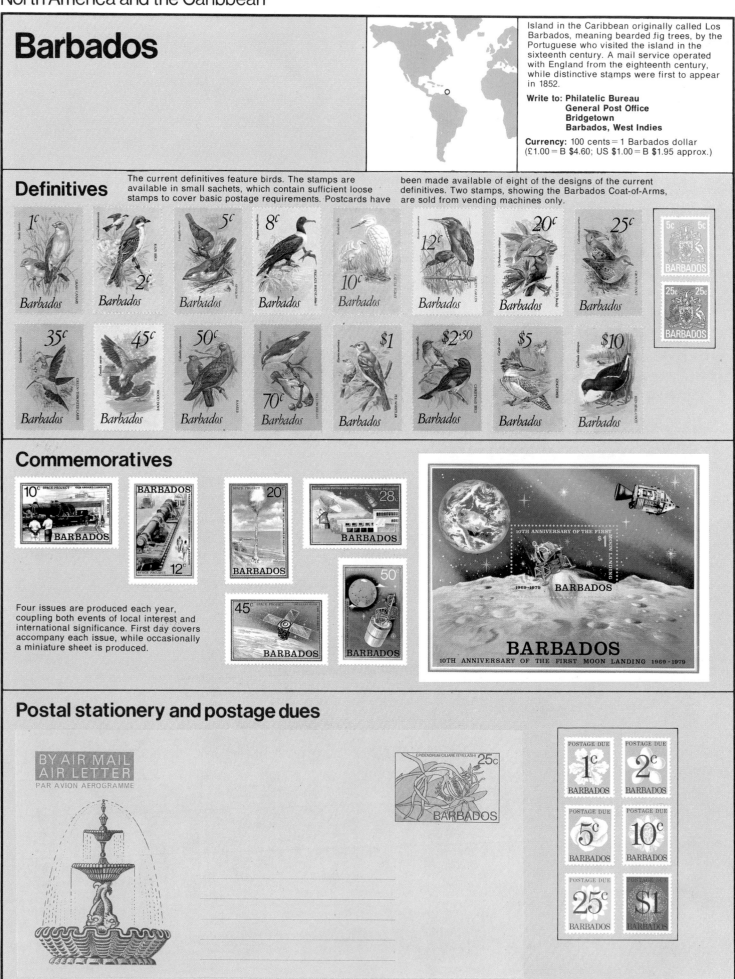

Island in the Caribbean originally called Los Barbados, meaning bearded fig trees, by the Portuguese who visited the island in the sixteenth century. A mail service operated with England from the eighteenth century, while distinctive stamps were first to appear in 1852.

Write to: Philatelic Bureau
General Post Office
Bridgetown
Barbados, West Indies

Currency: 100 cents = 1 Barbados dollar
(£1.00 = B $4.60; US $1.00 = B $1.95 approx.)

Definitives

The current definitives feature birds. The stamps are available in small sachets, which contain sufficient loose stamps to cover basic postage requirements. Postcards have been made available of eight of the designs of the current definitives. Two stamps, showing the Barbados Coat-of-Arms, are sold from vending machines only.

Commemoratives

Four issues are produced each year, coupling both events of local interest and international significance. First day covers accompany each issue, while occasionally a miniature sheet is produced.

Postal stationery and postage dues

Postal stationery available consists of an aerogramme, postcard and registered envelope. Postage due labels are in use.

Antigua

An island in the West Indies which was discovered in 1493 by Christopher Columbus and named by him after the Church of Santa Maria la Antigua in Seville. Its first stamps were issued in 1862, to be replaced for a short period by the issues of the Leeward Islands. For a time stamps of Antigua and Leeward Islands were used jointly.

Write to: Philatelic Bureau
GPO, St John's
Antigua
West Indies

Currency: 100 cents = 1 East Caribbean dollar
(£1.00 = EC $6.20; US $1.00 = EC $2.60 approx.)

Definitives

The current definitive series is a reflection of life on the island, depicting its flowers, birds, important buildings and so on.

Commemoratives and other items

Commemorative stamps are released on about seven occasions each year, mainly in honour of international events and frequently 'thematic' in their design. Miniature sheets are often issued. Coil stamps were introduced in Antigua a few years ago, but their use now seems to be very limited. Stamp booklets are available from time to time. An aerogramme is also in use.

Barbuda

and Redonda

Barbuda and Redonda are both small island dependencies of Antigua. All reports indicate that Redonda in uninhabited. Stamps for Barbuda, being overprints on the definitives of the Leeward Islands, appeared in 1922. Following a long period when Antigua stamps were used, the islands' own issues again appeared in 1968.

Write to: Philatelic Bureau
Barbuda Post Office
West Indies, via Antigua

Currency: 100 cents = 1 East Caribbean dollar
(£1.00 = EC $6.20; US $1.00 = EC $2.60 approx.)

Definitives

The present definitive series of Barbuda depicts birds. The current definitive of Antigua also exists overprinted 'Barbuda'.

Commemoratives and other items

Commemorative stamps frequently appear, either inscribed Barbuda, or as overprints on the commemoratives of Antigua. The events are international in their appeal, while the designs are aimed at 'thematic' collectors. Stamp booklets are occasionally made available.
Stamps are also issued inscribed Redonda, but their appearance seems hardly justified.

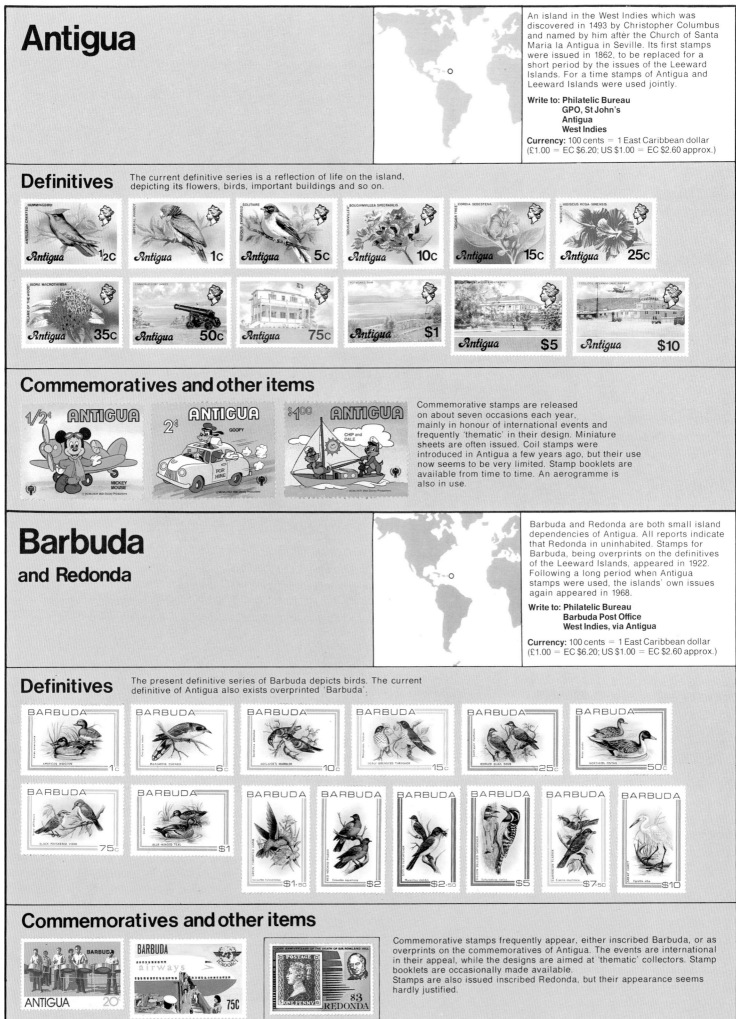

Trinidad and Tobago

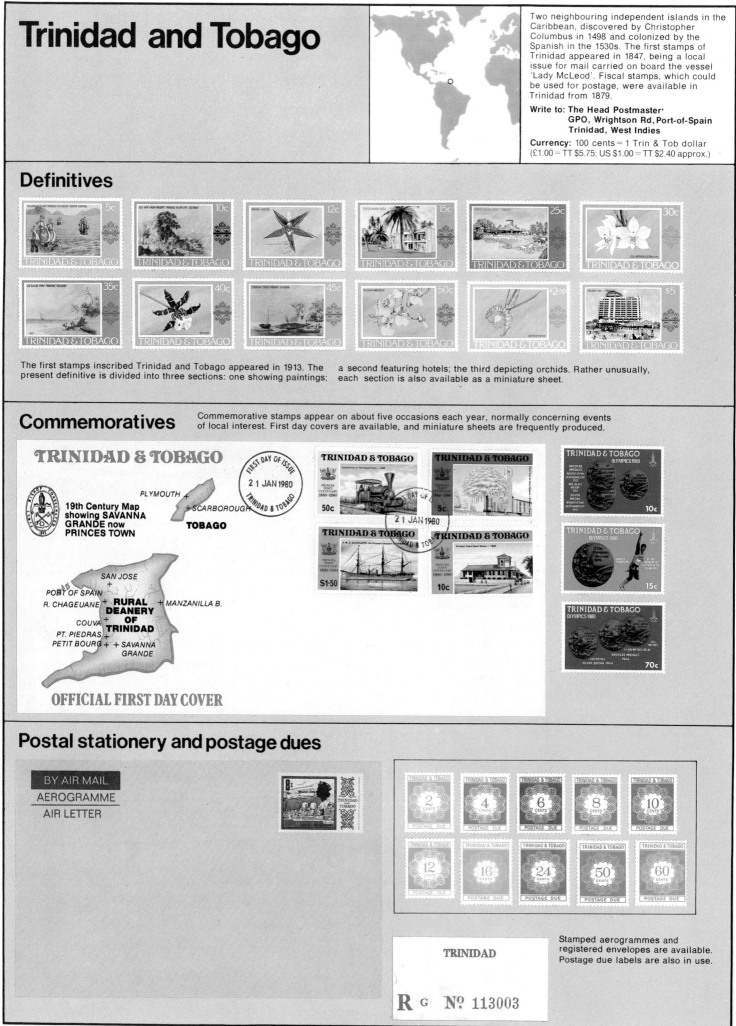

Two neighbouring independent islands in the Caribbean, discovered by Christopher Columbus in 1498 and colonized by the Spanish in the 1530s. The first stamps of Trinidad appeared in 1847, being a local issue for mail carried on board the vessel 'Lady McLeod'. Fiscal stamps, which could be used for postage, were available in Trinidad from 1879.

Write to: The Head Postmaster·
GPO, Wrightson Rd, Port-of-Spain
Trinidad, West Indies

Currency: 100 cents = 1 Trin & Tob dollar
(£1.00 = TT $5.75; US $1.00 = TT $2.40 approx.)

Definitives

The first stamps inscribed Trinidad and Tobago appeared in 1913. The present definitive is divided into three sections: one showing paintings; a second featuring hotels; the third depicting orchids. Rather unusually, each section is also available as a miniature sheet.

Commemoratives

Commemorative stamps appear on about five occasions each year, normally concerning events of local interest. First day covers are available, and miniature sheets are frequently produced.

Postal stationery and postage dues

Stamped aerogrammes and registered envelopes are available. Postage due labels are also in use.

Montserrat

A Caribbean island, frequently known as the 'Emerald Isle' thanks to the lush green appearance of its forests, and the Irish brogue of its inhabitants. The island was discovered by Christopher Columbus in 1493. Between 1858 and 1860 British stamps were used; in 1876 the stamps of Antigua overprinted 'Montserrat' appeared. Stamps inscribed Montserrat were introduced in 1903.

Write to: Montserrat Philatelic Bureau Ltd
GPO Plymouth, Montserrat
West Indies

Currency: 100 cents = 1 East Caribbean dollar (£1.00 = EC $6.20; US $1.00 = EC $2.60 approx.)

Definitives

A new definitive series was introduced early in 1981 depicting Caribbean fish.

Commemoratives and other items

About five commemorative stamp issues are released each year, mainly celebrating important international events. First day covers are available on each occasion. Frequently a miniature sheet is also produced, and from time to time a stamp booklet containing the special stamps also appears. Stamps overprinted 'O.H.M.S.' are used by the Philatelic Bureau on its correspondence.

Turks and Caicos Islands

Turks & Caicos Islands Philatelic Bureau

A group of islands in the Caribbean, of which the largest is Grand Turk. The Turks group was discovered in 1512 and initially inhabited in 1678 by settlers from Bermuda. Stamps for the Turks Islands were first issued in 1867: for the combined Turks and Caicos Islands, stamps appeared in 1900.

Write to: Turks & Caicos Islands
Philatelic Bureau
Grand Turk
Turks & Caicos Islands, West Indies

Currency: 100 cents = 1 US dollar (£1.00 = US $2.20 approx.)

Definitives

The present definitive series features fish.

Commemoratives and other items

The first commemorative set from the Turks and Caicos Islands appeared in 1948 to mark the centenary of the separation of the group from the Bahamas. Today about seven commemorative sets are produced each year, with an international flavour, most sets being accompanied by a miniature sheet. Booklets containing commemorative stamps are occasionally produced.

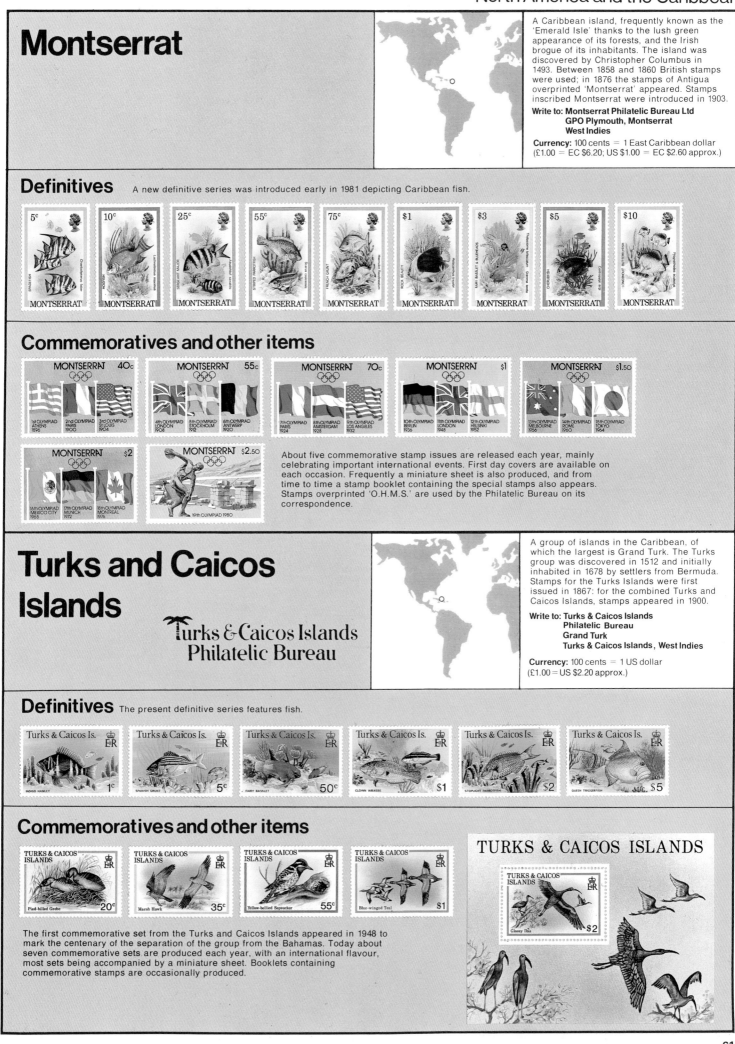

Anguilla

POSTMASTER ANGUILLA

A small group of islands in the West Indies settled by the British in 1650. It was politically attached to the larger grouping of St Kitts Nevis Anguilla, until this grouping was granted Associated Statehood, upon which Anguilla declared herself 'independent'. Anguilla was restored to British control by the Anguilla Act of 1971.

Write to: The Postmaster
Post Office
The Valley
Anguilla
West Indies

Currency: 100 cents = 1 East Caribbean dollar (£1.00 = EC $6.20; US $1.00 = EC $2.60 approx.)

Definitives

The first definitives for Anguilla were issued in 1967, being the then current issue of St Kitts Nevis Anguilla with the territory name obliterated and 'Independent Anguilla' added. The current definitives depict various aspects of life on the islands, including birds, fishes and flowers.

Commemoratives and other items

Commemorative stamps are issued about four to six times a year, celebrating both local and international events; there is usually a set for Christmas. Most commemorative sets are accompanied by a miniature sheet and a first day cover. Aerogrammes have appeared with special 'stamp' design inscribed Anguilla, but blank aerogrammes are also used to which the appropriate definitive stamps are attached. Stamp booklets are on sale.

Dominican Republic

República Dominicana

The eastern part of the island of San Domingo in the West Indies (the western part is known as Haiti), which became independent of Spanish control in 1865. In that same year it started issuing its own stamps. The island was first discovered by Christopher Columbus.

Write to: Dirección General de Correos
Sección Filatélica
Santo Domingo
Dominican Republic

Currency: 100 centavos = 1 Dominican peso (£1.00 = RD$2.25; US $1.00 = RD$1.00 approx.)

Definitives and commemoratives

The definitive series (not illustrated) depicts the National Shrine. There are about twenty commemorative sets released each year, which include an obligatory Tax stamp, this being used to raise money for such things as child welfare and tuberculosis relief.

Postal stationery and other items

Also available are special stamps for express delivery (first introduced in 1920), for registered mail (introduced in 1935) and postage due labels.

Jamaica

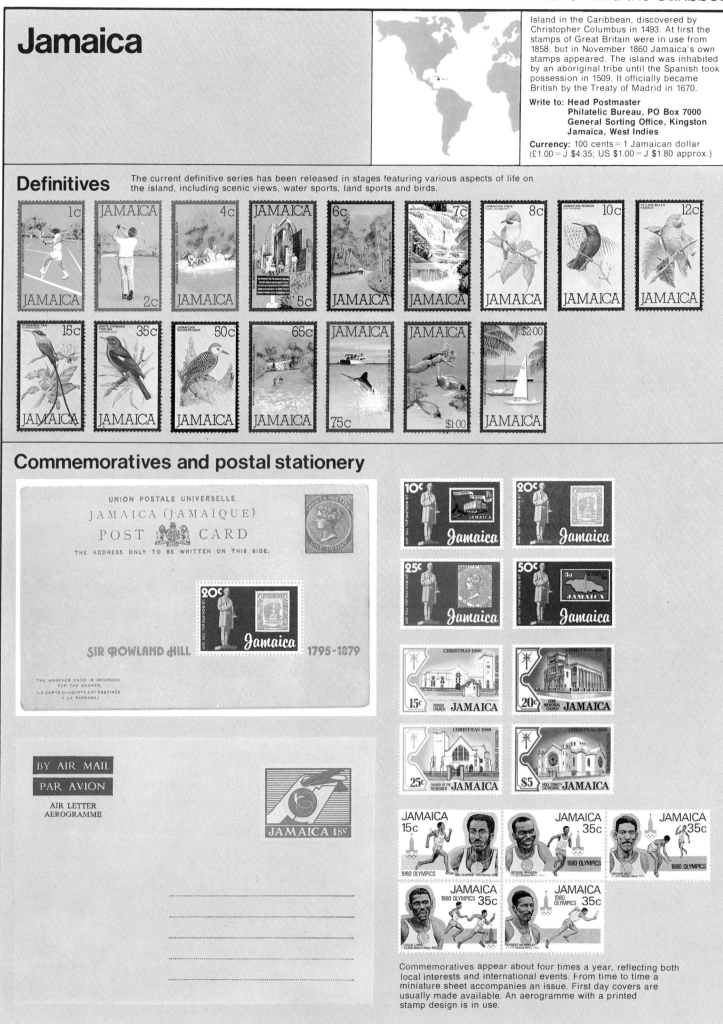

Island in the Caribbean, discovered by Christopher Columbus in 1493. At first the stamps of Great Britain were in use from 1858, but in November 1860 Jamaica's own stamps appeared. The island was inhabited by an aboriginal tribe until the Spanish took possession in 1509. It officially became British by the Treaty of Madrid in 1670.

Write to: Head Postmaster
Philatelic Bureau, PO Box 7000
General Sorting Office, Kingston
Jamaica, West Indies

Currency: 100 cents = 1 Jamaican dollar
(£1.00 = J $4.35; US $1.00 = J $1.80 approx.)

Definitives

The current definitive series has been released in stages featuring various aspects of life on the island, including scenic views, water sports, land sports and birds.

Commemoratives and postal stationery

UNION POSTALE UNIVERSELLE
JAMAICA (JAMAÏQUE)
POST CARD
THE ADDRESS ONLY TO BE WRITTEN ON THIS SIDE.

SIR ROWLAND HILL
1795-1879

THE ANNEXED CARD IS INTENDED
FOR THE ANSWER.
(LA CARTE CI-JOINTE EST DESTINÉE
À LA RÉPONSE.)

BY AIR MAIL
PAR AVION

AIR LETTER
AEROGRAMME

JAMAICA 18c

Commemoratives appear about four times a year, reflecting both local interests and international events. From time to time a miniature sheet accompanies an issue. First day covers are usually made available. An aerogramme with a printed stamp design is in use.

St. Vincent

An island in the Caribbean, discovered by Christopher Columbus on St Vincent's Day in 1498. At first British stamps were in use – from 1855 until 1861 – although St Vincent's own stamps were introduced in 1861.

Write to: Philatelic Services
General Post Office
Kingstown, St Vincent
West Indies

Currency: 100 cents = 1 East Caribbean dollar
(£1.00 = EC $6.20; US $1.00 = EC $2.60 approx.)

Definitives, commemoratives and other items

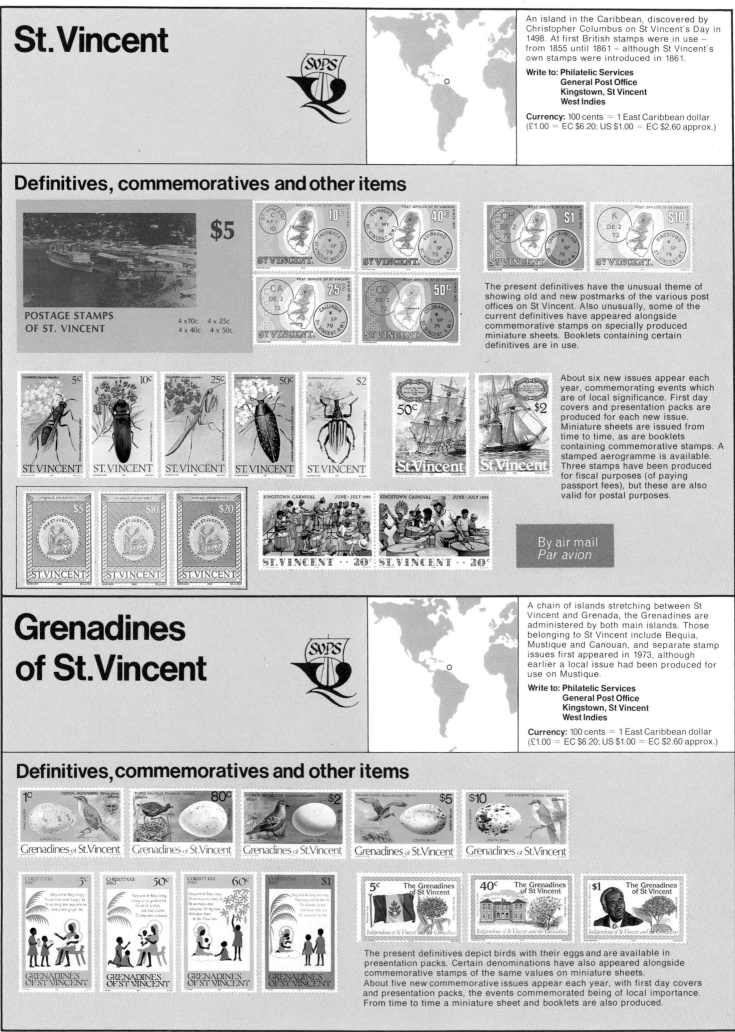

POSTAGE STAMPS
OF ST. VINCENT

4 x 10c.   4 x 25c.
4 x 40c.   4 x 50c.

The present definitives have the unusual theme of showing old and new postmarks of the various post offices on St Vincent. Also unusually, some of the current definitives have appeared alongside commemorative stamps on specially produced miniature sheets. Booklets containing certain definitives are in use.

About six new issues appear each year, commemorating events which are of local significance. First day covers and presentation packs are produced for each new issue. Miniature sheets are issued from time to time, as are booklets containing commemorative stamps. A stamped aerogramme is available. Three stamps have been produced for fiscal purposes (of paying passport fees), but these are also valid for postal purposes.

By air mail
Par avion

Grenadines of St. Vincent

A chain of islands stretching between St Vincent and Grenada, the Grenadines are administered by both main islands. Those belonging to St Vincent include Bequia, Mustique and Canouan, and separate stamp issues first appeared in 1973, although earlier a local issue had been produced for use on Mustique.

Write to: Philatelic Services
General Post Office
Kingstown, St Vincent
West Indies

Currency: 100 cents = 1 East Caribbean dollar
(£1.00 = EC $6.20; US $1.00 = EC $2.60 approx.)

Definitives, commemoratives and other items

The present definitives depict birds with their eggs and are available in presentation packs. Certain denominations have also appeared alongside commemorative stamps of the same values on miniature sheets.
About five new commemorative issues appear each year, with first day covers and presentation packs, the events commemorated being of local importance. From time to time a miniature sheet and booklets are also produced.

Grenada

An island in the West Indies which is now independent. It was discovered in 1498 by Christopher Columbus, who called the island 'La Concepcion'. British stamps were used from 1858, but three years later distinctive stamps for Grenada were introduced.

Write to: The Postmaster General
General Post Office
St. George's, Grenada
West Indies

Currency: 100 cents = 1 East Caribbean dollar (£1.00 = EC $6.20; US $1.00 = EC $2.60 approx.)

Definitives The definitives at present in use show ships.

Commemoratives and other items

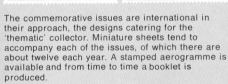

The commemorative issues are international in their approach, the designs catering for the 'thematic' collector. Miniature sheets tend to accompany each of the issues, of which there are about twelve each year. A stamped aerogramme is available and from time to time a booklet is produced.

Grenadines of Grenada
Grenada Grenadines

The Grenadines are a string of islands which lie between the West Indian islands of Grenada and St Vincent. Both Grenada and St Vincent have in recent years produced separate stamp issues for their respective sections of the Grenadines. The most important island in the Grenada Grenadines group is Carriacou.

Write to: The Postmaster General
General Post Office
St. George's, Grenada
West Indies

Currency: 100 cents = 1 East Caribbean dollar (£1.00 = EC $6.20; US $1.00 = EC $2.60 approx.)

Definitives The current definitives are in designs depicting fish.

Commemoratives

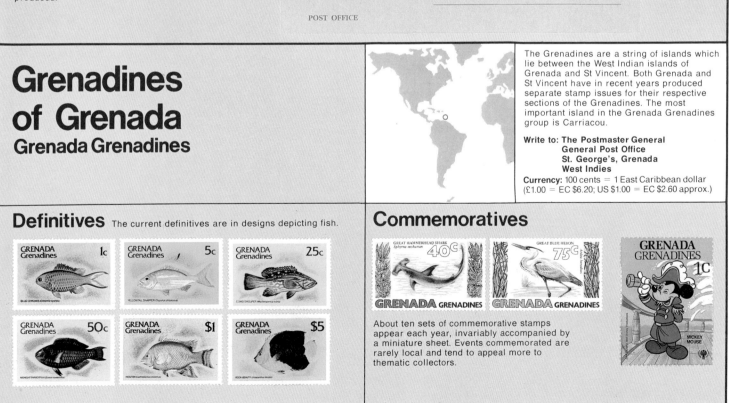

About ten sets of commemorative stamps appear each year, invariably accompanied by a miniature sheet. Events commemorated are rarely local and tend to appeal more to thematic collectors.

British Virgin Islands

A group of islands in the West Indies, of which eight inhabited islands form the British Virgin Islands, the remainder being administered by the United States of America. The group was discovered by Christopher Columbus, who called the largest island St Ursula and the others, the 11,000 Virgins.

Write to: **British Virgin Islands**
Chief Postmaster
GPO, Road Town
Tortola, British Virgin Islands

Currency: 100 cents = 1 United States dollar (£1.00 = US $2.20 approx.)

Definitives

The first stamps of the group were issued in 1866 and depict St Ursula. The current definitives feature marine life.

Commemoratives and postal stationery

About four to five commemorative sets are released each year, usually with a local significance. First day covers are prepared. On occasions a miniature sheet is also produced. A pictorial aerogramme is in use, bearing a 'printed' stamp.

Official First Day Cover

British Virgin Islands

Drake Commemorative

By Air Mail - Air Letter
Par Avion - Aerogramme

Caribbean

Treasure Chest

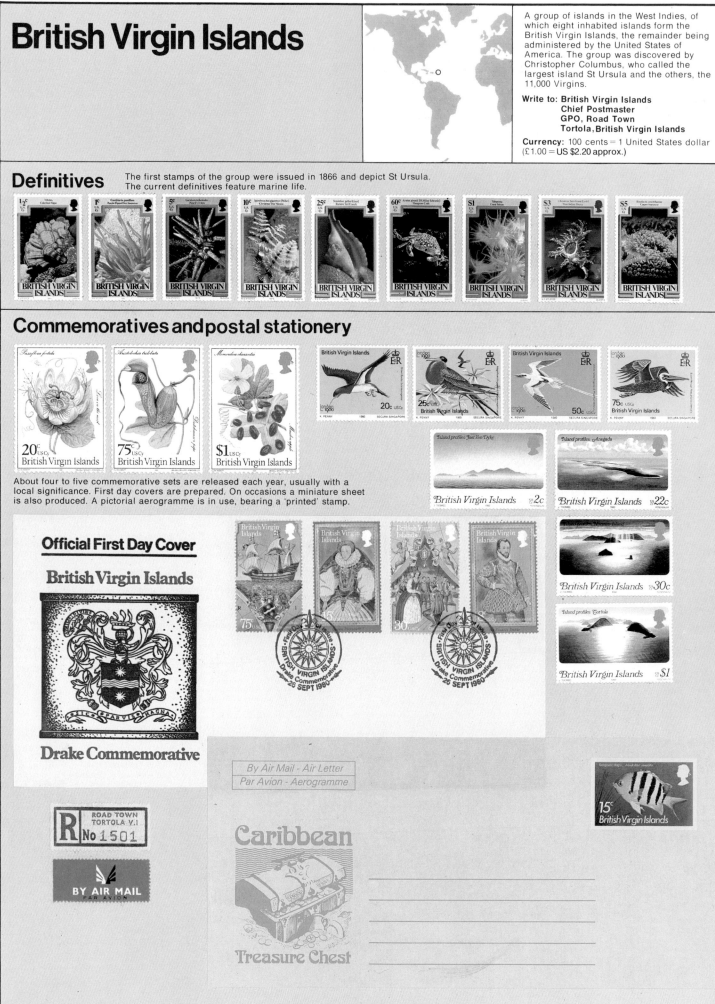

Nevis

A West Indian island, discovered by Christopher Columbus in 1493, which has formed part of the Associated State of St Kitts Nevis. A post office was established in 1710 and at first British stamps were used. From 1861 until 1890 stamps inscribed Nevis were issued, being replaced by stamps inscribed St Kitts-Nevis in 1903, and by St Christopher Nevis Anguilla from 1952.

Write to: Nevis Philatelic Bureau
Head Post Office
Nevis
West Indies

Currency: 100 cents = 1 East Caribbean dollar (£1.00 = EC $6.20; US $1.00 = EC $2.60 approx.)

Definitives

With the re-introduction of separate stamp issues for Nevis in 1980, the former definitives of St Christopher Nevis Anguilla were issued with the words 'St Christopher' and 'Anguilla' blacked out. These overprinted stamps also exist with the further overprint 'Official' for use by the Philatelic Bureau. A new definitive series, released in 1981, shows local scenes. The stamps are overprinted for Official use.

Commemoratives and other items

About four to five new issues are planned each year, all available on first day cover. It is expected that miniature sheets and presentation packs will be produced. A booklet is already in use, as well as maximum cards.

St. Kitts

A Caribbean island which has formed part of St Christopher (known locally as St Kitts) Nevis Anguilla grouping. Separate stamp issues inscribed St Christopher appeared from 1870 to 1890, when they were discontinued in favour of stamps inscribed Leeward Islands. Stamps inscribed St Kitts Nevis first appeared in 1903. St Kitts again issued its own stamps in 1980.

Write to: St. Kitts Philatelic Bureau
General Post Office, Basseterre
St Kitts
West Indies

Currency: 100 cents = 1 East Caribbean dollar (£1.00 = EC $6.20; US $1.00 = EC $2.60 approx.)

Definitives

The definitives of St Christopher Nevis Anguilla, with the old territory name obliterated and the legend 'St Kitts' overprinted, were introduced. The same stamps were also overprinted 'Official' for use by the Philatelic Bureau. A new series released in 1981 depicts birds. These are also overprinted 'Official'

Commemoratives and other items

The intention is to release four new issues each year of local significance or international importance. First day covers and presentation packs will be provided. It is expected that miniature sheets will also be produced.

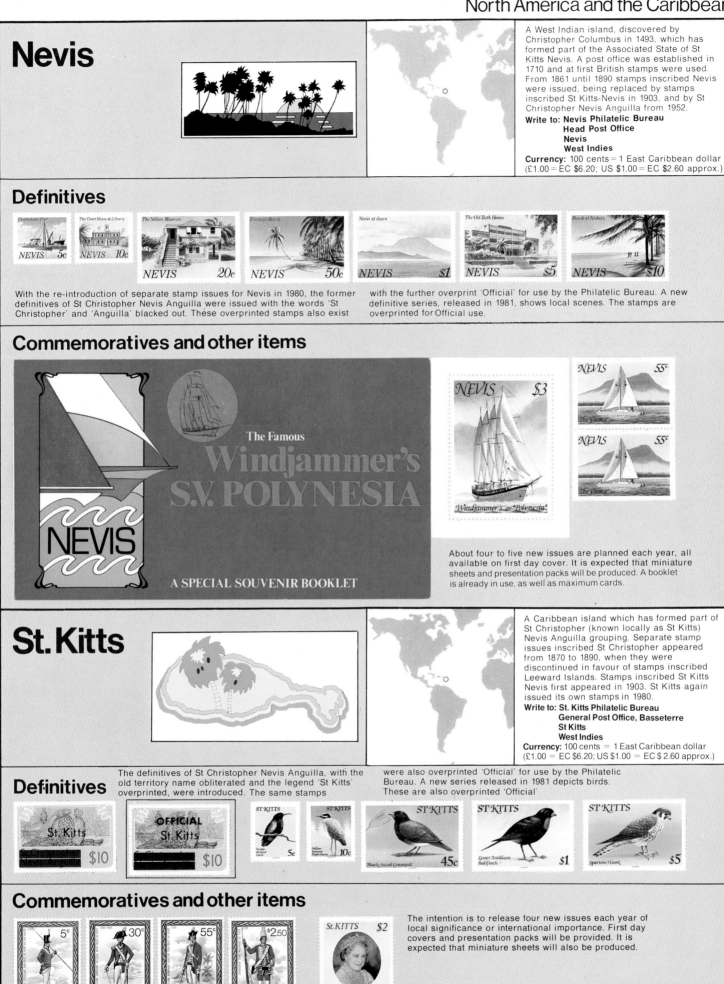

Netherlands Antilles

Nederlandse Antillen

POSTERIJEN NEDERLANDSE ANTILLEN

A group of islands in the Caribbean under Dutch control, which were given their present name in 1948, stamps inscribed thus first appearing the following year. Previously they had been known as Curacao, and the previous stamp issues had been so inscribed.

Write to: The Postmaster
Philatelic Department
Willemstad, Curaçao
Netherlands Antilles

Currency: 100 cents = 1 Antillian Guilder
(£1.00 = fl 4.03; US $1.00 = fl 1.80 approx.)

Definitives

The present definitive series in use features Queen Juliana together with local scenes.

Commemoratives

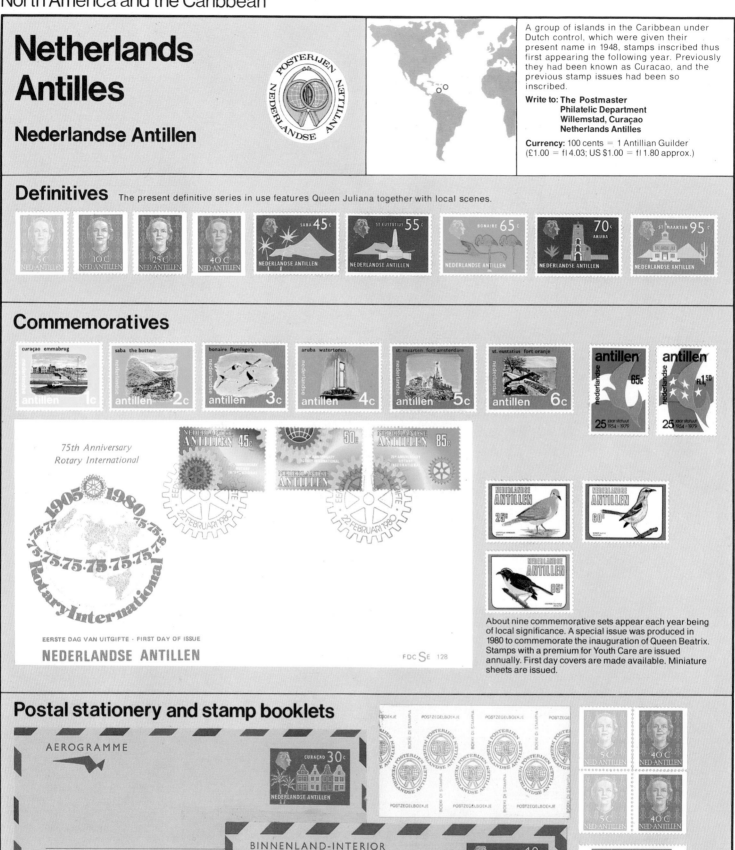

About nine commemorative sets appear each year being of local significance. A special issue was produced in 1980 to commemorate the inauguration of Queen Beatrix. Stamps with a premium for Youth Care are issued annually. First day covers are made available. Miniature sheets are issued.

Postal stationery and stamp booklets

Stamped aerogrammes are available (one for inland, another for overseas usage). Booklets are also in use, containing definitives or commemoratives and sometimes both.

Central · South America

Mexico

CORREOS MEXICO

This Republic in Central America was the home of the Aztecs, probably the greatest of America's ancient civilisations. Prior to the issue of her own stamps in 1856, there had been British postal agencies at Vera Cruz and Tampico, using British stamps.

Write to: Departamento Filatélico
Dirección General de Correos
Palacio Postal 2° Piso
Tacuba 1, Mexico1, D.F, Mexico

Currency: 100 centavos = 1 Mexican peso
(£1.00 = M $51.30; US $1.00 = M $23.60 approx.)

Definitives, commemoratives and other items

Definitive stamps showing Mexican exports are in use. Although there are, on average, thirty commemorative sets each year, these tend to be of low face value. Express Letter and Insured Letter stamps are in use. Items of postal stationery available include aerogrammes, postcards, stamped envelopes and letter cards.

Bolivia

Bolivia, in South America, was invaded by the Spanish in the sixteenth century, who made slaves of the Incas, the previous inhabitants. An internal postal service was established in 1866 for which stamps were produced, although the first stamps for international mail did not appear until the following year. A British postal agency did operate at Cobija until 1878.

Write to: Seccion Filatélica
Dirección General de Correos
La Paz
Bolivia

Currency: 100 centavos = 1 Bolivian peso
(£1.00 = $b56.00; US $1.00 = $b25.00 approx.)

Definitives and commemoratives

Few definitive stamps have been issued in recent times, although a 'numeral' design is in use, as are three values depicting landmarks. There are on average five commemorative sets each year, these related to events applicable to Bolivia. A postcard is in use.

Belize

This country in Central America, bounded by Mexico and Guatemala, was colonized by the Jamaicans in 1662. Once known as Belize, it then became British Honduras, reverting to Belize in 1973. The stamps of Great Britain were used from 1857, with stamps inscribed British Honduras being introduced in 1866. Stamps inscribed Belize first appeared in 1973.

**Write to: Belize Philatelic Bureau
PO Box 485
Belize City, Belize
Central America**

Currency: 100 cents = 1 Belize dollar
(£1.00 = B $4.80; US $1.00 = B $2.00 approx.)

Definitives and other items

Commemoratives

The current series depicts shells; rather unusually, miniature sheets accompany the current definitives, obviously aimed at stamp collectors. A series of postage dues is in use. Stationery ranges from newspaper wrappers to unstamped postcards, registered envelopes and two different aerogrammes.

A recent change of policy has produced about six commemorative issues a year, mostly thematic in nature, including high denominations, miniature sheets and first day covers.

Honduras

República de Honduras

A Republic in Central America which was discovered by Christopher Columbus in 1502 and later became a colony of Spain. An attempt to establish a postal service was made in 1866 and stamps were issued, but they did not really see regular use until 1877 when a further attempt was made to organize the post.

**Write to: Departamento Filatélico
Dirección General de Correos
Tegucigalpa DC, Republic of Honduras
Central America**

Currency: 100 centavos = 1 lempira
(£1.00 = L4.80; US $1.00 = L2.00 approx.)

Commemoratives and other items

About seven commemorative sets appear each year, being of local significance. No definitive stamps have been issued in recent times. Stamps to promote the Red Cross, stamps for Official use, and for letters to be sent by Express Post have been made available. A stamped aerogramme is in use.

El Salvador

A Republic in Central America which was invaded by Spain in 1524, the name becoming El Salvador in 1841. The first stamps were issued in 1867, but between 1890 and 1898 there was a period of philatelic exploitation, resulting in a multitude of stamp issues which are still philatelically worthless.

Write to: Departamento de Filatelia
Dirección General de Correos
San Salvador
El Salvador, Central America

Currency: 100 centavos = 1 colón
(£1.00 = ₡6.00; US $1.00 = ₡2.50 approx.)

Commemoratives and postal stationery

The last series of definitive stamps, issued several years ago, depict architecture. There are about twelve commemorative issues each year, mainly honouring local events, although the designs are frequently 'thematic' in character. An aerogramme is in use.

Panama

Panama, in Central America, gained independence in 1903, having formerly been part of the Republic of Colombia. The first stamps, in 1878, were therefore issued as part of Colombia, until stamps were issued for independent Panama in 1903.

Write to: Departamento de Filatelia
Dirección General Correos y
Telecomunicaciones, Apartado 3421
Panama 1, Republic of Panama
Central America

Currency: 100 centesimos = 1 balboa
(£1.00 = B2.39; US $1.00 = B1.00 approx.)

Commemoratives and other items

No definitive series as such is available, use being made of commemorative issues, particularly those of a 'thematic' nature. International events are commemorated by about five issues each year. Miniature sheets are frequently produced. The designs are often 'thematic' in nature. A stamped aerogramme is in use. Obligatory tax stamps are in use.

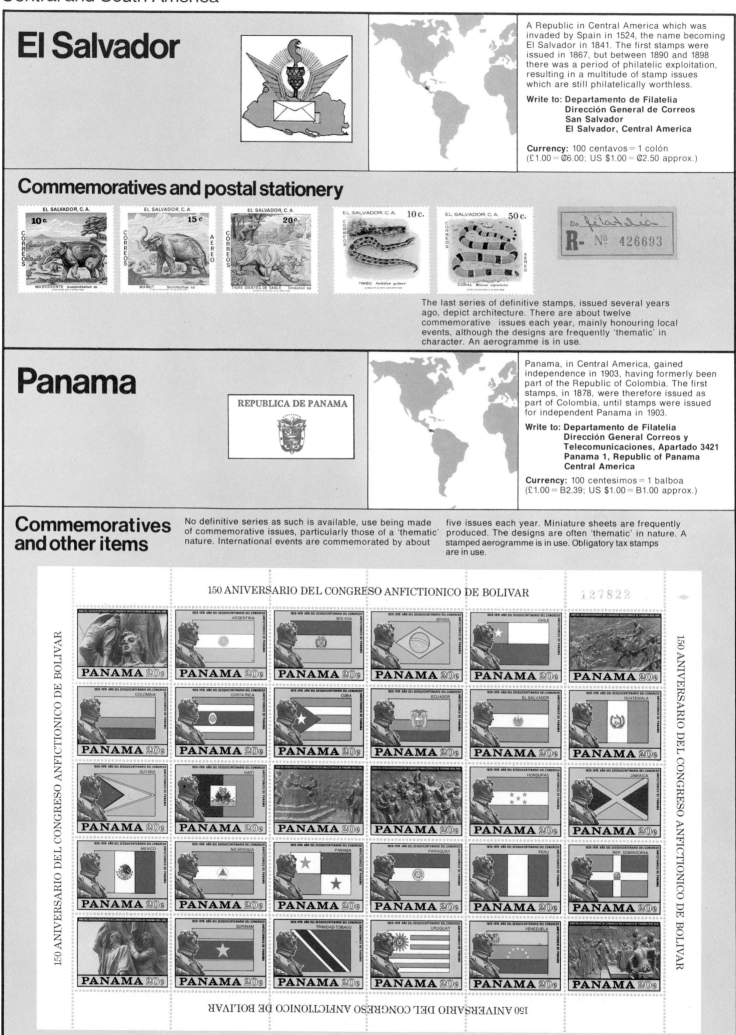

Nicaragua

A Republic in Central America, Nicaragua was colonized by the Spanish following the landing by Gil Gonzales de Avila. The first stamps were issued in 1862, although there were periods in the mid 1800s when British stamps were used in parts of the country.

Write to: Oficina de Control des
Especies Postales y Filatelia
Apartado Postal 325
Palacio Nacional
Managua, DN
Nicaragua, Central America

Currency: 100 centavos = 1 cordoba
(£1.00 = ₡23.90: US $1.00 = ₡10.00 approx.)

Commemoratives

A change in policy in 1980 has produced a surfeit of stamps, many of which are overprints on previous issues, commemorating a wide range of subjects. There are no definitive stamps at present in use.

Costa Rica

A Republic in Central America, which has both the Caribbean and the Pacific Ocean as its borders. It was visited by Christopher Columbus in 1502, and its name arose during the sixteenth century when gold was found, Costa Rica meaning 'Rich Coast'. The first stamps appeared in 1863.

Write to: 'CORTEL'
Oficina Filatélica de Costa Rica
San José, Costa Rica
Central America

Currency: 100 céntimos = 1 colón
(£1.00 = ₡20.56: US $1.00 = ₡8.57 approx.)

Definitives, commemoratives and other items

Definitive stamps are in use. There are about fifteen commemorative sets each year of local interest. First day covers are made available. Special stamps are issued for items sent by 'Express Post' and for 'Special Delivery' and obligatory tax stamps are in use for Christmas post. Stamped aerogrammes and envelopes are also available.

Surinam

Suriname

POSTERIJEN
SURINAME

Once a Netherlands colony in South America (also known as Netherlands, or Dutch, Guiana), until independence in 1975, Surinam issued her first stamps in 1873.

Write to: Dienst der Posterijen
Filatelistische Dienst
Wanicaplein
Paramaribo
Surinam

Currency: 100 cents = 1 Surinam guilder
(£1.00 = Sf4.03; US $1.00 = Sf1.80 approx.)

Definitives and commemoratives

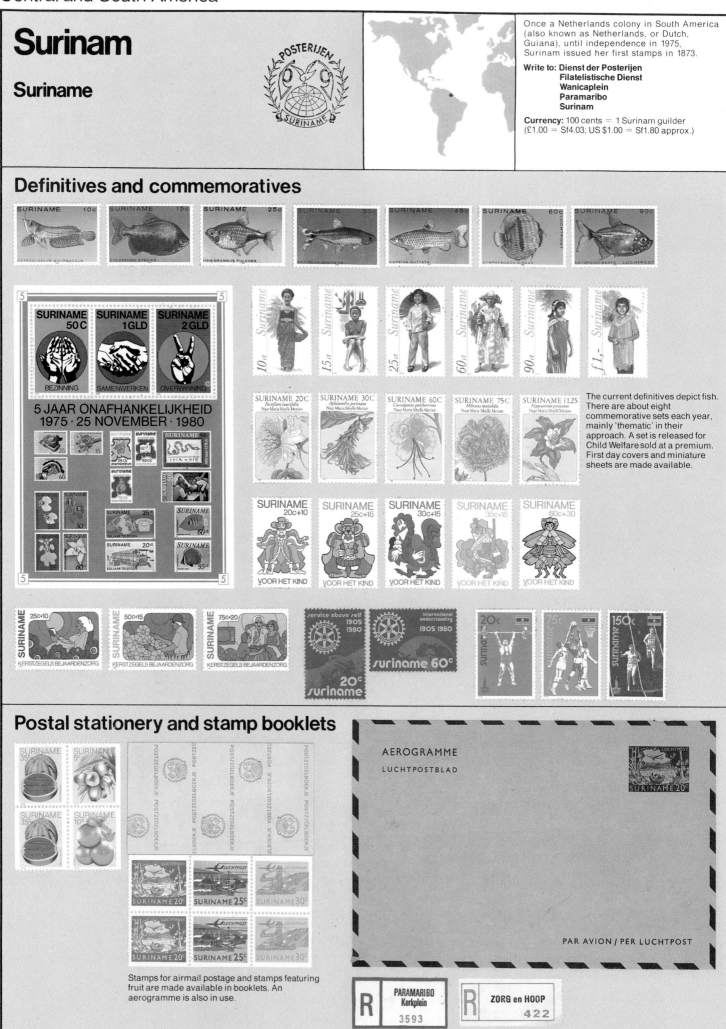

The current definitives depict fish. There are about eight commemorative sets each year, mainly 'thematic' in their approach. A set is released for Child Welfare sold at a premium. First day covers and miniature sheets are made available.

Postal stationery and stamp booklets

Stamps for airmail postage and stamps featuring fruit are made available in booklets. An aerogramme is also in use.

AEROGRAMME
LUCHTPOSTBLAD

SURINAME 20c

PAR AVION / PER LUCHTPOST

R PARAMARIBO Kerkplein 3593

R ZORG en HOOP 422

Venezuela

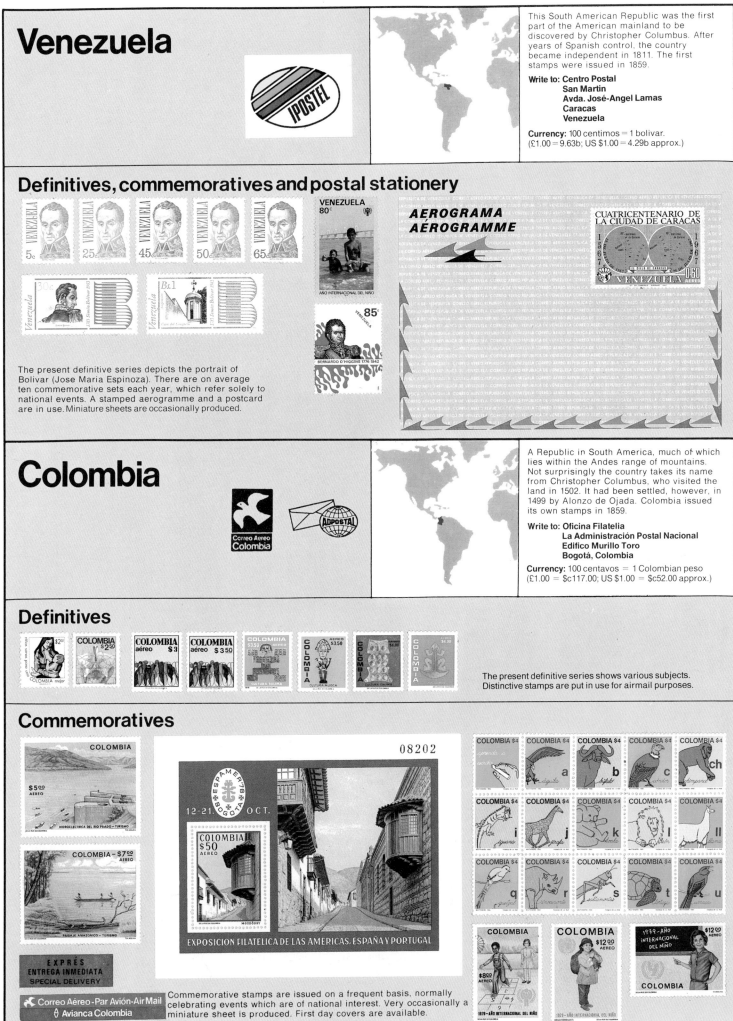

IPOSTEL

This South American Republic was the first part of the American mainland to be discovered by Christopher Columbus. After years of Spanish control, the country became independent in 1811. The first stamps were issued in 1859.

Write to: Centro Postal
San Martin
Avda. José-Angel Lamas
Caracas
Venezuela

Currency: 100 centimos = 1 bolivar.
(£1.00 = 9.63b; US $1.00 = 4.29b approx.)

Definitives, commemoratives and postal stationery

The present definitive series depicts the portrait of Bolivar (Jose Maria Espinoza). There are on average ten commemorative sets each year, which refer solely to national events. A stamped aerogramme and a postcard are in use. Miniature sheets are occasionally produced.

Colombia

Correo Aereo Colombia

ADPOSTAL

A Republic in South America, much of which lies within the Andes range of mountains. Not surprisingly the country takes its name from Christopher Columbus, who visited the land in 1502. It had been settled, however, in 1499 by Alonzo de Ojada. Colombia issued its own stamps in 1859.

Write to: Oficina Filatelia
La Administración Postal Nacional
Edifico Murillo Toro
Bogotá, Colombia

Currency: 100 centavos = 1 Colombian peso
(£1.00 = $c117.00; US $1.00 = $c52.00 approx.)

Definitives

The present definitive series shows various subjects. Distinctive stamps are put in use for airmail purposes.

Commemoratives

Commemorative stamps are issued on a frequent basis, normally celebrating events which are of national interest. Very occasionally a miniature sheet is produced. First day covers are available.

Guyana

Guyana is an independent Republic in South America previously known as British Guiana. Guiana was the name given to the area of land between the Amazon and Orinoco rivers. British stamps were used, although the country's own stamps appeared in 1850. The most famous is the 1856 1c black on magenta, the world's rarest stamp.

Write to: Philatelic Bureau
General Post Office
Georgetown
Guyana

Currency: 100 cents = 1 Guyanese dollar
(£1.00 = G $6.20; US $1.00 = G $2.48 approx.)

Definitives

The first definitives for Guyana as such appeared in 1966. The current definitives show butterflies.

Commemoratives

These appear about four times a year, normally confined to commemorating local events and anniversaries. From time to time a miniature sheet accompanies a set. First day covers are available.

Postal stationery and postage dues

Postal stationery currently available consists of newspaper wrappers, stamped envelopes, registered envelopes and aerogrammes, the last three having distinctive 'Coat-of-Arms' stamp designs. Postage due labels are in use.

AIRLETTER-AEROGRAMME

25c Postage Paid

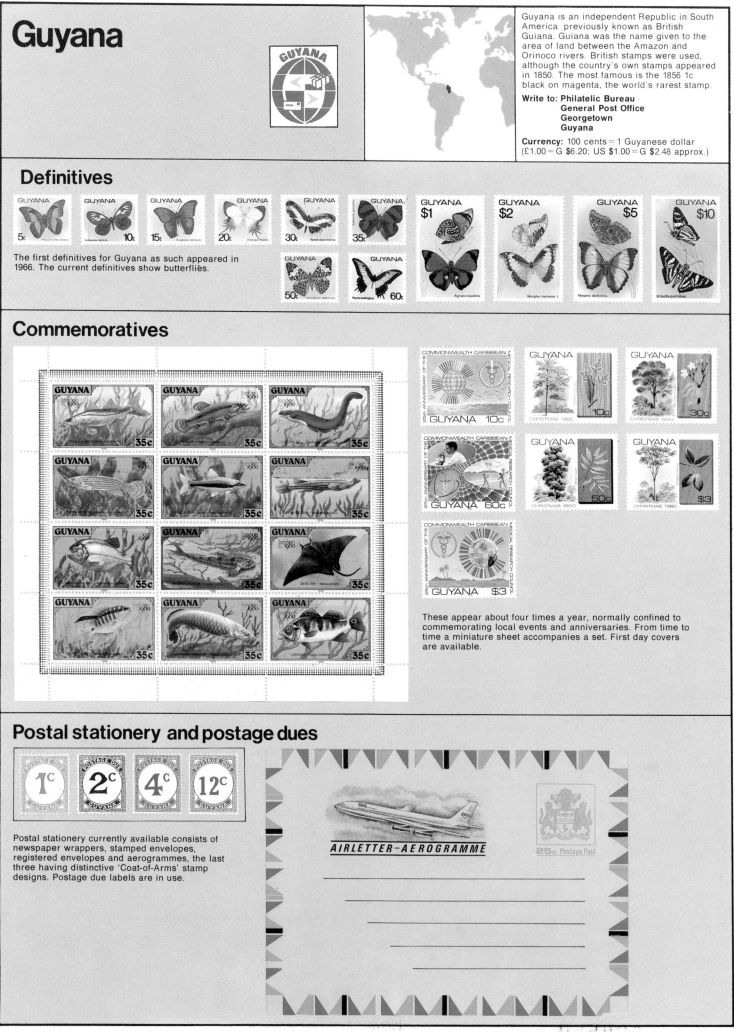

Peru

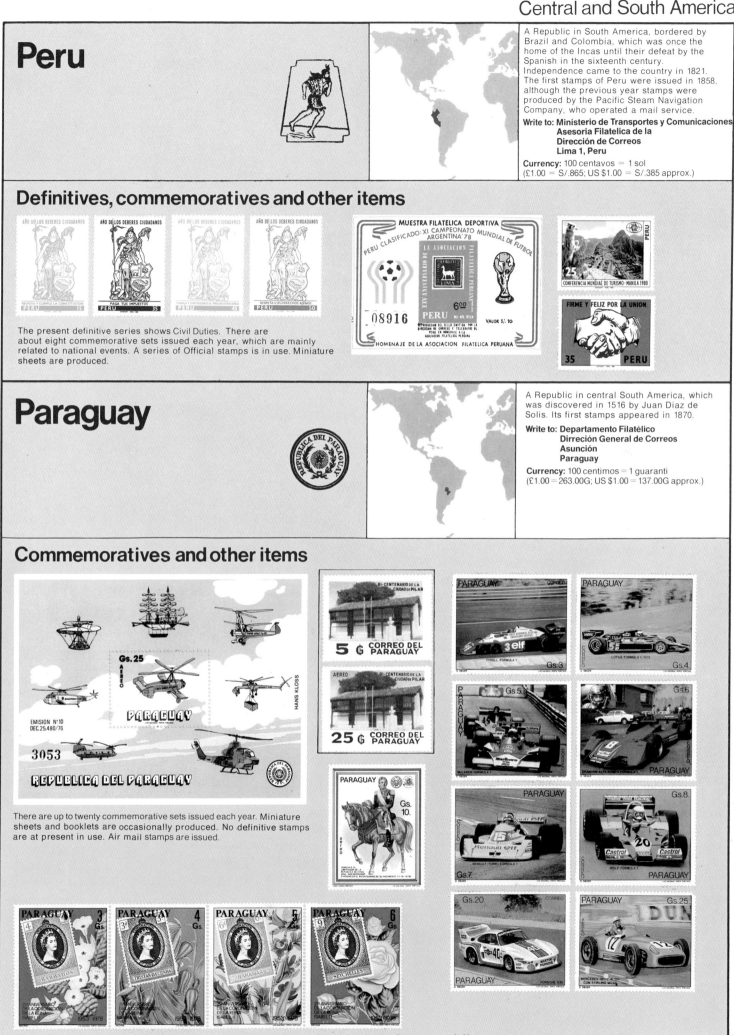

A Republic in South America, bordered by Brazil and Colombia, which was once the home of the Incas until their defeat by the Spanish in the sixteenth century. Independence came to the country in 1821. The first stamps of Peru were issued in 1858, although the previous year stamps were produced by the Pacific Steam Navigation Company, who operated a mail service.

Write to: Ministerio de Transportes y Comunicaciones
Asesoria Filatelica de la
Dirección de Correos
Lima 1, Peru

Currency: 100 centavos = 1 sol
(£1.00 = S/.865; US $1.00 = S/.385 approx.)

Definitives, commemoratives and other items

The present definitive series shows Civil Duties. There are about eight commemorative sets issued each year, which are mainly related to national events. A series of Official stamps is in use. Miniature sheets are produced.

Paraguay

A Republic in central South America, which was discovered in 1516 by Juan Diaz de Solis. Its first stamps appeared in 1870.

Write to: Departamento Filatélico
Dirreción General de Correos
Asunción
Paraguay

Currency: 100 centimos = 1 guaranti
(£1.00 = 263.00G; US $1.00 = 137.00G approx.)

Commemoratives and other items

There are up to twenty commemorative sets issued each year. Miniature sheets and booklets are occasionally produced. No definitive stamps are at present in use. Air mail stamps are issued.

Brazil

Brasil

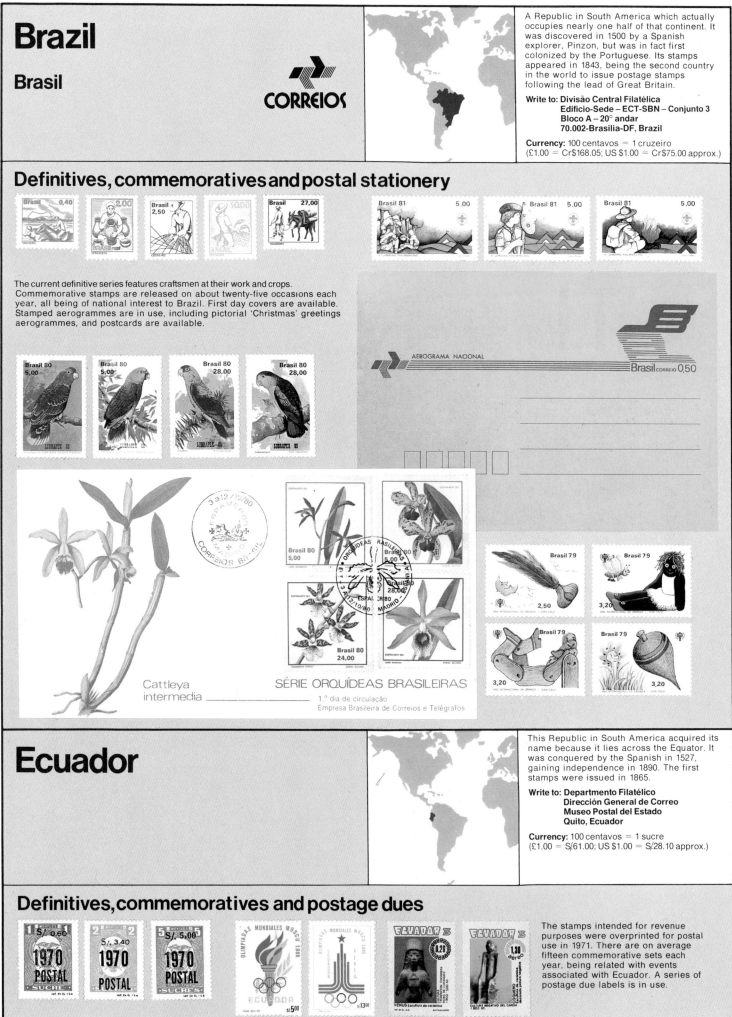

CORREIOS

A Republic in South America which actually occupies nearly one half of that continent. It was discovered in 1500 by a Spanish explorer, Pinzon, but was in fact first colonized by the Portuguese. Its stamps appeared in 1843, being the second country in the world to issue postage stamps following the lead of Great Britain.

Write to: Divisão Central Filatélica
Edificio-Sede – ECT-SBN – Conjunto 3
Bloco A – 20° andar
70.002-Brasilia-DF, Brazil

Currency: 100 centavos = 1 cruzeiro
(£1.00 = Cr$168.05; US $1.00 = Cr$75.00 approx.)

Definitives, commemoratives and postal stationery

The current definitive series features craftsmen at their work and crops. Commemorative stamps are released on about twenty-five occasions each year, all being of national interest to Brazil. First day covers are available. Stamped aerogrammes are in use, including pictorial 'Christmas' greetings aerogrammes, and postcards are available.

Cattleya
intermedia

SÉRIE ORQUÍDEAS BRASILEIRAS
1.° dia de circulação
Empresa Brasileira de Correios e Telégrafos

Ecuador

This Republic in South America acquired its name because it lies across the Equator. It was conquered by the Spanish in 1527, gaining independence in 1890. The first stamps were issued in 1865.

Write to: Departmento Filatélico
Dirección General de Correo
Museo Postal del Estado
Quito, Ecuador

Currency: 100 centavos = 1 sucre
(£1.00 = S/.61.00; US $1.00 = S/.28.10 approx.)

Definitives, commemoratives and postage dues

The stamps intended for revenue purposes were overprinted for postal use in 1971. There are on average fifteen commemorative sets each year, being related with events associated with Ecuador. A series of postage due labels is in use.

Argentina

República Argentina

encotel ARGENTINA

The second largest country in South America, which derives its name from the Latin word for silver. It was colonized by the Spanish in the sixteenth century. However there was a period when British stamps were used in Buenos Aires. Its own stamps first appeared in 1858, the country's first commemorative being issued 34 years later in 1892.

Write to: Sección Filatelia
Correo Central
1000 Buenos Aires
Argentina

Currency: 100 centavos = 1 Argentine peso
(£1.00 = 4760.00P; US $1.00 = 1954.50P approx.)

Definitives

Definitives from several series are available concurrently, and many additions are made each year. Among current designs are Argentine buildings and monuments, historical figures, postal coding publicity and the national 'football rosette'.

Commemoratives and other items

Frequent commemorative issues are released, mostly just of single values and appertaining to local interests. First day covers are made available. A stamped aerogramme and postcard are on sale. Miniature sheets are also issued. Stamps are sold at a premium for charitable purposes.

Uruguay

One of the smallest of the Republics in South America, Uruguay became independent in 1828. The first stamps were issued in 1856, these being known as 'Montevideo suns' on account of their design, showing a small, smiling face surrounding by rays.

Write to: Dirección Nacional de Correos
del Uruguay
Departamento de Filatelia
Casilla de Correo No. 1296
Montevideo, Uruguay

Currency: 100 centesimos = 1 Uruguay peso
(£1.00 = N $23.25; US $1.00 = N $10.34 approx.)

Definitives, commemoratives and other items

The definitive series comprises a mixture of designs, including the Teru bird, local flowers, paintings and a portrait of José Artigas. The commemorative issues relate to national events, and are released on about twelve occasions each year. A miniature sheet is sometimes produced, and an aerogramme is also available.

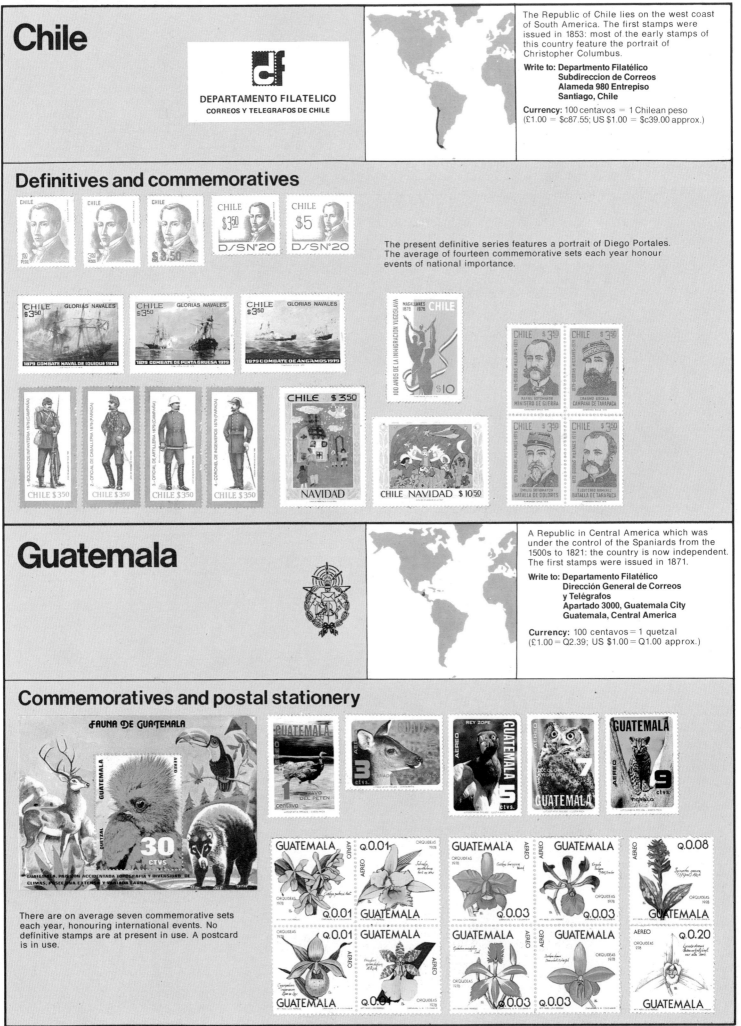

Chile

DEPARTAMENTO FILATELICO
CORREOS Y TELEGRAFOS DE CHILE

The Republic of Chile lies on the west coast of South America. The first stamps were issued in 1853: most of the early stamps of this country feature the portrait of Christopher Columbus.

**Write to: Departmento Filatélico
Subdireccion de Correos
Alameda 980 Entrepiso
Santiago, Chile**

Currency: 100 centavos = 1 Chilean peso
(£1.00 = $c87.55; US $1.00 = $c39.00 approx.)

Definitives and commemoratives

The present definitive series features a portrait of Diego Portales. The average of fourteen commemorative sets each year honour events of national importance.

Guatemala

A Republic in Central America which was under the control of the Spaniards from the 1500s to 1821: the country is now independent. The first stamps were issued in 1871.

**Write to: Departmento Filatélico
Dirección General de Correos
y Telégrafos
Apartado 3000, Guatemala City
Guatemala, Central America**

Currency: 100 centavos = 1 quetzal
(£1.00 = Q2.39; US $1.00 = Q1.00 approx.)

Commemoratives and postal stationery

There are on average seven commemorative sets each year, honouring international events. No definitive stamps are at present in use. A postcard is in use.

Falkland Islands

Group of islands in the South Atlantic, including the two main islands of East Falkland and West Falkland. The first stamps appeared in 1869, comprising hand franks reading 'Falkland Islands Paid' impressed onto envelopes. Actual stamps inscribed Falkland Islands first appeared in 1878.

**Write to: Philatelic Bureau
Post Office, Port Stanley
Falkland Islands, South Atlantic**

Currency: 100 pence = 1 pound sterling
(US $1.00 = £0.45 approx.)

Definitives

The current definitives were released in 1978 and depict mail ships.

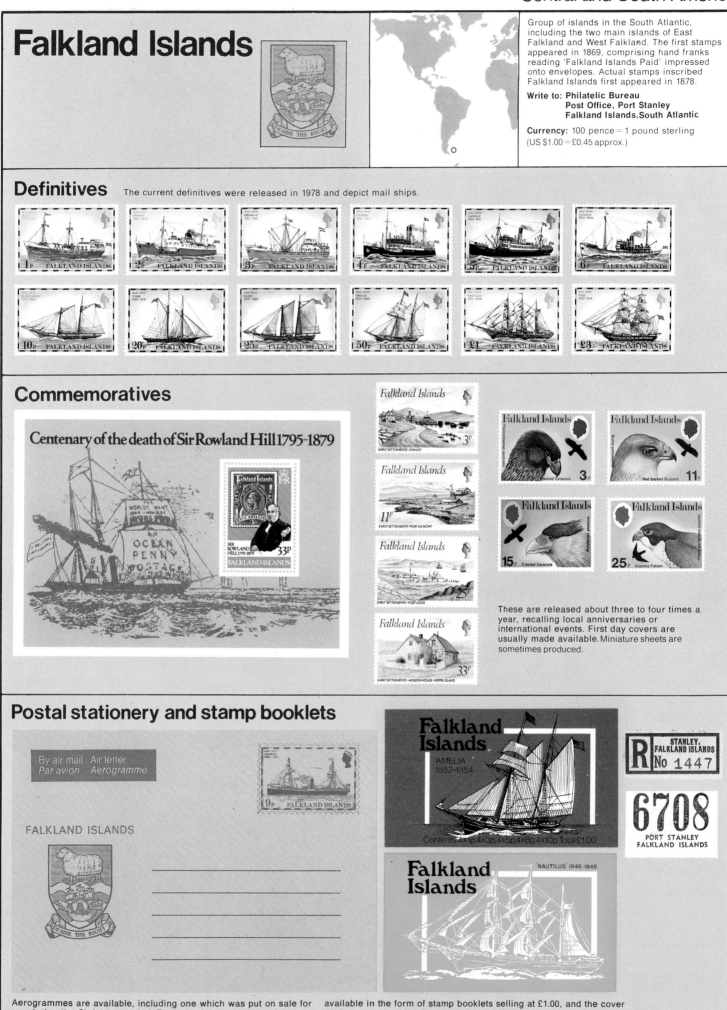

Commemoratives

Centenary of the death of Sir Rowland Hill 1795-1879

These are released about three to four times a year, recalling local anniversaries or international events. First day covers are usually made available. Miniature sheets are sometimes produced.

Postal stationery and stamp booklets

Aerogrammes are available, including one which was put on sale for use during the Christmas period. There is also an envelope for registered mail. Certain denominations of definitives have been made available in the form of stamp booklets selling at £1.00, and the cover design of the booklets is changed from time to time.

Falkland Islands Dependencies

A group of Antarctic islands originally consisting of South Georgia, the South Orkneys, the South Shetlands and Graham Land. Stamps for these areas first appeared in 1944. In 1963 separate stamp issues were prepared for South Georgia, the remaining islands having stamps under the heading of British Antarctic Territory. In 1980 stamps inscribed 'Falkland Islands Dependencies' again appeared.

Write to: Philatelic Bureau
Post Office, Port Stanley
Falkland Islands, South Atlantic
Currency: 100 pence = 1 pound sterling
(US $1.00 = £0.45 approx.)

Definitives and commemoratives

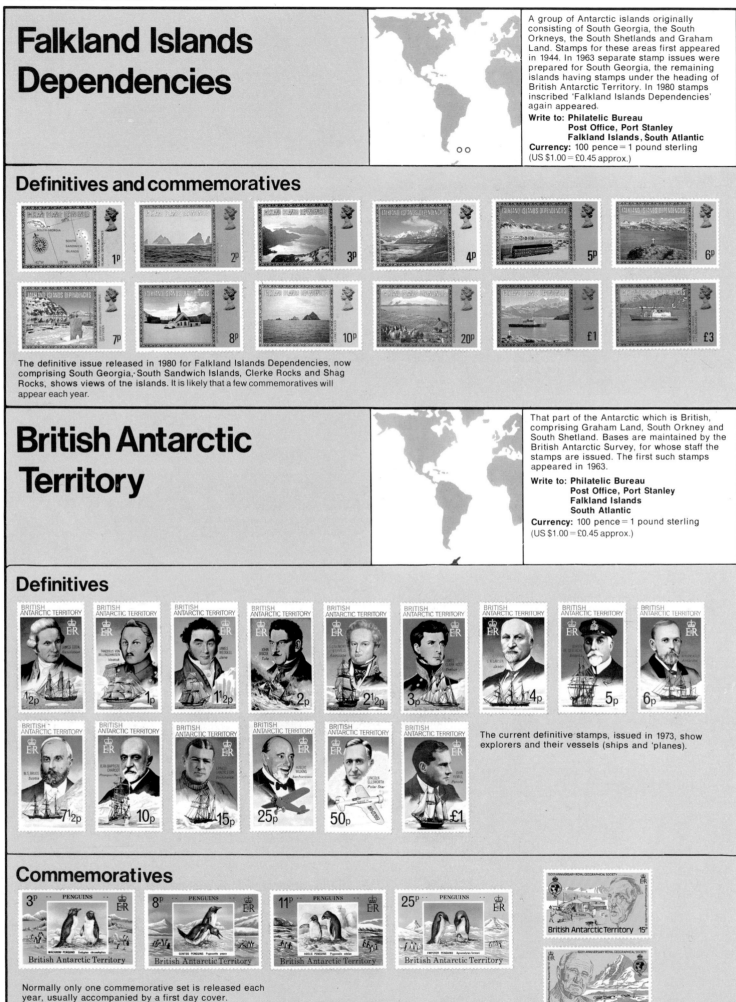

The definitive issue released in 1980 for Falkland Islands Dependencies, now comprising South Georgia, South Sandwich Islands, Clerke Rocks and Shag Rocks, shows views of the islands. It is likely that a few commemoratives will appear each year.

British Antarctic Territory

That part of the Antarctic which is British, comprising Graham Land, South Orkney and South Shetland. Bases are maintained by the British Antarctic Survey, for whose staff the stamps are issued. The first such stamps appeared in 1963.

Write to: Philatelic Bureau
Post Office, Port Stanley
Falkland Islands
South Atlantic
Currency: 100 pence = 1 pound sterling
(US $1.00 = £0.45 approx.)

Definitives

The current definitive stamps, issued in 1973, show explorers and their vessels (ships and 'planes).

Commemoratives

Normally only one commemorative set is released each year, usually accompanied by a first day cover.

Middle East

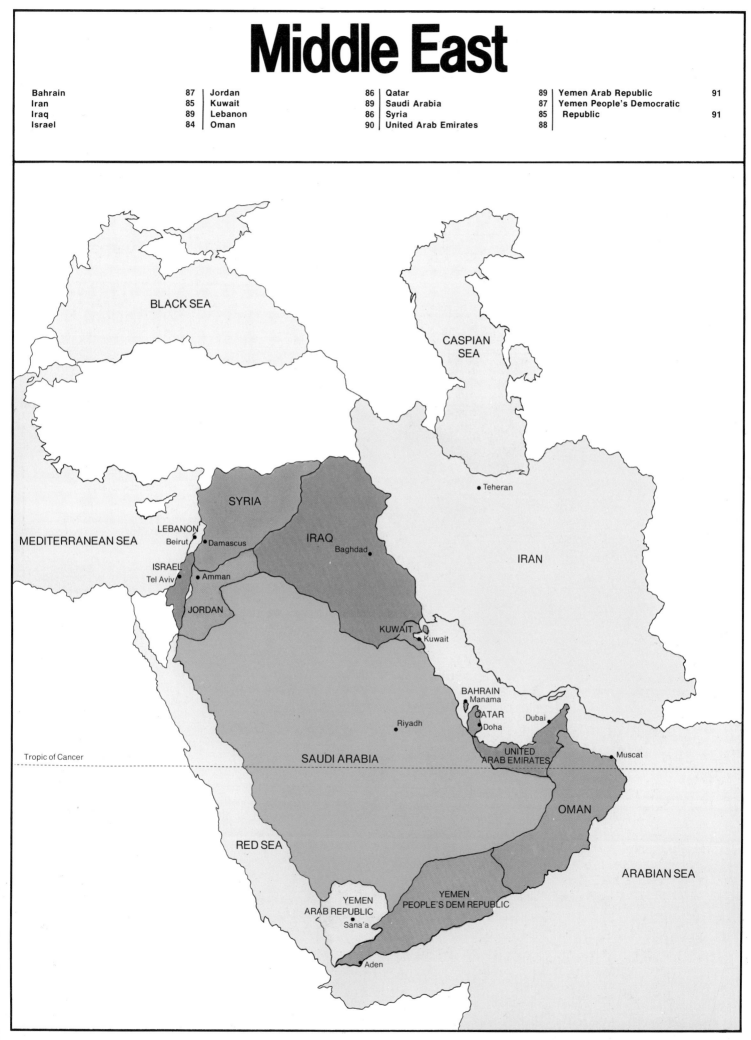

BLACK SEA

CASPIAN SEA

MEDITERRANEAN SEA

SYRIA

LEBANON
Beirut • Damascus

IRAQ
Baghdad •

• Teheran

IRAN

ISRAEL
Tel Aviv • • Amman

JORDAN

KUWAIT
• Kuwait

BAHRAIN
Manama •

QATAR
• Doha

Dubai •

UNITED
ARAB EMIRATES

• Muscat

Tropic of Cancer

SAUDI ARABIA
• Riyadh

OMAN

RED SEA

ARABIAN SEA

YEMEN
ARAB REPUBLIC
• Sana'a

YEMEN
PEOPLE'S DEM REPUBLIC

• Aden

Israel

ישראל اسرائيل

A Jewish Republic in the former territory of Palestine, which came into being in 1948, following a period from 1917 when the area was governed by Britain. The first stamps for Israel appeared in 1948, although there had been earlier issues for Palestine, as a British Military Administration, a British Civil Administration and a British Mandated Territory.

Write to: Philatelic Services
Ministry of Communications
Tel Aviv – Yafo 61 080
State of Israel

Currency: 100 agorot = 1 shekel
(£1.00 = 19.95Sh; US $1.00 = 8.58Sh approx.)

Definitives

A new series of definitives, featuring the shekel currency, was issued in December 1980. The design is uniform, apart from the value panels. Israeli stamps are noted for their decorative sheet margins known as 'tabs'; stamps are collected with these tabs attached.

Commemoratives

There are about fifteen commemorative sets each year, all of national significance. The Jewish New Year normally forms the subject for one issue annually. First day covers are available. Miniature sheets are also available.

Postal stationery

Stamped aerogrammes and postcards are in use.

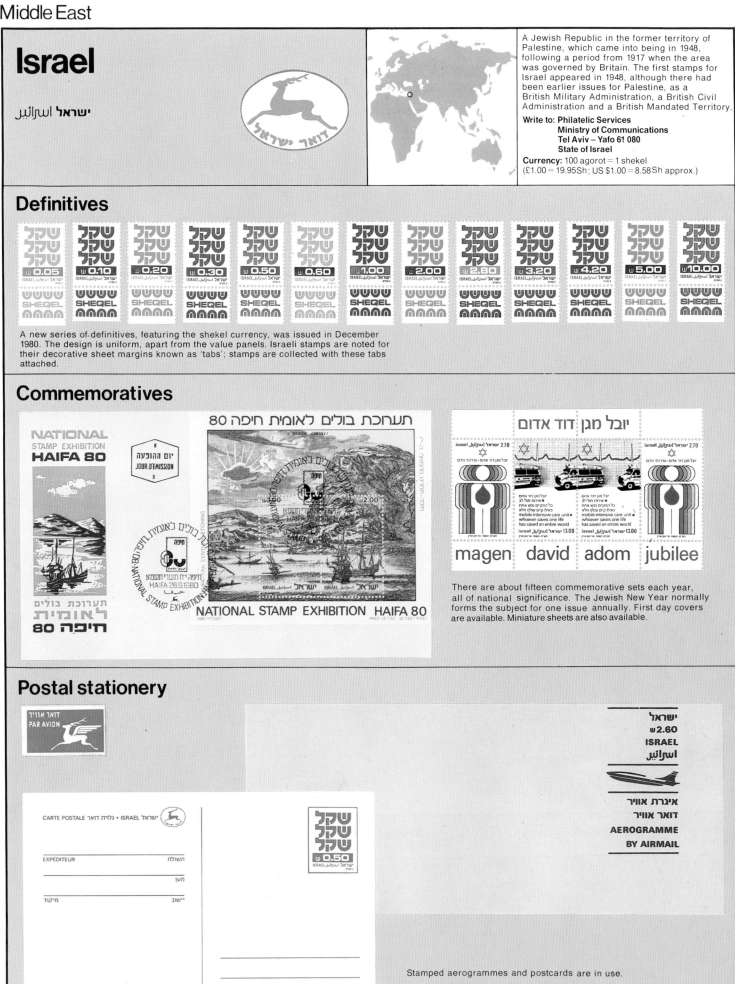

Iran

République Islamique de l'Iran

جمهوری اسلامی ایران

This country in Asia was formerly known as Persia. The first stamps were introduced in 1868, although as Iran the first issue appeared in 1935.

Write to: Ministry of Post, Telegraph and
Telephone of Iran
Directorate General of Posts
Philatelic Bureau
Teheran, Iran

Currency: 100 dinars = 1 rial
(£1.00 = 168.50R; US $1.00 = 70.00R approx.)

Definitives

The present definitive series features a symbolic design.

Commemoratives and other items

The commemorative issues tend to be of a propaganda nature. A stamped aerogramme is in use. Official stamps are issued.

Syria

Syrian A.R.

الجمهورية العربية السورية

The history of Syria includes Turkish control, and French Military Administration and a French Mandate. In 1958 Egypt and Syria joined to form the United Arab Republic, but this was split up in 1961 and the Syrian Arab Republic was formed. The first stamps, in 1919, were overprints on France. Stamps inscribed for Syria were issued in 1920.

Write to: General Post Establishment
Philatelic Office
Damascus
Syrian Arab Republic

Currency: 100 piastres = 1 Syrian pound
(£1.00 = 8.80PS; US $1.00 = 3.93PS approx.)

Definitives

The present definitive stamps feature antiquities.

Commemoratives and postal stationery

There are about twelve commemorative sets each year, which reflect either national events, or are purely 'thematic'. A postcard is available. Miniature sheets are produced.

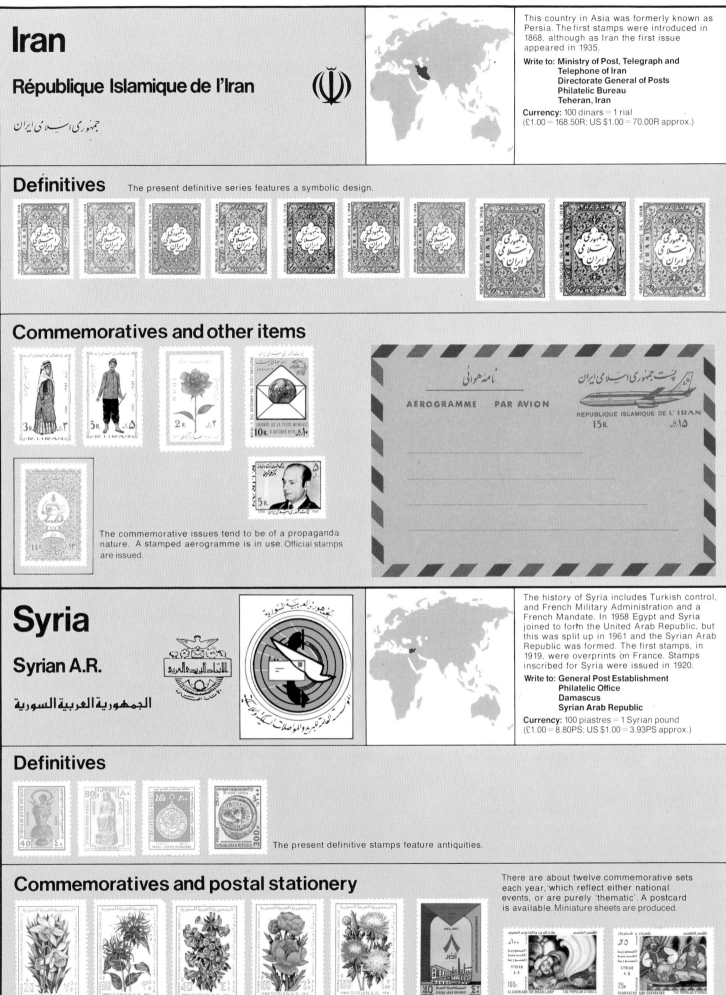

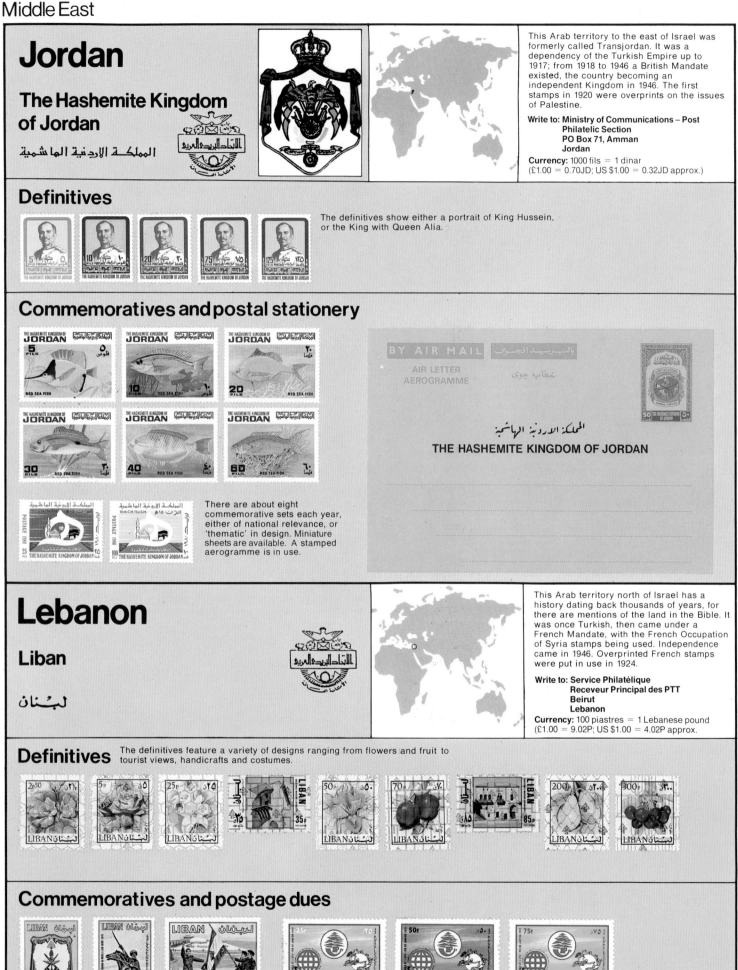

Jordan

The Hashemite Kingdom of Jordan

المملكة الاردنية الهاشمية

This Arab territory to the east of Israel was formerly called Transjordan. It was a dependency of the Turkish Empire up to 1917; from 1918 to 1946 a British Mandate existed, the country becoming an independent Kingdom in 1946. The first stamps in 1920 were overprints on the issues of Palestine.

Write to: Ministry of Communications – Post
Philatelic Section
PO Box 71, Amman
Jordan
Currency: 1000 fils = 1 dinar
(£1.00 = 0.70JD; US $1.00 = 0.32JD approx.)

Definitives

The definitives show either a portrait of King Hussein, or the King with Queen Alia.

Commemoratives and postal stationery

There are about eight commemorative sets each year, either of national relevance, or 'thematic' in design. Miniature sheets are available. A stamped aerogramme is in use.

BY AIR MAIL   بالبريد الجوى
AIR LETTER
AEROGRAMME   خطاب جوى

المملكة الاردنية الهاشمية
THE HASHEMITE KINGDOM OF JORDAN

Lebanon

Liban

لبنان

This Arab territory north of Israel has a history dating back thousands of years, for there are mentions of the land in the Bible. It was once Turkish, then came under a French Mandate, with the French Occupation of Syria stamps being used. Independence came in 1946. Overprinted French stamps were put in use in 1924.

Write to: Service Philatélique
Receveur Principal des PTT
Beirut
Lebanon
Currency: 100 piastres = 1 Lebanese pound
(£1.00 = 9.02P; US $1.00 = 4.02P approx.)

Definitives

The definitives feature a variety of designs ranging from flowers and fruit to tourist views, handicrafts and costumes.

Commemoratives and postage dues

Few commemorative sets are released, those that are being of national significance. A series of postage due labels bearing the portrait of the Emir is in use.

Bahrain

State of Bahrain

دولة البحرين

An independent Sheikdom and island in the Persian Gulf, whose postal affairs have been administered both from India and Great Britain until Bahrain took over in 1966. Indian stamps overprinted were introduced in 1933; British stamps overprinted appeared in 1948, while stamps actually inscribed Bahrain did not appear until 1960.

Write to: Philatelic Bureau
PO Box 1212
State of Bahrain

Currency: 1000 fils = 1 dinar
(£1.00 = 0.85BD; US $1.00 = 0.38BD approx.)

Definitives, commemoratives and other items

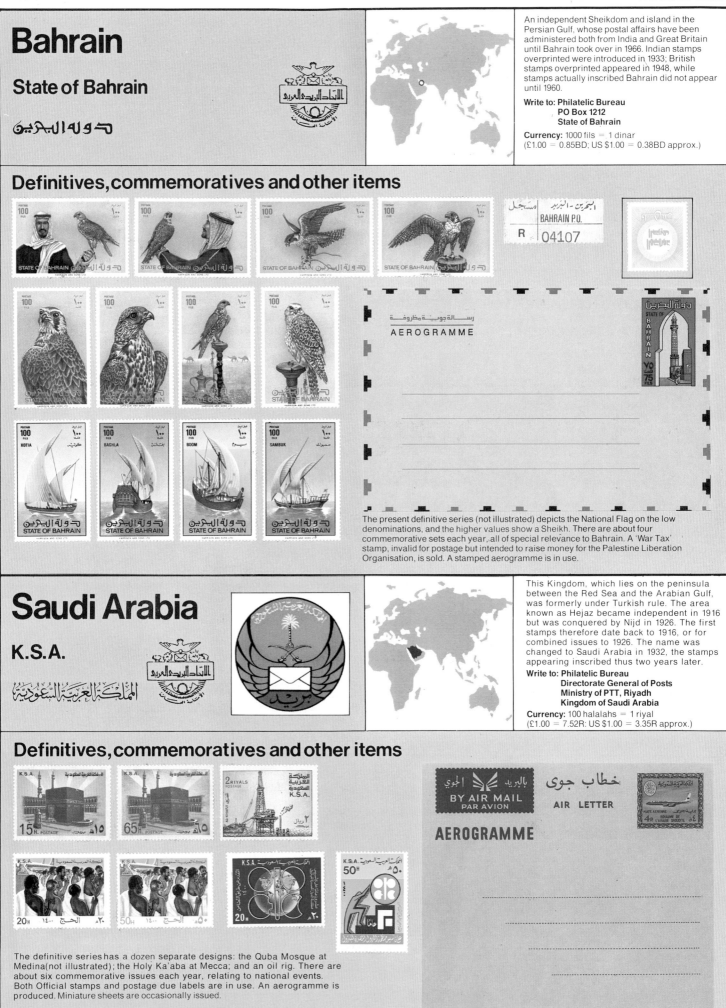

The present definitive series (not illustrated) depicts the National Flag on the low denominations, and the higher values show a Sheikh. There are about four commemorative sets each year, all of special relevance to Bahrain. A 'War Tax' stamp, invalid for postage but intended to raise money for the Palestine Liberation Organisation, is sold. A stamped aerogramme is in use.

Saudi Arabia

K.S.A.

المملكة العربية السعودية

This Kingdom, which lies on the peninsula between the Red Sea and the Arabian Gulf, was formerly under Turkish rule. The area known as Hejaz became independent in 1916 but was conquered by Nijd in 1926. The first stamps therefore date back to 1916, or for combined issues to 1926. The name was changed to Saudi Arabia in 1932, the stamps appearing inscribed thus two years later.

Write to: Philatelic Bureau
Directorate General of Posts
Ministry of PTT, Riyadh
Kingdom of Saudi Arabia

Currency: 100 halalahs = 1 riyal
(£1.00 = 7.52R: US $1.00 = 3.35R approx.)

Definitives, commemoratives and other items

The definitive series has a dozen separate designs: the Quba Mosque at Medina (not illustrated); the Holy Ka'aba at Mecca; and an oil rig. There are about six commemorative issues each year, relating to national events. Both Official stamps and postage due labels are in use. An aerogramme is produced. Miniature sheets are occasionally issued.

United Arab Emirates

دولة الامارات العربية المتحدة

A union established by seven of the Trucial States in the Arabian Gulf following the withdrawal of British troops in 1971. The separate stamp issues of the individual States were replaced by the stamps of United Arab Emirates. The first such stamps comprised the overprint 'UAE' on the definitives of Abu Dhabi, released in 1972.

Write to: Philatelic Section
Postal Headquarters
Dubai
United Arab Emirates

Currency: 100 fils = 1 UAE dirham
(£1.00 = Dh8.25; US $1.00 = Dh3.65 approx.)

Definitives
The present definitive series features the Crest of the United Arab Emirates.

Commemoratives and postal stationery

PAR AVION
البريد الجوي

About four commemorative stamp issues are prepared each year, each referring to events of local interest. An aerogramme is available. Miniature sheets are produced.

Kuwait

State of Kuwait

دولة الكويت

An independent Arab State in the Persian Gulf, the postal service at which has been administered by India, then Great Britain, until Kuwait itself took over in 1959. Consequently, the first stamps were overprints on India in 1923, followed by overprints on Great Britain, and Kuwait's own stamps in 1958.

Write to: The Director
Post Office Department
(Philatelic Bureau)
Safat Post Office, Kuwait

Currency: 1000 fils = 1 dinar
(£1.00 = KD0.62; US $1.00 = KD0.27 approx.)

Definitives and commemoratives
definitives feature a portrait of the Ruler. There are about ten commemorative issues each year, relating to events of direct importance to Kuwait.

Postal stationery and postage dues

AEROGRAMME

PAR AVION
بالبريد الجوي

A stamped aerogramme and a series of postage due labels are in use.

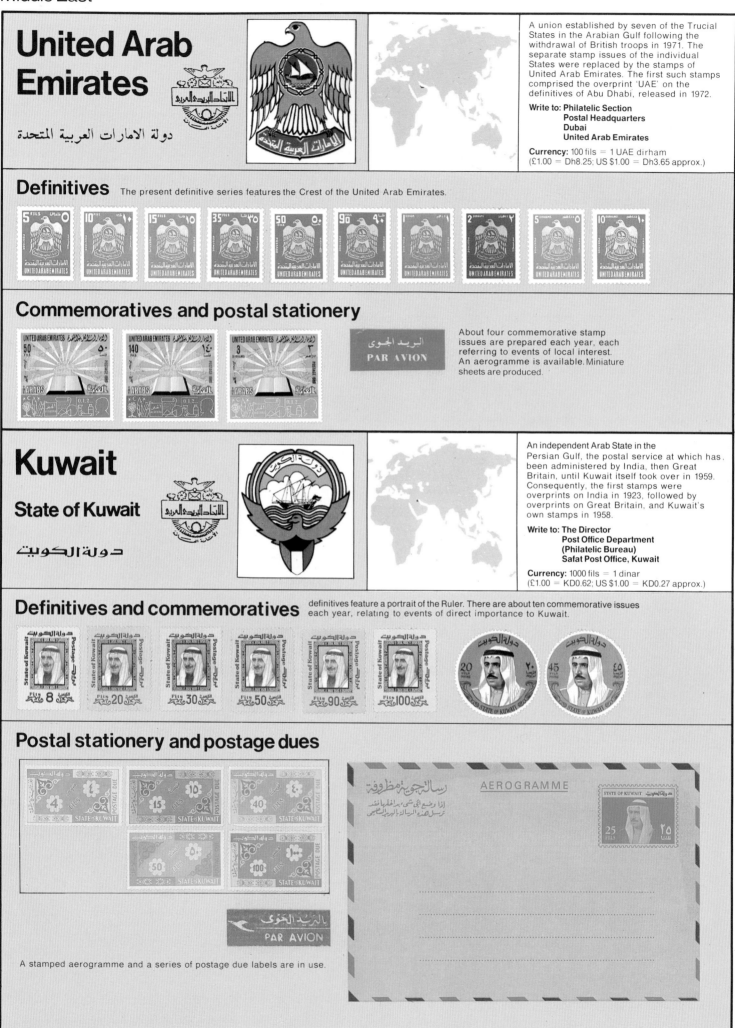

Qatar

State of Qatar

دولة قطر

An independent Arab State whose wealth has come from oil. There was a British postal administration from 1950 to 1963, with British stamps used from 1950. British stamps were overprinted 'Qatar' in 1957, while stamps inscribed with the name were introduced in 1961.

**Write to: Philatelic Bureau
Department of Posts
Doha
State of Qatar**

Currency: 100 dirhams = 1 riyal
(£1.00 = 8.78R; US $1.00 = 3.64R approx.)

Definitives

The current definitive series features the portrait of Sheikh Khalifa. Booklets of definitives sold from vending machines are available: these definitives have a similar design to those issued in normal sheets, but are smaller in format and in different colours.

Commemoratives and other items

International events are commemorated on an average of five special issues each year. A stamped aerogramme and registered envelope are in use, as are postage due labels.

Iraq

Republic of Iraq

الجمهورية العراقية

A country to the west of Iran, Iraq was formerly under Turkish control, until a British Mandate was declared following the First World War. It became a Republic in 1958. The first stamps appeared in 1918, being overprints on the stamps of Turkey, reading 'Iraq in British Occupation'. Stamps inscribed Iraq appeared in 1923.

**Write to: Ministry of Transport & Communications, PTT State Organization
Posts Administration, Stamp Department
Baghdad, Republic of Iraq**

Currency: 1000 fils = 1 dinar
(£1.00 = 0.68d; US $1.00 = 0.30d approx.)

Definitives, commemoratives and other items

The current definitive series features a range of designs including a view of a power station and dam, statues, a harp and a minaret.

The commemorative issues relate to national events and there are about twelve such issues each year. First day covers are made available. A set of Official stamps is in use, the design featuring an eagle. An aerogramme is also in use.

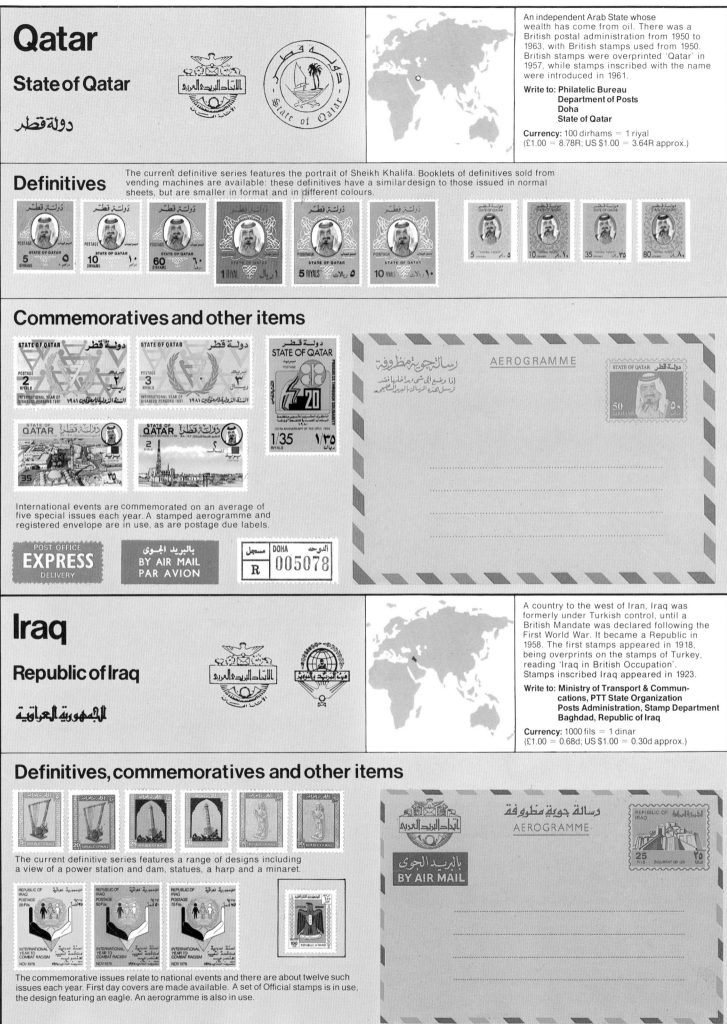

Oman
Sultanate of Oman

سلطنة عُمان

This Sultanate in Arabia was formerly known as Muscat and Oman. As the postal administration has been in the hands of both India and Great Britain, the stamps of East Africa, Pakistan and Great Britain have been used. The first stamps inscribed Muscat and Oman appeared in 1966; stamps designated Oman were first issued in 1971.

Write to: Philatelic Bureau
Ministry of Posts, Telegraphs & Telephones
Directorate General of Posts
Muscat
Sultanate of Oman

Currency: 1000 biazas = 1 Omani rial
(£1.00 = RO 0.78; US $1.00 = RO 0.35 approx.)

Definitives

The current definitive series features historic scenes of the Sultanate.

Commemoratives

There are only about three or four commemorative sets each year, honouring local events and anniversaries. First day covers are available.

Postal stationery

Two different stamped aerogrammes are in use.

Yemen Arab Republic

الجمهورية العربية اليمنية

Yemen is part of Arabia, which was formerly part of the Ottoman Empire. In 1958 it entered into a union with Egypt and Syria for a brief period. Stamps for Yemen appeared from 1926 to 1962. In 1962 the first stamps for the Yemen Arab Republic appeared.

Write to: Philatelic Bureau
Ministry of Communications
General Department of Post
Sana'a, Yemen Arab Republic

Currency: 100 fils = 1 riyal
(£1.00 = 10.16R; US $1.00 = 4.57R approx.)

Definitives, commemoratives and postal stationery

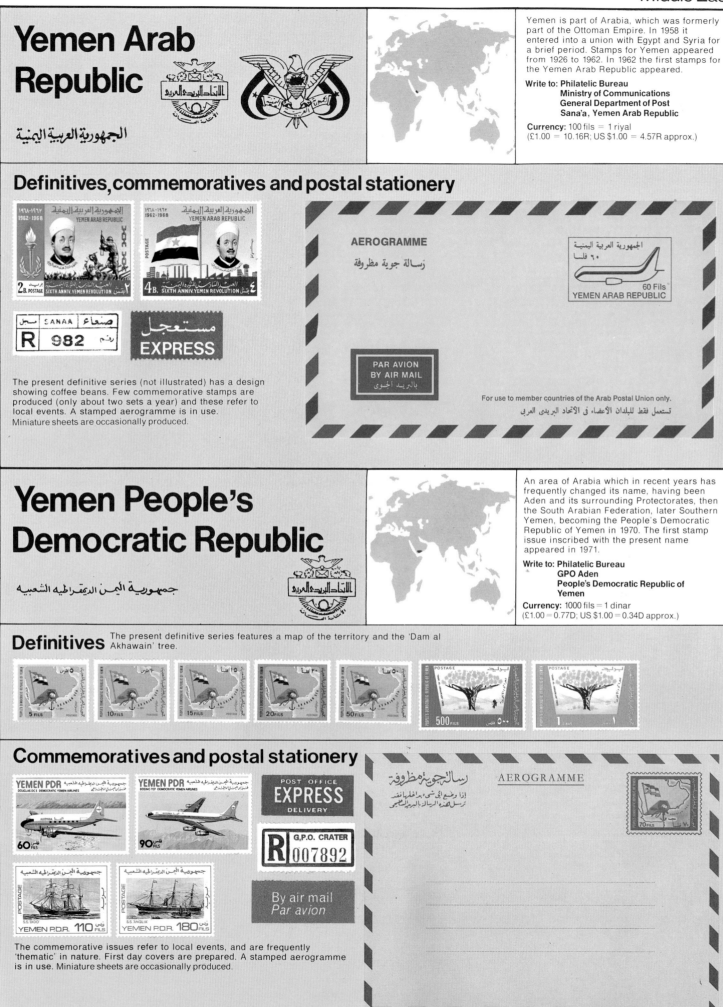

The present definitive series (not illustrated) has a design showing coffee beans. Few commemorative stamps are produced (only about two sets a year) and these refer to local events. A stamped aerogramme is in use. Miniature sheets are occasionally produced.

Yemen People's Democratic Republic

جمهورية اليمن الديمقراطيه الشعبيه

An area of Arabia which in recent years has frequently changed its name, having been Aden and its surrounding Protectorates, then the South Arabian Federation, later Southern Yemen, becoming the People's Democratic Republic of Yemen in 1970. The first stamp issue inscribed with the present name appeared in 1971.

Write to: Philatelic Bureau
GPO Aden
People's Democratic Republic of Yemen

Currency: 1000 fils = 1 dinar
(£1.00 = 0.77D; US $1.00 = 0.34D approx.)

Definitives

The present definitive series features a map of the territory and the 'Dam al Akhawain' tree.

Commemoratives and postal stationery

The commemorative issues refer to local events, and are frequently 'thematic' in nature. First day covers are prepared. A stamped aerogramme is in use. Miniature sheets are occasionally produced.

Asia

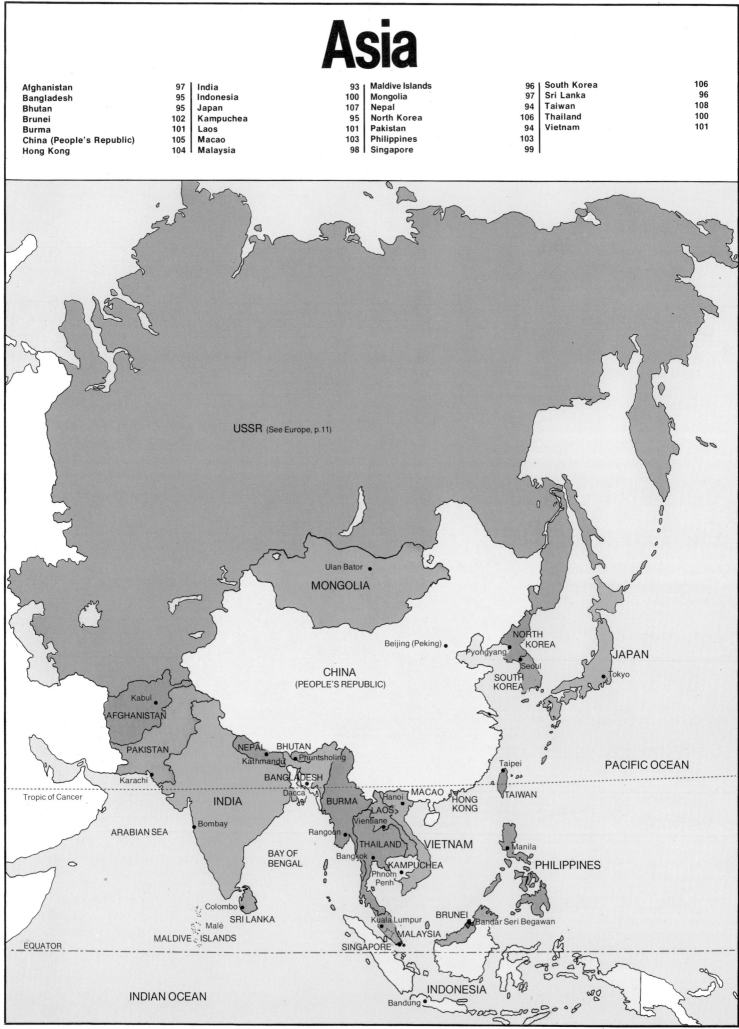

India

भारत

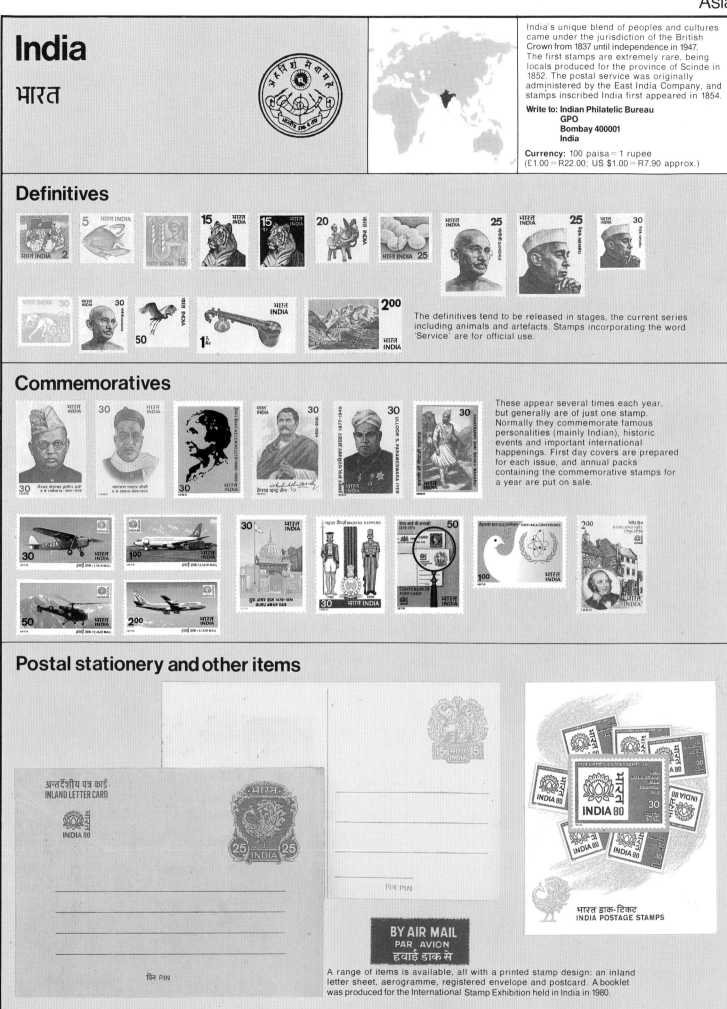

India's unique blend of peoples and cultures came under the jurisdiction of the British Crown from 1837 until independence in 1947. The first stamps are extremely rare, being locals produced for the province of Scinde in 1852. The postal service was originally administered by the East India Company, and stamps inscribed India first appeared in 1854.

Write to: Indian Philatelic Bureau
GPO
Bombay 400001
India

Currency: 100 paisa = 1 rupee
(£1.00 = R22.00; US $1.00 = R7.90 approx.)

Definitives

The definitives tend to be released in stages, the current series including animals and artefacts. Stamps incorporating the word 'Service' are for official use.

Commemoratives

These appear several times each year, but generally are of just one stamp. Normally they commemorate famous personalities (mainly Indian), historic events and important international happenings. First day covers are prepared for each issue, and annual packs containing the commemorative stamps for a year are put on sale.

Postal stationery and other items

A range of items is available, all with a printed stamp design: an inland letter sheet, aerogramme, registered envelope and postcard. A booklet was produced for the International Stamp Exhibition held in India in 1980.

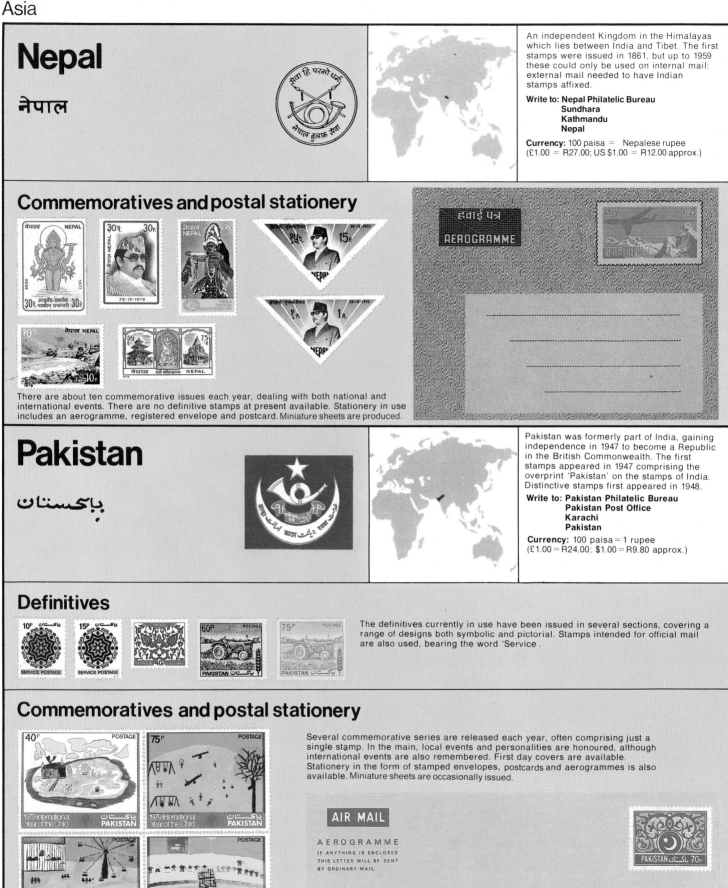

Nepal

नेपाल

An independent Kingdom in the Himalayas which lies between India and Tibet. The first stamps were issued in 1861, but up to 1959 these could only be used on internal mail: external mail needed to have Indian stamps affixed.

Write to: Nepal Philatelic Bureau
Sundhara
Kathmandu
Nepal

Currency: 100 paisa = Nepalese rupee
(£1.00 = R27.00; US $1.00 = R12.00 approx.)

Commemoratives and postal stationery

There are about ten commemorative issues each year, dealing with both national and international events. There are no definitive stamps at present available. Stationery in use includes an aerogramme, registered envelope and postcard. Miniature sheets are produced.

Pakistan

پاکستان

Pakistan was formerly part of India, gaining independence in 1947 to become a Republic in the British Commonwealth. The first stamps appeared in 1947 comprising the overprint 'Pakistan' on the stamps of India. Distinctive stamps first appeared in 1948.

Write to: Pakistan Philatelic Bureau
Pakistan Post Office
Karachi
Pakistan

Currency: 100 paisa = 1 rupee
(£1.00 = R24.00; $1.00 = R9.80 approx.)

Definitives

The definitives currently in use have been issued in several sections, covering a range of designs both symbolic and pictorial. Stamps intended for official mail are also used, bearing the word 'Service.'

Commemoratives and postal stationery

Several commemorative series are released each year, often comprising just a single stamp. In the main, local events and personalities are honoured, although international events are also remembered. First day covers are available. Stationery in the form of stamped envelopes, postcards and aerogrammes is also available. Miniature sheets are occasionally issued.

Bhutan

হ্ম্‌যা

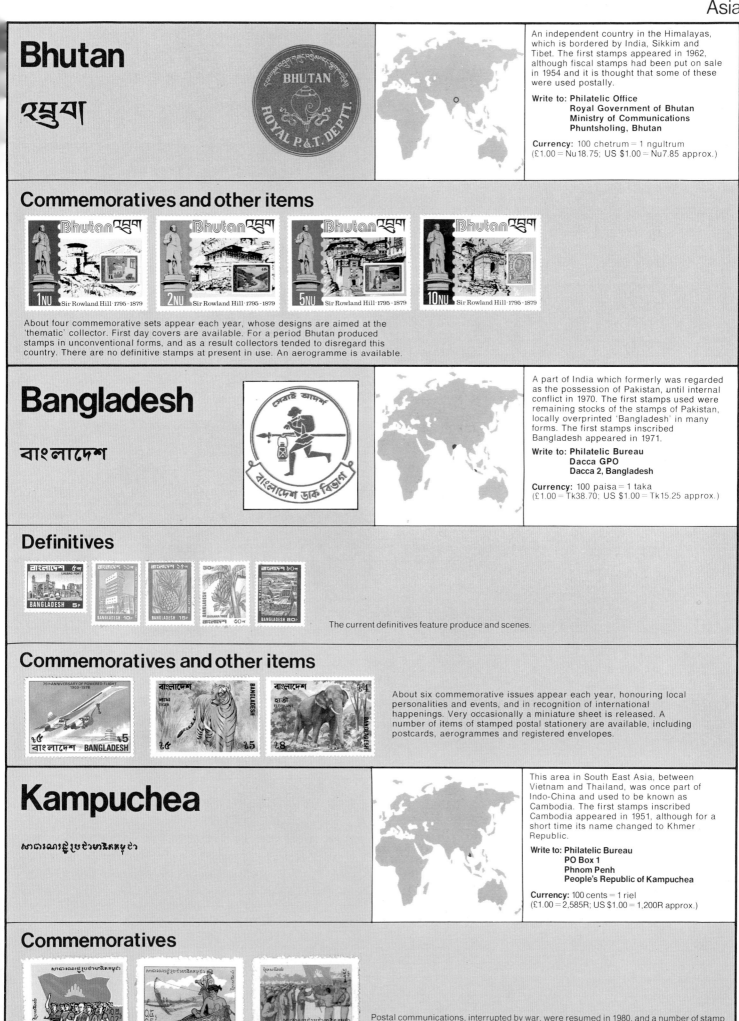

An independent country in the Himalayas, which is bordered by India, Sikkim and Tibet. The first stamps appeared in 1962, although fiscal stamps had been put on sale in 1954 and it is thought that some of these were used postally.

Write to: Philatelic Office
Royal Government of Bhutan
Ministry of Communications
Phuntsholing, Bhutan

Currency: 100 chetrum = 1 ngultrum
(£1.00 = Nu 18.75; US $1.00 = Nu7.85 approx.)

Commemoratives and other items

1NU Sir Rowland Hill · 1795 - 1879
2NU Sir Rowland Hill · 1795 - 1879
5NU Sir Rowland Hill · 1795 - 1879
10NU Sir Rowland Hill · 1795 - 1879

About four commemorative sets appear each year, whose designs are aimed at the 'thematic' collector. First day covers are available. For a period Bhutan produced stamps in unconventional forms, and as a result collectors tended to disregard this country. There are no definitive stamps at present in use. An aerogramme is available.

Bangladesh

বাংলাদেশ

A part of India which formerly was regarded as the possession of Pakistan, until internal conflict in 1970. The first stamps used were remaining stocks of the stamps of Pakistan, locally overprinted 'Bangladesh' in many forms. The first stamps inscribed Bangladesh appeared in 1971.

Write to: Philatelic Bureau
Dacca GPO
Dacca 2, Bangladesh

Currency: 100 paisa = 1 taka
(£1.00 = Tk38.70; US $1.00 = Tk15.25 approx.)

Definitives

The current definitives feature produce and scenes.

Commemoratives and other items

About six commemorative issues appear each year, honouring local personalities and events, and in recognition of international happenings. Very occasionally a miniature sheet is released. A number of items of stamped postal stationery are available, including postcards, aerogrammes and registered envelopes.

Kampuchea

ស្ថាធរណរដ្ឋ ្រ ់ ប្រ ជាមានិត កម្ពុជា

This area in South East Asia, between Vietnam and Thailand, was once part of Indo-China and used to be known as Cambodia. The first stamps inscribed Cambodia appeared in 1951, although for a short time its name changed to Khmer Republic.

Write to: Philatelic Bureau
PO Box 1
Phnom Penh
People's Republic of Kampuchea

Currency: 100 cents = 1 riel
(£1.00 = 2,585R; US $1.00 = 1,200R approx.)

Commemoratives

Postal communications, interrupted by war, were resumed in 1980, and a number of stamp issues are now appearing.

Sri Lanka

ශ්‍රී ලංකා இலங்கை

A tropical island to the south of India, known as Ceylon until 1972. The civilisation on the island dates back to the time of Vijaya who was exiled on the island, about 2,500 years ago, and became King Lanka. Stamps inscribed Ceyon first appeared in 1857 to be replaced by stamps inscribed Sri Lanka in 1972.

Write to: Department of Posts
Philatelic Bureau
4th Floor, Ceylinco House
Colombo-1, Sri Lanka

Currency: 100 cents = 1 Sri Lanka rupee
(£1.00 = R40.00; US $1.00 = R18.00 approx.)

Definitives

The definitive series of Sri Lanka consists of a number of different sets, each comprising about four or six values and each with its own theme. One has featured flowers, another butterflies. In addition, the definitives have frequently been produced as miniature sheets.

Commemoratives and postal stationery

Commemorative issues appear about six times a year, normally associated with local events. First day covers are made available, and occasionally a miniature sheet is issued. A stamped aerogramme and a postcard are on sale.

Maldives

Republic of Maldives

An independent Republic to the south-west of Sri Lanka, the Maldives comprise some 2,000 coral islands, which, until 1965, were part of the British Commonwealth. A post office opened in 1906 using the stamps of Ceylon suitably overprinted. Stamps inscribed Maldive Islands appeared in 1909.

Write to: Philatelic Bureau
General Post Office
Male'
Republic of Maldives

Currency: 100 larees = 1 Maldive rupee
(£1.00 = 8.82R; $1.00 = 3.93R approx.)

Commemoratives and postal stationery

There are about eight or nine commemorative sets each year, mostly of an international nature with thematic designs, frequently including a miniature sheet. The last definitive issue appeared in 1966 featuring seashells, flowers and birds. Stamps for everyday use are now satisfied by commemorative issues. An aerogramme is in use.

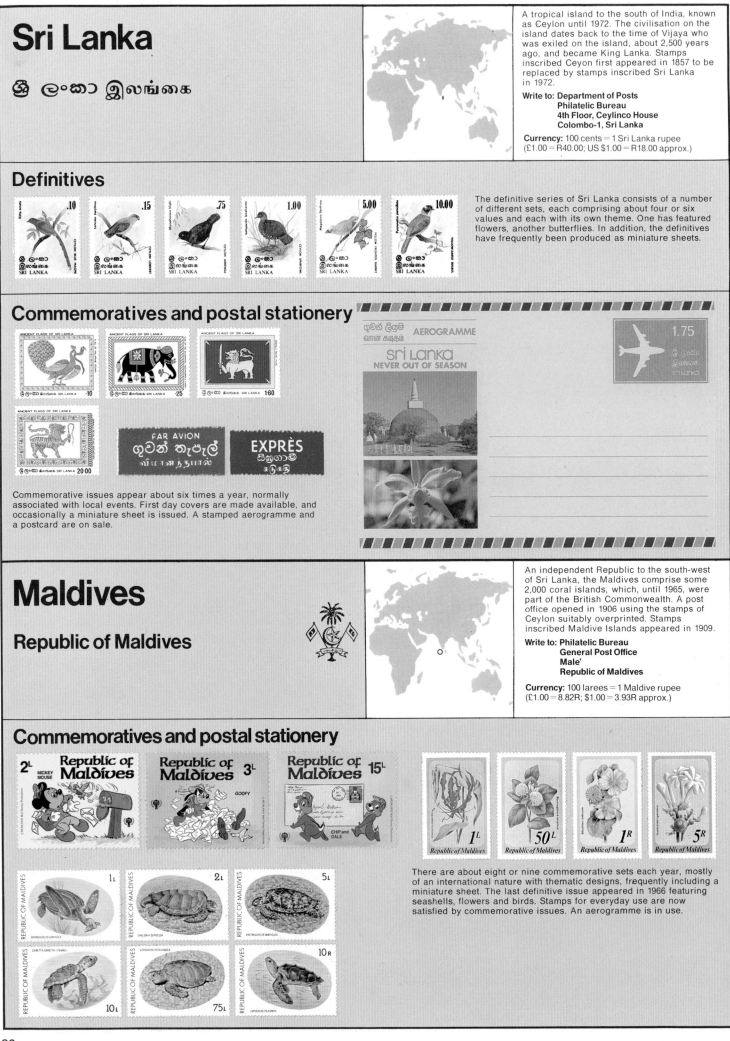

Mongolia

МОНГОЛ ШУУДАН

A People's Republic in Asia which lies between Russia and China. It was once the head of a large empire which stretched over much of Asia and Europe. The first stamps were issued in 1924: the early stamps were inscribed in both Mongol and English.

Write to: Bureau of Stamps
Ministry of Communications
Ulan Bator, Mongolia
(Philatelia Hungarica – see p.33 – will also supply Mongolian stamps)

Currency: 100 mung = 1 tugrik
(£1.00 = 7.05T; US $1.00 = 3.36T approx.)

Definitives, commemoratives and other items

Definitive stamps issued in 1975, show important buildings.
The commemorative sets issued, of which there are about twelve each year, are 'thematic' in their design, relating to international events. Miniature sheets are produced fairly frequently. First day covers are available. A stamped aerogramme and postcards are in use.

Afghanistan

Postes Afghanes

داافغانستان پُست

A barren, mountainous country in Asia, which for just over 200 years was a monarchy, becoming an independent Republic in 1973. The first stamps appeared in 1893, having the rare distinction that the method of 'cancelling' was to tear the stamps. Equally unusual is the fact that many of the early stamps were round.

Write to: Ministry of Communications
Postal Department
Philatelic Section, Kabul
Democratic Republic of Afghanistan

Currency: 100 puls = 1 afghani
(£1.00 = AFS115.00; US $1.00 = AFS44.00 approx.)

Commemoratives and other items

The commemorative issues relate to national events, there being about ten such issues each year, although these normally only comprise one or two stamps. No definitives have been released in recent times. An aerogramme and postcard are available. Stamps are sold at a premium for charitable purposes.

AEROGRAMME

REPUBLIQUE D'AFGHANISTAN

EXPRES   PAR AVION

Malaysia

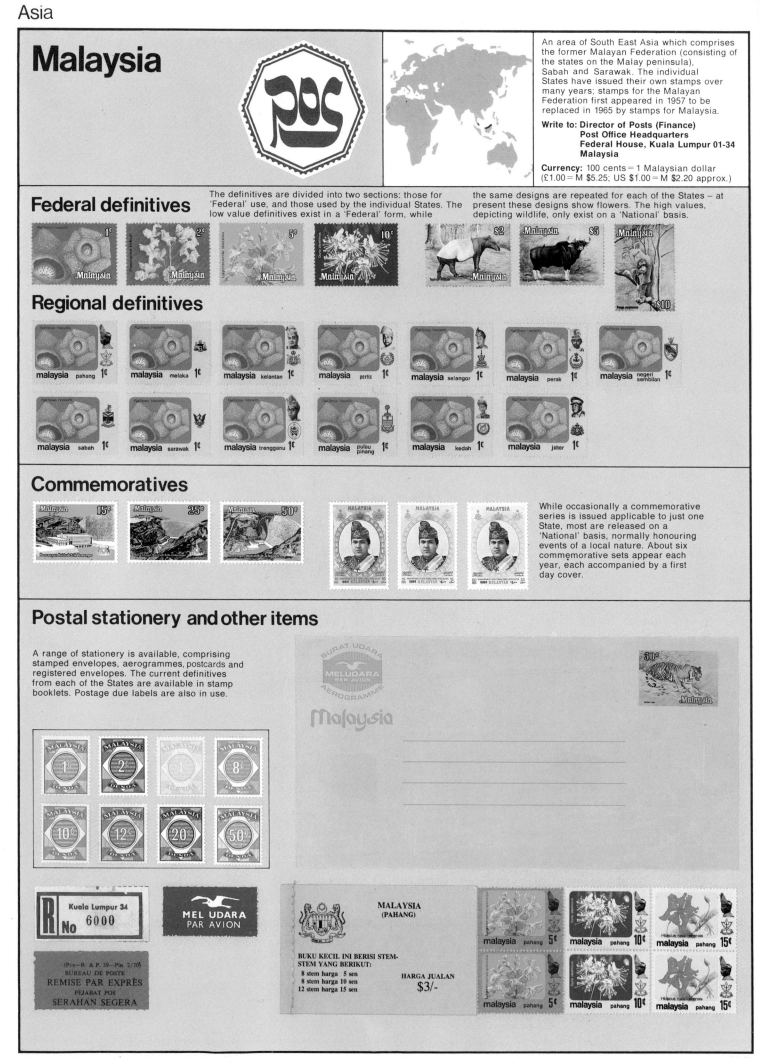

An area of South East Asia which comprises the former Malayan Federation (consisting of the states on the Malay peninsula), Sabah and Sarawak. The individual States have issued their own stamps over many years; stamps for the Malayan Federation first appeared in 1957 to be replaced in 1965 by stamps for Malaysia.

Write to: Director of Posts (Finance)
Post Office Headquarters
Federal House, Kuala Lumpur 01-34
Malaysia

Currency: 100 cents = 1 Malaysian dollar
(£1.00 = M $5.25; US $1.00 = M $2.20 approx.)

Federal definitives

The definitives are divided into two sections: those for 'Federal' use, and those used by the individual States. The low value definitives exist in a 'Federal' form, while the same designs are repeated for each of the States – at present these designs show flowers. The high values, depicting wildlife, only exist on a 'National' basis.

Regional definitives

Commemoratives

While occasionally a commemorative series is issued applicable to just one State, most are released on a 'National' basis, normally honouring events of a local nature. About six commemorative sets appear each year, each accompanied by a first day cover.

Postal stationery and other items

A range of stationery is available, comprising stamped envelopes, aerogrammes, postcards and registered envelopes. The current definitives from each of the States are available in stamp booklets. Postage due labels are also in use.

Singapore

A Republic comprising a group of islands on the southern tip of the Malay peninsula – named after the largest island in the group – which became an important sea port and trading centre, thanks to its position between India and China. It became a separate colony in 1948 when the Straits Settlements were dissolved.

Write to: Philatelic Bureau
Postal Services Department
8th Floor, World Trade Centre
Maritime Square, Singapore 0409
Republic of Singapore
Currency: 100 cents = 1 Singapore dollar
(£1.00 = S $4.72; US $1.00 = S $2.08 approx.)

Definitives

Singapore has used a variety of stamp issues, including those of India and the Straits Settlements [also Straits Settlements stamps overprinted 'BMA (*British Military Administration*) Malaya']. Singapore's own stamps appeared in 1948. The present definitives show sailing vessels.

Commemoratives

About six issues of local significance appear each year. First day covers and presentation packs are produced. Occasionally a miniature sheet is issued.

Postal stationery and other items

Postal stationery available includes picture postcards with a printed stamp, a stamped aerogramme and a registered envelope with the registration fee pre-paid, but not the postage charge. Postage dues and stamp booklets, containing definitives, are in use.

AIR MAIL
AEROGRAMME

SINGAPORE 35¢

SINGAPORE 59
No 9089

BY AIR MAIL
PAR AVION

Pos-R & P 39
POST OFFICE
EXPRESS

SINGAPORE POSTAGE DUE 1 CENT	SINGAPORE POSTAGE DUE 4 CENTS
SINGAPORE POSTAGE DUE 10 CENTS	SINGAPORE POSTAGE DUE 20 CENTS
SINGAPORE POSTAGE DUE 50 CENTS	

POSTAL SERVICES DEPARTMENT
SINGAPORE

STAMP BOOKLET PRICE $1

speedpost
SINGAPORE

Indonesia

Republik Indonesia

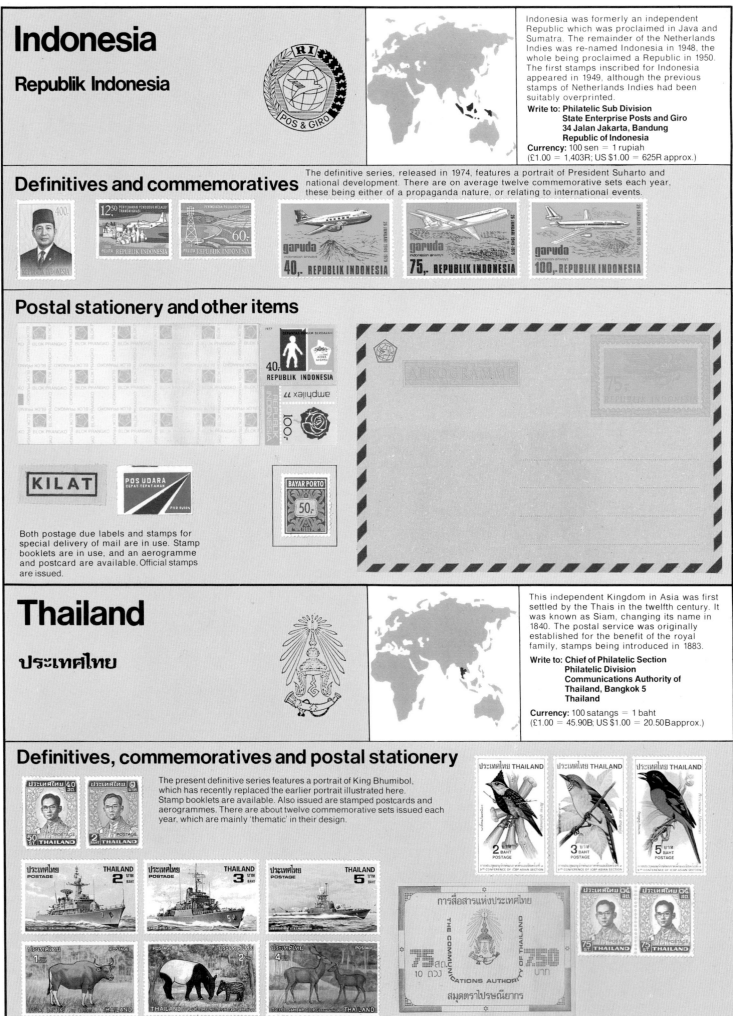

Indonesia was formerly an independent Republic which was proclaimed in Java and Sumatra. The remainder of the Netherlands Indies was re-named Indonesia in 1948, the whole being proclaimed a Republic in 1950. The first stamps inscribed for Indonesia appeared in 1949, although the previous stamps of Netherlands Indies had been suitably overprinted.

**Write to: Philatelic Sub Division
State Enterprise Posts and Giro
34 Jalan Jakarta, Bandung
Republic of Indonesia**

Currency: 100 sen = 1 rupiah
(£1.00 = 1,403R; US $1.00 = 625R approx.)

Definitives and commemoratives

The definitive series, released in 1974, features a portrait of President Suharto and national development. There are on average twelve commemorative sets each year, these being either of a propaganda nature, or relating to international events.

Postal stationery and other items

Both postage due labels and stamps for special delivery of mail are in use. Stamp booklets are in use, and an aerogramme and postcard are available. Official stamps are issued.

Thailand

ประเทศไทย

This independent Kingdom in Asia was first settled by the Thais in the twelfth century. It was known as Siam, changing its name in 1840. The postal service was originally established for the benefit of the royal family, stamps being introduced in 1883.

**Write to: Chief of Philatelic Section
Philatelic Division
Communications Authority of
Thailand, Bangkok 5
Thailand**

Currency: 100 satangs = 1 baht
(£1.00 = 45.90B; US $1.00 = 20.50B approx.)

Definitives, commemoratives and postal stationery

The present definitive series features a portrait of King Bhumibol, which has recently replaced the earlier portrait illustrated here. Stamp booklets are available. Also issued are stamped postcards and aerogrammes. There are about twelve commemorative sets issued each year, which are mainly 'thematic' in their design.

Vietnam

Viêt Nam

Buu Chinh

Formerly part of French Indo-China, the first stamps comprised overprints issued in 1945. Since that date there have been several changes: independence in 1949 was followed by partitioning in 1954, with separate stamp issues for South and North Vietnam. Separate issues ended with the formation of the Socialist Republic of Vietnam in 1976.

Write to: Philatelic Department
Xunhasaba
32 Hai Bà Trung, Hanoi
Socialist Republic of Vietnam

Currency: 100 xu = 1 dong
(£1.00 = 5.16 D; US $1.00 = 2.18D approx.)

Definitives and commemoratives

Definitive stamps (not illustrated) are in use, and military frank stamps are issued. The commemorative issues tend to be of a propaganda nature and are frequently 'thematic' in design. There are about twelve such issues each year.

Laos

République Democratique Populaire Lao

ສາທາລະນະລັດປະຊາທິປະໄຕປະຊາຊົນລາວ

A Republic in South East Asia which gained independence from France in 1949, and since that time has had a rather violent history. The stamps of French Indo-China were used until 1951, when the stamps of Laos first appeared.

Write to: Service Philatélique
Direction des Postes
Ministère des PTT
Vientiane
Lao People's Democratic Republic

Currency: 100 cents = 1 kip
(£1.00 = 23.85K; US $1.00 = 10.00K approx.)

Commemoratives and other items

There are on average four commemorative sets each year, mostly of a propaganda nature. No definitive stamps have been issued in recent years. Postage due labels have been in use. Miniature sheets are issued.

Burma

Socialist Republic of the Union of Burma

ပြည်ထောင်စုဆိုရှယ်လစ်သမ္မတမြန်မာနိုင်ငံတော်

A country lying to the east of India, which was once part of India until it separated in 1937. Thence it was a British Crown Colony until independence in 1948. From 1942 to 1945, the Japanese occupied the country. Indian stamps overprinted for Burma appeared in 1937, followed by stamps inscribed Burma the following year.

Write to: Myanma Export Import Corporation
Export Division, Philatelic Section
No. 622/624 Merchant St, Rangoon
The Socialist Republic
of the Union of Burma

Currency: 100 pyas = 1 kyat
(£1.00 = 15.10K; US $1.00 = 6.72K approx.)

Definitives, commemoratives and postal stationery

Local events are commemorated by about three special stamp issues each year. The definitives show the national races of Burma. Items of postal stationery are available.

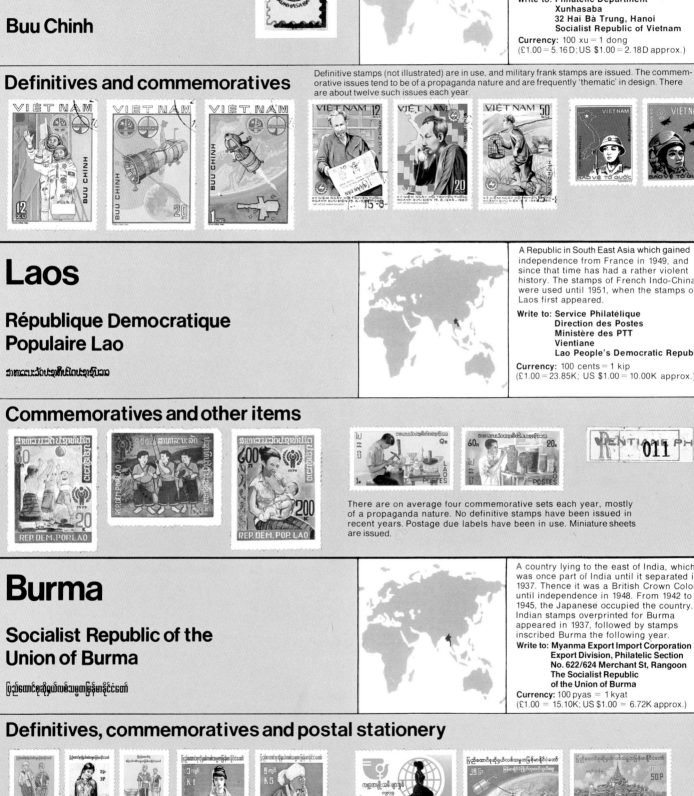

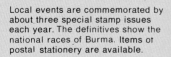

Brunei

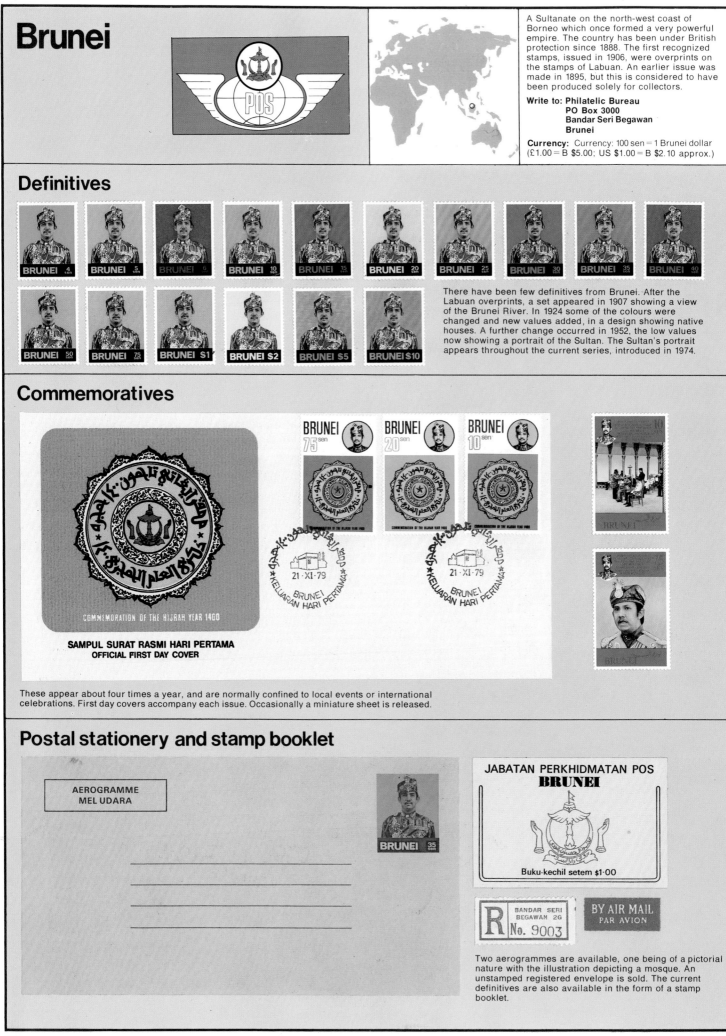

A Sultanate on the north-west coast of Borneo which once formed a very powerful empire. The country has been under British protection since 1888. The first recognized stamps, issued in 1906, were overprints on the stamps of Labuan. An earlier issue was made in 1895, but this is considered to have been produced solely for collectors.

Write to: Philatelic Bureau
PO Box 3000
Bandar Seri Begawan
Brunei

Currency: Currency: 100 sen = 1 Brunei dollar
(£1.00 = B $5.00; US $1.00 = B $2.10 approx.)

Definitives

There have been few definitives from Brunei. After the Labuan overprints, a set appeared in 1907 showing a view of the Brunei River. In 1924 some of the colours were changed and new values added, in a design showing native houses. A further change occurred in 1952, the low values now showing a portrait of the Sultan. The Sultan's portrait appears throughout the current series, introduced in 1974.

Commemoratives

These appear about four times a year, and are normally confined to local events or international celebrations. First day covers accompany each issue. Occasionally a miniature sheet is released.

Postal stationery and stamp booklet

Two aerogrammes are available, one being of a pictorial nature with the illustration depicting a mosque. An unstamped registered envelope is sold. The current definitives are also available in the form of a stamp booklet.

Philippines

Pilipinas

A group of over 7,000 islands in the China Sea, which were discovered by Ferdinand Magellan in 1521 and named in honour of King Philip II of Spain. After a history of control by various countries, they became independent in 1946. The first stamps appeared in 1854 while the islands were under Spanish Occupation.

Write to: Stamp and Philatelic Section
Bureau of Posts
Manila
Republic of the Philippines

Currency: 100 centavos = 1 Philippine peso
(£1.00 = 16.90P; US $1.00 = 7.65P approx.)

Definitives, commemoratives and other items

The present definitive series (not illustrated) depicts celebrities from the history of the Philippines. There are about twenty commemorative issues each year, but these mainly comprise just a single value. The events concerned are both national and international. An Official stamp is in use. An aerogramme and postcard are also available.

Macao

Macau

A Portuguese colony which lies on the Chinese coast at the mouth of the Canton River. The first stamps were issued in 1884, but definitives distinctively designed for Macao did not appear until 1934.

Write to: Service Postal, Da Direcções dos
Serviços de Correios e Telecomunicações
Macao
Asia

Currency: 100 avos = 1 pataca
(£1.00 = $12.00; US $1.00 = $5.30 approx.)

Definitives, commemoratives and other items

Very few commemorative stamps are issued, while those that do appear relate to local events. Definitives, a stamped aerogramme and postage due labels are in use.

Hong Kong

香港

Hong Kong is a British Crown Colony, situated at the mouth of the Canton River, consisting of the island of Hong Kong and the peninsula of Kowloon. Postage stamps were first issued on 8th December, 1862, featuring the portrait of Queen Victoria.

Write to: The Philatelic Bureau
General Post Office
Hong Kong

Currency: 100 cents = 1 Hong Kong dollar
(£1.00 = HK $11.85; US $1.00 = HK $5.20 approx.)

Definitives

The current definitives show the portrait of Queen Elizabeth II. They were released in 1973. The designs of the definitives are changed approximately every seven years.

Commemoratives

Commemorative issues are released about three times a year: for each a first day cover is made available. For certain issues souvenir folders are also sold, as are miniature sheets.

Postal stationery and postage dues

Hong Kong makes use of stamp booklets and aerogrammes, while postage due labels and registered envelopes are also available.

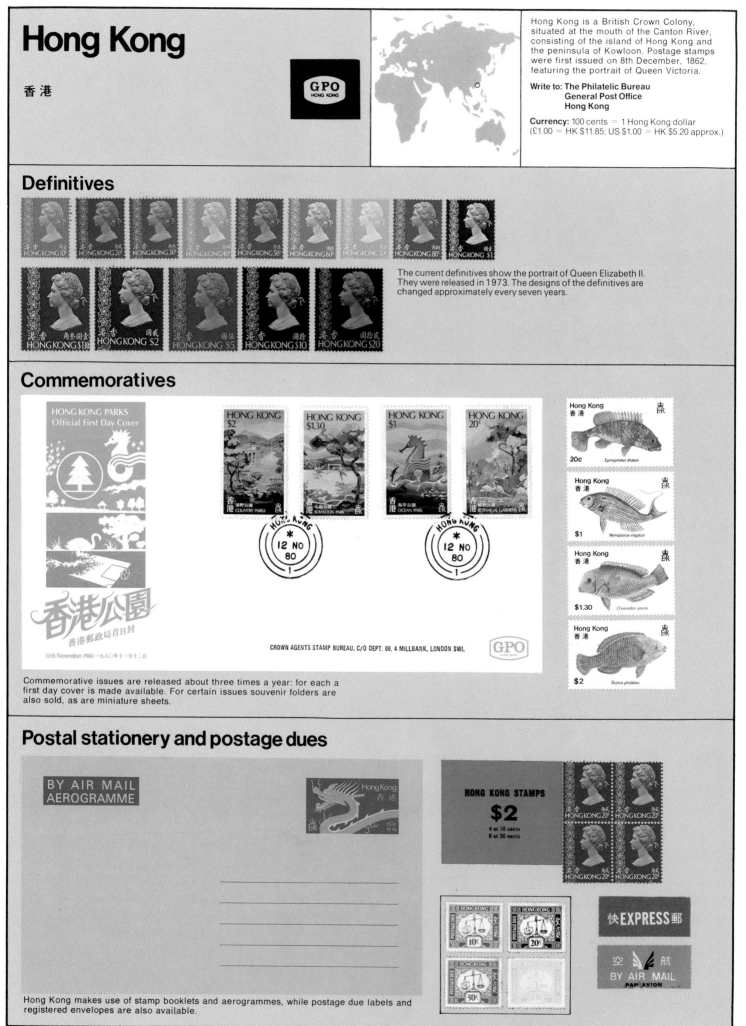

China

中国人民邮政

A Communist Republic in Asia which was proclaimed in 1949, after twenty years of war between the nationalists and communists. The first stamps of the Republic were issued in 1949, although there had been earlier private and local issues from China, including stamps issued by the communists during the war.

Write to: China National Stamp Corporation
28 Tung An Men Street
Beijing
People's Republic of China

Currency: 100 fen = 1 renminbi yuan
(£1.00 = ¥3.64; US $1.00 = ¥1.60 approx.)

Definitives
The definitive series currently in use features local industry and, on the higher values, local views.

Commemoratives

Commemorative issues appear about twenty-five times a year, although are usually of low face value. National events are commemorated, although many designs are thematic in nature. First day covers are available. Miniature sheets are occasionally produced.

首日封 F. D. C.

Postal stationery and other items

Stamp booklets are occasionally produced.
A postcard is also in use.

105

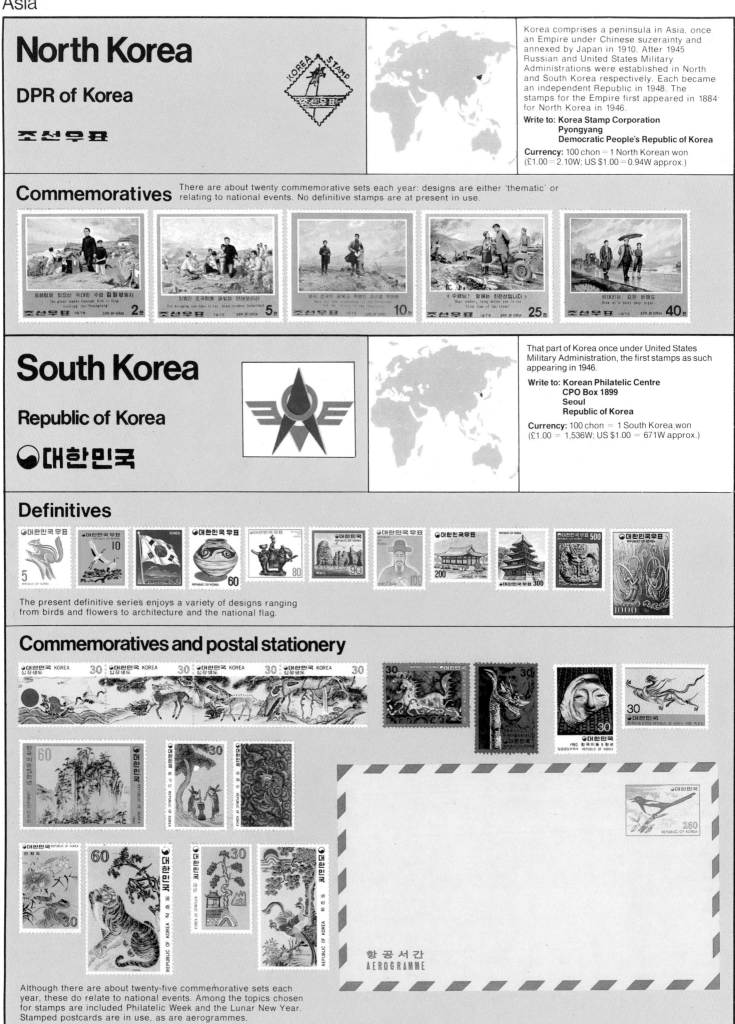

North Korea

DPR of Korea

조선우표

Korea comprises a peninsula in Asia, once an Empire under Chinese suzerainty and annexed by Japan in 1910. After 1945 Russian and United States Military Administrations were established in North and South Korea respectively. Each became an independent Republic in 1948. The stamps for the Empire first appeared in 1884 for North Korea in 1946.

Write to: **Korea Stamp Corporation**
Pyongyang
Democratic People's Republic of Korea

Currency: 100 chon = 1 North Korean won
(£1.00 = 2.10W; US $1.00 = 0.94W approx.)

Commemoratives

There are about twenty commemorative sets each year: designs are either 'thematic' or relating to national events. No definitive stamps are at present in use.

South Korea

Republic of Korea

대한민국

That part of Korea once under United States Military Administration, the first stamps as such appearing in 1946.

Write to: **Korean Philatelic Centre**
CPO Box 1899
Seoul
Republic of Korea

Currency: 100 chon = 1 South Korea won
(£1.00 = 1,536W; US $1.00 = 671W approx.)

Definitives

The present definitive series enjoys a variety of designs ranging from birds and flowers to architecture and the national flag.

Commemoratives and postal stationery

Although there are about twenty-five commemorative sets each year, these do relate to national events. Among the topics chosen for stamps are included Philatelic Week and the Lunar New Year. Stamped postcards are in use, as are aerogrammes.

Japan

Nippon

日本郵便

A chain of islands which comprise the Empire of Japan in Asia. While Japan can trace its history as far back as 500 AD, it was not really until the nineteenth century that Japan as it is known today developed. The first stamps were issued in 1871.

Write to: Tokyo Central Post Office
Philatelic Section
CPO Box 888
Tokyo, 100-91 Japan

Currency: yen
(£1.00 = ¥469.00; US $1.00 = ¥206.00 approx.)

Definitives
The current definitive series involves a range of designs.

Commemoratives

PHILATELY WEEK 1980
April 21, 1980

There are about twenty-five commemorative sets each year, these being related solely to Japan. Included in the annual programme are stamps for the New Year and Philatelic Week. First day covers are prepared.

Postal stationery and other items

Items of postal stationery are in use, including aerogrammes, postcards and parcel tags. An Official stamp is in use. Stamp booklets are available

Taiwan

票郵國民華中

Taiwan is one of a group of islands which have been occupied by the National Government since their expulsion from mainland China in 1949. Formerly known as Formosa, it was ceded to Japan in 1895, but handed back to China in 1945.

Write to: Philatelic Bureau
    Director General of Posts
    Taipei 106
    Taiwan

Currency: 100 cents = 1 new Taiwan dollar
(£1.00 = $t81.00; US $1.00 = $t36.00 approx.)

Definitives

The current definitives show flags, national development and a double carp.

Commemoratives and other items

There are about twenty commemorative sets released each year, being of a local nature, and frequently thematic in design. First day covers are prepared.
A stamped aerogramme is in use, as are registered envelopes and postcards. Stamp booklets are made available and official stamps are issued.

North Africa - Africa

Algeria	110	Equatorial Guinea	125	Mauritania	125	Sudan	112
Angola	129	Ethiopia	113	Mauritius	134	Swaziland	133
Ascension	142	Gabon	118	Morocco	110	Tanzania	129
Benin	121	The Gambia	124	Mozambique	126	Togo	121
Bophuthatswana	139	Ghana	139	Niger	113	Transkei	139
Botswana	132	Guinea	132	Nigeria	119	Tristan da Cunha	141
Burundi	115	Guinea-Bissau	115	Rwanda	127	Tunisia	111
Cameroon	128	Ivory Coast	121	St Thomas and Prince Islands	127	Uganda	114
Cape Verde	126	Kenya	116	St Helena	141	Upper Volta	123
Central African Republic	119	Lesotho	135	Senegal	128	Venda	139
Chad	119	Liberia	122	Seychelles	137	Zaire	117
Comoro Islands	127	Libya	111	Sierra Leone	122	Zambia	136
Congo Republic	117	Malagasy Republic	130	Somalia	114	Zil Eloigne Sesel	137
Djibouti	134	Malaŵi	130	South Africa	138	Zimbabwe	131
Egypt	112	Mali	123	South West Africa	140		

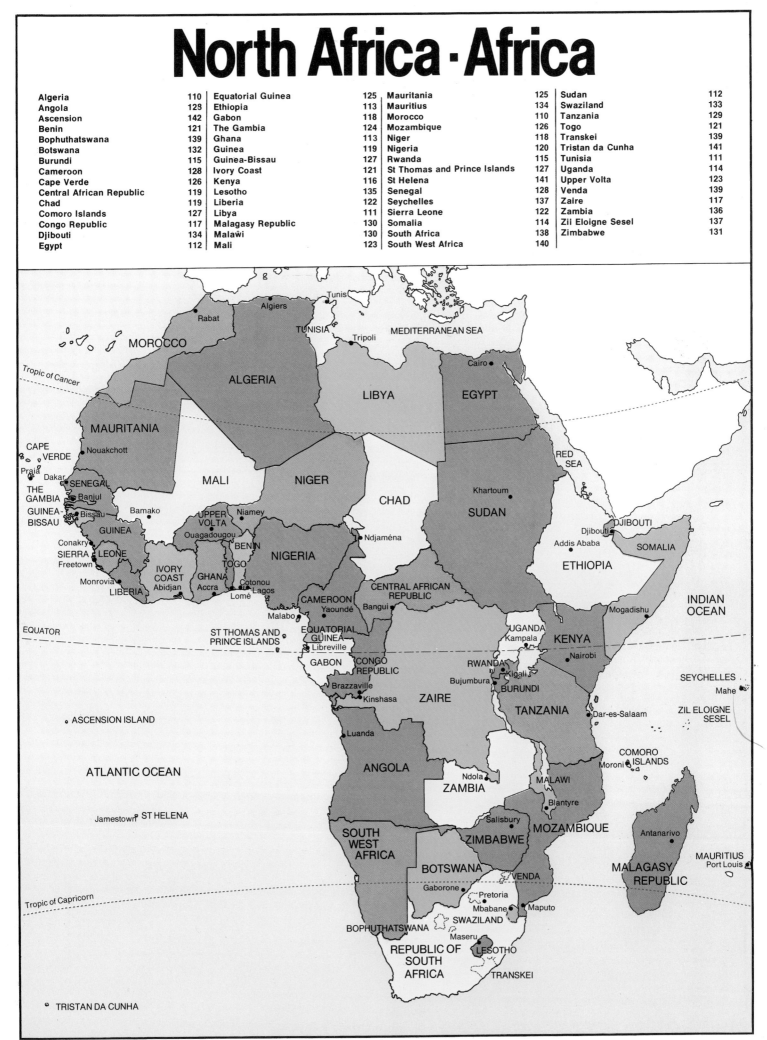

109

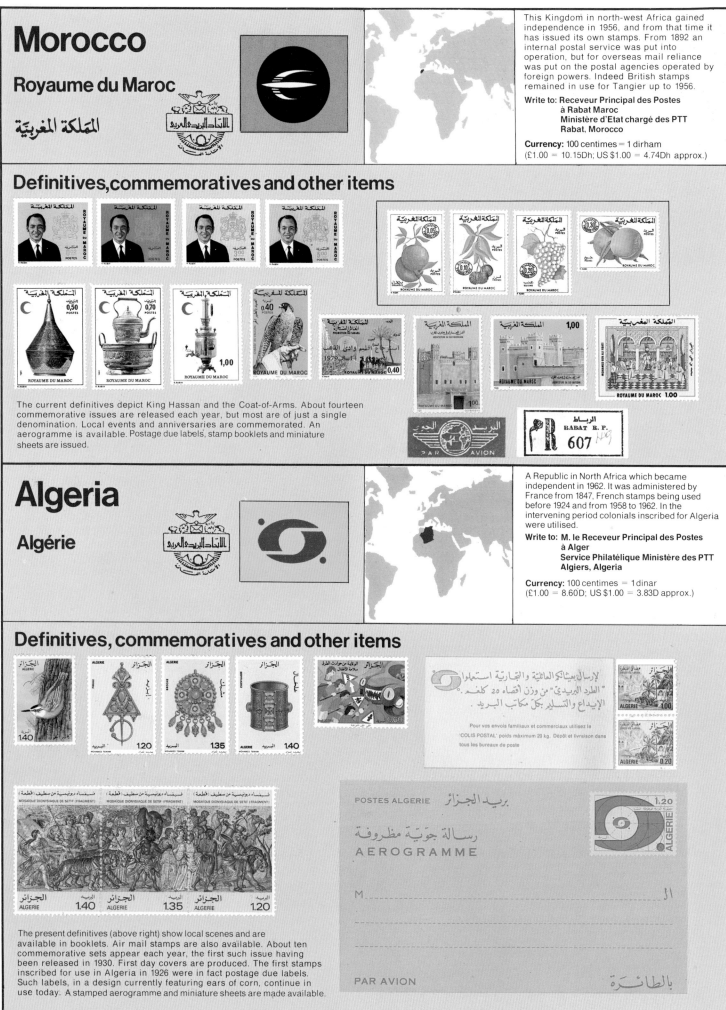

Morocco

Royaume du Maroc

المملكة المغربية

This Kingdom in north-west Africa gained independence in 1956, and from that time it has issued its own stamps. From 1892 an internal postal service was put into operation, but for overseas mail reliance was put on the postal agencies operated by foreign powers. Indeed British stamps remained in use for Tangier up to 1956.

Write to: Receveur Principal des Postes à Rabat Maroc
Ministère d'Etat chargé des PTT Rabat, Morocco

Currency: 100 centimes = 1 dirham
(£1.00 = 10.15Dh; US $1.00 = 4.74Dh approx.)

Definitives, commemoratives and other items

The current definitives depict King Hassan and the Coat-of-Arms. About fourteen commemorative issues are released each year, but most are of just a single denomination. Local events and anniversaries are commemorated. An aerogramme is available. Postage due labels, stamp booklets and miniature sheets are issued.

Algeria

Algérie

A Republic in North Africa which became independent in 1962. It was administered by France from 1847, French stamps being used before 1924 and from 1958 to 1962. In the intervening period colonials inscribed for Algeria were utilised.

Write to: M. le Receveur Principal des Postes à Alger
Service Philatélique Ministère des PTT Algiers, Algeria

Currency: 100 centimes = 1 dinar
(£1.00 = 8.60D; US $1.00 = 3.83D approx.)

Definitives, commemoratives and other items

The present definitives (above right) show local scenes and are available in booklets. Air mail stamps are also available. About ten commemorative sets appear each year, the first such issue having been released in 1930. First day covers are produced. The first stamps inscribed for use in Algeria in 1926 were in fact postage due labels. Such labels, in a design currently featuring ears of corn, continue in use today. A stamped aerogramme and miniature sheets are made available.

Tunisia

République Tunisienne

الجمهورية التونسية

A Republic in North Africa which was formerly a French Protectorate. A postal service was established by the Sardinians in 1853, and Sardinian stamps were at first used. Later, Italian stamps were in use, until Tunisia produced her own stamps in 1888. Stamps for air mail post were introduced in 1919.

Write to: **Service Philatélique, Direction des Services Postaux, Ministère des Transports et des Communications, Tunis, Tunisia.**

Currency: 1000 millimes = 1 dinar
(£1.00 = 0.95D; US $1.00 = 0.40D approx.)

Definitives and commemoratives

The definitive stamps show Tunisian work and life. About fourteen commemorative sets appear each year, honouring international events. First day covers and miniature sheets are made available.

Libya

Socialist People's Libyan Arab Jamahiriya

الجماهيرية العربية الليبية الشعبية الاشتراكية

Libya is in fact the Greek name for North Africa. Libya was formerly an Italian colony: following a revolution the country became the Libyan Arab Republic. Stamps of Italy suitably overprinted were issued in 1912, followed by distinctive stamps in 1921.

Write to: **Post and Telecommunications Corporation Philatelic Service – Tripoli Socialist People's Libyan Arab Jamahiriya**

Currency: 100 dirhams = 1 Libyan dinar
(£1.00 = 0.67d; US $1.00 = 0.30d approx.)

Definitives, commemoratives and other items

Definitive stamps issued in 1979 show a Libyan torch. Coil stamps are available, showing a hunting trophy. An average of fifteen commemorative stamps appear each year, honouring events of local importance, sometimes supported by miniature sheets. A series of postage due labels, depicting men in a boat, is in use. An aerogramme is available and, from time to time, a booklet is produced.

Egypt

AR Egypt

جمهورية مصر العربية

An Arab Republic in north-east Africa. The civilisation in Egypt dates back some 6,000 years, and indeed a postal service, by pigeons, was in use as long ago as 1,300 BC. The first stamps as such did not appear until 1866.

Write to: Philatelic Office
Postal Organization
Cairo
Arab Republic of Egypt

Currency: 100 piastres = 1 Egyptian pound
(£1.00 = £E1.67; US $1.00 = £E0.70 approx.)

Definitives and other items

The current definitive in use features architecture. Official stamps are issued.

Commemoratives\postal stationery

There are at least twenty commemorative stamp issues each year, but most tend to be of just one denomination. Events of national importance are commemorated. Miniature sheets are occasionally produced. First day covers are also available. Stamped aerogrammes and envelopes are in use.

Sudan

Democratic Republic of the Sudan

جمهورية السودان الديمقراطية

An independent Republic in Africa, south of Egypt, whose population comprises both Arabs and Negroes. The post office was established in 1867 and at first Egyptian stamps were used. Sudan's first stamps comprised overprints on Egypt issued in 1897, replaced in 1898 by stamps in a design showing a Camel Postman.

Write to: Director of Posts and Telegraphs
Philatelic Section
Khartoum
Democratic Republic of the Sudan

Currency: 100 piastres = 1 Sudanese pound
(£1.00 = £S1.19; US $1.00 = £S0.80 approx.)

Definitives and commemoratives

The current definitive series has a mixture of designs, some symbolic, some featuring local industry, and others depicting buildings of note. There are normally only about four commemorative sets each year, and these are of local significance.

Postal stationery

Stamped postcards and aerogrammes are in use.

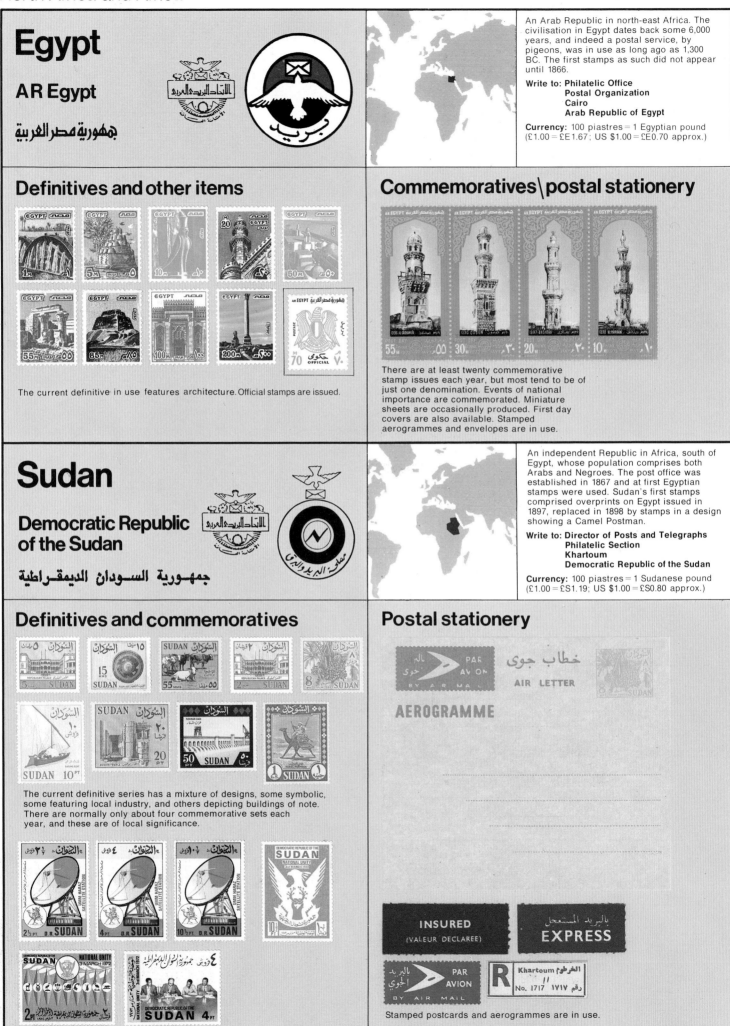

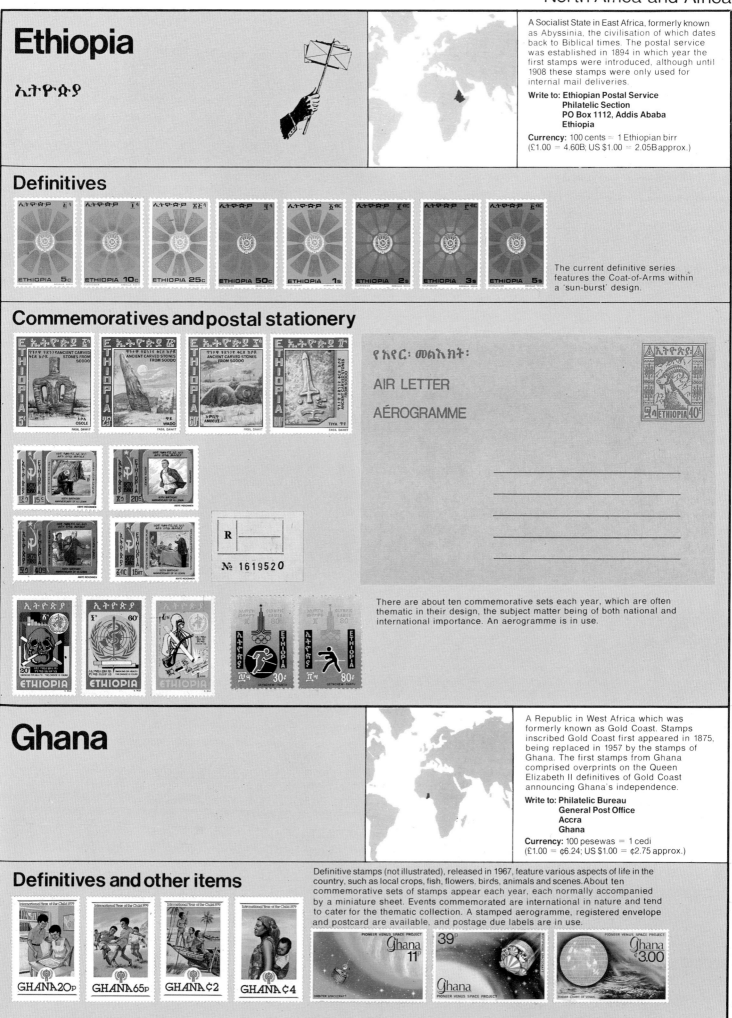

Ethiopia

ኢትዮጵያ

A Socialist State in East Africa, formerly known as Abyssinia, the civilisation of which dates back to Biblical times. The postal service was established in 1894 in which year the first stamps were introduced, although until 1908 these stamps were only used for internal mail deliveries.

Write to: Ethiopian Postal Service
Philatelic Section
PO Box 1112, Addis Ababa
Ethiopia

Currency: 100 cents = 1 Ethiopian birr
(£1.00 = 4.60B; US $1.00 = 2.05B approx.)

Definitives

The current definitive series features the Coat-of-Arms within a 'sun-burst' design.

Commemoratives and postal stationery

AIR LETTER

AÉROGRAMME

There are about ten commemorative sets each year, which are often thematic in their design, the subject matter being of both national and international importance. An aerogramme is in use.

Ghana

A Republic in West Africa which was formerly known as Gold Coast. Stamps inscribed Gold Coast first appeared in 1875, being replaced in 1957 by the stamps of Ghana. The first stamps from Ghana comprised overprints on the Queen Elizabeth II definitives of Gold Coast announcing Ghana's independence.

Write to: Philatelic Bureau
General Post Office
Accra
Ghana

Currency: 100 pesewas = 1 cedi
(£1.00 = ¢6.24; US $1.00 = ¢2.75 approx.)

Definitives and other items

Definitive stamps (not illustrated), released in 1967, feature various aspects of life in the country, such as local crops, fish, flowers, birds, animals and scenes. About ten commemorative sets of stamps appear each year, each normally accompanied by a miniature sheet. Events commemorated are international in nature and tend to cater for the thematic collection. A stamped aerogramme, registered envelope and postcard are available, and postage due labels are in use.

Somalia

Jamhuuriyadda Dimoqraadiga Soomaaliya

الجمهورية الديموقراطية الصومالية

A Republic formed in 1960 by the amalgamation of Italian-administered Somalia and the British-administered Somaliland Protectorate. The first (colonial) stamps were issued in 1903. The present country name was introduced in October 1969.

Write to: Ministry of Posts & Telecommunications
Philatelic Service
Mogadishu
Somali Democratic Republic

Currency: 100 centesimi = 1 Somali shilling
(£1.00 = SH SO13.50; US 1.00 = SH SO6.02 approx.)

Commemoratives and postal stationery

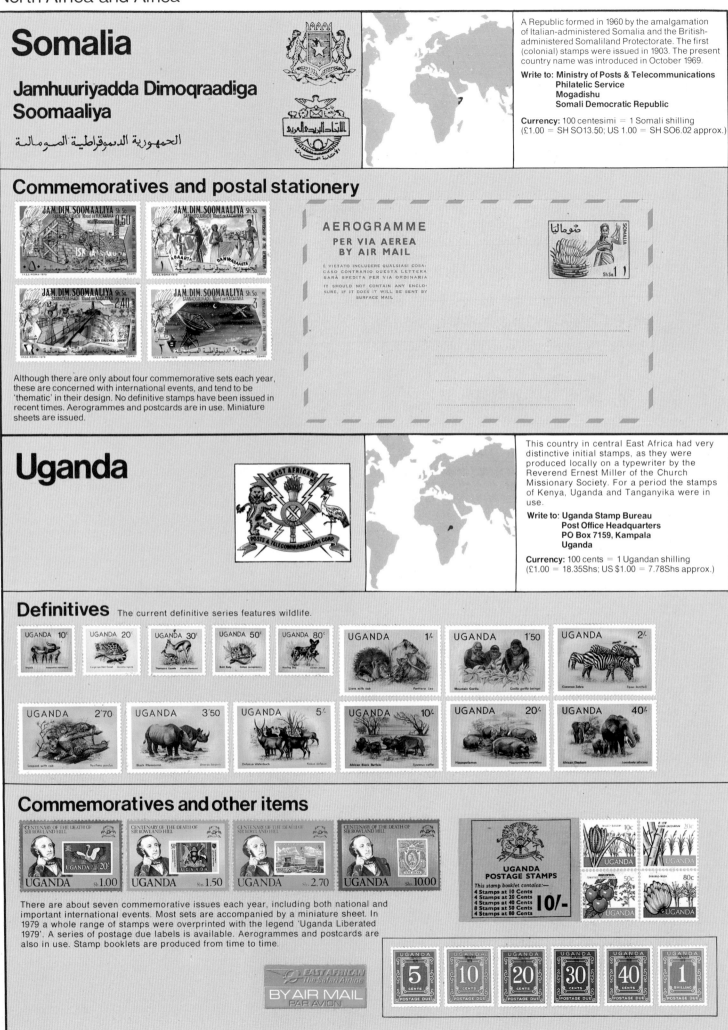

AEROGRAMME
PER VIA AEREA
BY AIR MAIL

È VIETATO INCLUDERE QUALSIASI COSA: CASO CONTRARIO QUESTA LETTERA SARÀ SPEDITA PER VIA ORDINARIA

IT SHOULD NOT CONTAIN ANY ENCLO-SURE, IF IT DOES IT WILL BE SENT BY SURFACE MAIL

Although there are only about four commemorative sets each year, these are concerned with international events, and tend to be 'thematic' in their design. No definitive stamps have been issued in recent times. Aerogrammes and postcards are in use. Miniature sheets are issued.

Uganda

This country in central East Africa had very distinctive initial stamps, as they were produced locally on a typewriter by the Reverend Ernest Miller of the Church Missionary Society. For a period the stamps of Kenya, Uganda and Tanganyika were in use.

Write to: Uganda Stamp Bureau
Post Office Headquarters
PO Box 7159, Kampala
Uganda

Currency: 100 cents = 1 Ugandan shilling
(£1.00 = 18.35Shs; US $1.00 = 7.78Shs approx.)

Definitives The current definitive series features wildlife.

Commemoratives and other items

There are about seven commemorative issues each year, including both national and important international events. Most sets are accompanied by a miniature sheet. In 1979 a whole range of stamps were overprinted with the legend 'Uganda Liberated 1979'. A series of postage due labels is available. Aerogrammes and postcards are also in use. Stamp booklets are produced from time to time.

Rwanda

République Rwandaise

An independent Republic in central Africa which was established in 1962, having been previously part of the Belgian controlled territory of Ruánda-Urundi. The first stamps were issued in 1962.

Write to: Direction Générale des PTT
Section Philatélique
Kigali
Rwanda

Currency: 100 centimes = 1 Rwanda franc
(£1.00 = 202.53RF; US $1.00 = 92.84RF approx.)

Commemoratives and postal stationery

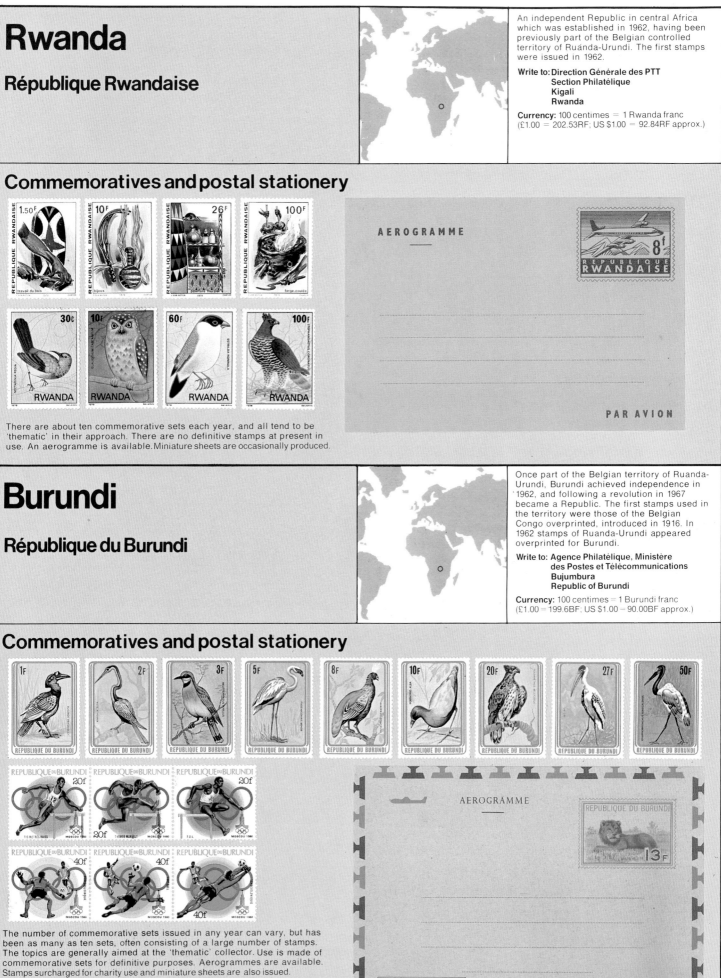

There are about ten commemorative sets each year, and all tend to be 'thematic' in their approach. There are no definitive stamps at present in use. An aerogramme is available. Miniature sheets are occasionally produced.

Burundi

République du Burundi

Once part of the Belgian territory of Ruanda-Urundi, Burundi achieved independence in 1962, and following a revolution in 1967 became a Republic. The first stamps used in the territory were those of the Belgian Congo overprinted, introduced in 1916. In 1962 stamps of Ruanda-Urundi appeared overprinted for Burundi.

Write to: Agence Philatélique, Ministère des Postes et Télécommunications
Bujumbura
Republic of Burundi

Currency: 100 centimes = 1 Burundi franc
(£1.00 = 199.6BF; US $1.00 = 90.00BF approx.)

Commemoratives and postal stationery

The number of commemorative sets issued in any year can vary, but has been as many as ten sets, often consisting of a large number of stamps. The topics are generally aimed at the 'thematic' collector. Use is made of commemorative sets for definitive purposes. Aerogrammes are available. Stamps surcharged for charity use and miniature sheets are also issued.

Kenya

Stamps inscribed Kenya have only appeared since this East African Republic became independent in 1963. Earlier stamps were either overprinted 'British East Africa Company' on Great Britain or inscribed as such; or inscribed British East Africa Protectorate, East Africa and Uganda Protectorate, Kenya and Uganda, or Kenya, Uganda and Tanganyika.

Write to: **The Stamp Bureau, Posts and Telecommunications Corporation, PO Box 30368, Nairobi, Kenya**

Currency: 100 cents = 1 Kenya shilling (£1.00 = 20.00s; US $1.00 = 7.50s approx.)

Definitives

The latest definitives show minerals, being also available in the form of stamp booklets and coils.

Commemoratives

These appear about four times a year, commemorating local events. Issues are sometimes accompanied by a miniature sheet and first day covers are available. Even after independence, there was a period when commemorative stamps were inscribed either Kenya, Uganda, Tanganyika and Zanzibar or Kenya, Uganda and Tanzania. Later the three country groups of Kenya, Uganda and Tanzania issued stamps in similar designs but individually inscribed. Today, the commemorative sets tend to be entirely separate from those of the neighbouring countries.

Postal stationery and other items

Aerogrammes and registered envelopes, without stamps, are made available. Postage due stamps are in use.

Zaire

République du Zaïre

This country in South Africa was formerly known as the Belgian Congo and Congo Republic, the change in name taking place in 1971. The first stamps inscribed Zaire therefore date from 1971, although stamps for Belgian Congo had existed since 1886.

Write to: Service Philatélique
Director General des Postes
Kinshasa
Republic of Zaire

Currency: 100 makuta = 1 zaire
(£1.00 = 6.98Z; US $1.00 = 3.46Z approx.)

Definitives
The present definitive series features a portrait of President Mobutu.

Commemoratives and other items
There are about five commemorative sets each year, which are mainly 'thematic' in their approach. Official stamps, in the design of the definitives, but suitably overprinted, are in use. Miniature sheets are produced.

Congo Republic

République Populaire du Congo

This independent Republic within the French Community was formerly known as Middle Congo, being part of French Equatorial Africa. The first stamps inscribed Congo Republic appeared in 1959 to mark the first anniversary of gaining republic status.

Write to: Le Directeur des Services Postaux et Financiers, Office National des P. et T. et de la C.N.D. le Brazzaville People's Republic of Congo

Currency: 100 centimes = 1 CFA franc
(£1.00 = 553F CFA; US $1.00 = 243F CFA approx.)

Commemoratives and other items

There are about twenty commemorative sets each year, honouring international events, aimed at the 'thematic' stamp collector. There are no definitive stamps in use. A series of postage due labels depicting flowers is in use. Miniature sheets are produced.

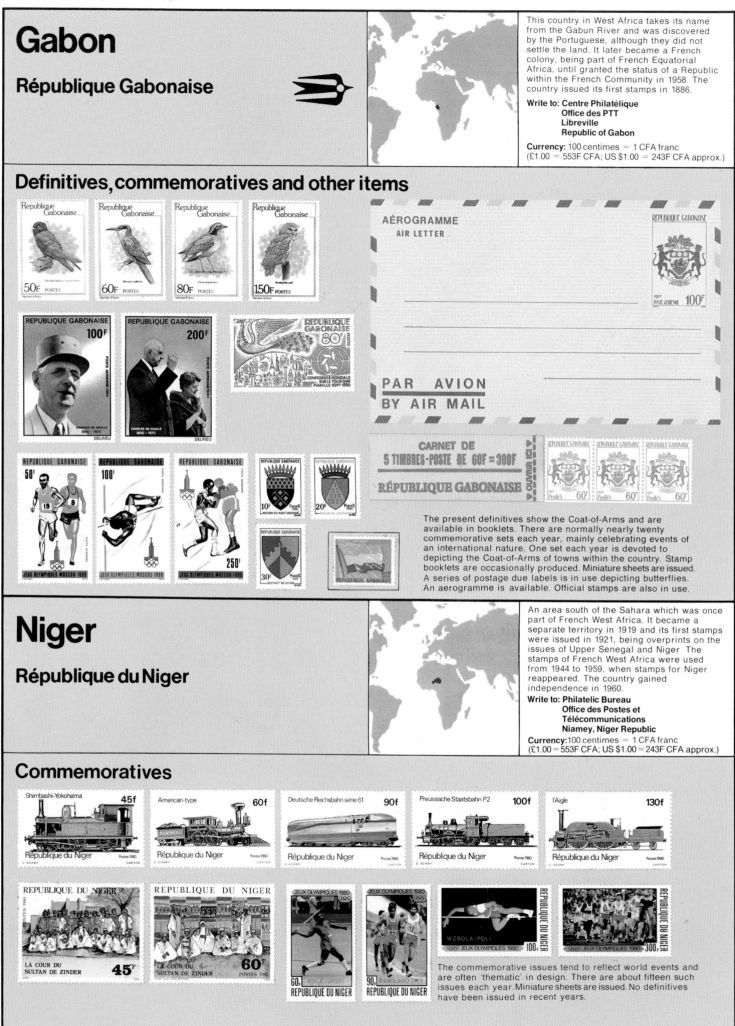

Gabon

République Gabonaise

This country in West Africa takes its name from the Gabun River and was discovered by the Portuguese, although they did not settle the land. It later became a French colony, being part of French Equatorial Africa, until granted the status of a Republic within the French Community in 1958. The country issued its first stamps in 1886.

Write to: Centre Philatélique
Office des PTT
Libreville
Republic of Gabon

Currency: 100 centimes = 1 CFA franc
(£1.00 = 553F CFA; US $1.00 = 243F CFA approx.)

Definitives, commemoratives and other items

The present definitives show the Coat-of-Arms and are available in booklets. There are normally nearly twenty commemorative sets each year, mainly celebrating events of an international nature. One set each year is devoted to depicting the Coat-of-Arms of towns within the country. Stamp booklets are occasionally produced. Miniature sheets are issued. A series of postage due labels is in use depicting butterflies. An aerogramme is available. Official stamps are also in use.

Niger

République du Niger

An area south of the Sahara which was once part of French West Africa. It became a separate territory in 1919 and its first stamps were issued in 1921, being overprints on the issues of Upper Senegal and Niger The stamps of French West Africa were used from 1944 to 1959, when stamps for Niger reappeared. The country gained independence in 1960.

Write to: Philatelic Bureau
Office des Postes et
Télécommunications
Niamey, Niger Republic

Currency:100 centimes = 1 CFA franc
(£1.00 =553F CFA; US $1.00 = 243F CFA approx.)

Commemoratives

The commemorative issues tend to reflect world events and are often 'thematic' in design. There are about fifteen such issues each year. Miniature sheets are issued. No definitives have been issued in recent years.

Chad

République du Tchad

One of the French territories in central Africa, a dependency of Ubangui-Chari, Chad became a Republic within the French Community in 1958. Stamps of French Congo were first used, before the stamps of Middle Congo suitably overprinted were introduced in 1922. Stamps inscribed for Chad were issued in 1950.

Write to: Service Philatélique
PTT
N'djamena
Republic of Chad

Currency: 100 centimes = 1 CFA franc
(£1.00 = 553F CFA; US $1.00 = 243F CFA approx.)

Commemoratives

International events are commemorated, there being about seven such issues each year. Designs are 'thematic' in their approach. There are no definitive stamps at present in use. Miniature sheets are issued.

Central African Republic

République Centrafricaine

Formerly known as Ubangui-Chari, part of French Equatorial Africa, this independent country within the French community became an Empire in 1976, but reverted to being a Republic in 1979 on the overthrow of the President. The Republic's first stamps appeared in 1959, with stamps for the Empire being issued from 1977 until 1979.

Write to: Service Philatélique des PTT
Bangui
Central African Republic

Currency: 100 centimes = 1 CFA franc
(£1.00 = 553F CFA; US $1.00 = 243F CFA approx.)

Commemoratives and other items

Several commemorative sets appear each year, in the main honouring international events. No definitive stamps are at present in use. A series of Official stamps was introduced in 1978, featuring the Coat-of-Arms. Miniature sheets are produced.

Guinea

République de Guinée

This former French colony on the west coast of Africa became independent in 1958. The first stamps were introduced the following year, initially consisting of the stamps of French West Africa suitably overprinted. Stamps inscribed Guinea appeared the same year.

Write to: Agence Philatélique de la
République de Guinée
Boîte Postale 814
Conakry, Republic of Guinea

Currency: 100 cauri = 1 syli
(£1.00 = 44.65S; US $1.00 = 19.90S approx.)

Commemoratives

The commemorative stamps are of a propaganda nature, many of the designs appealing to 'thematic' collectors. There are about five such issues each year. There have been no definitive stamps issued in recent years.

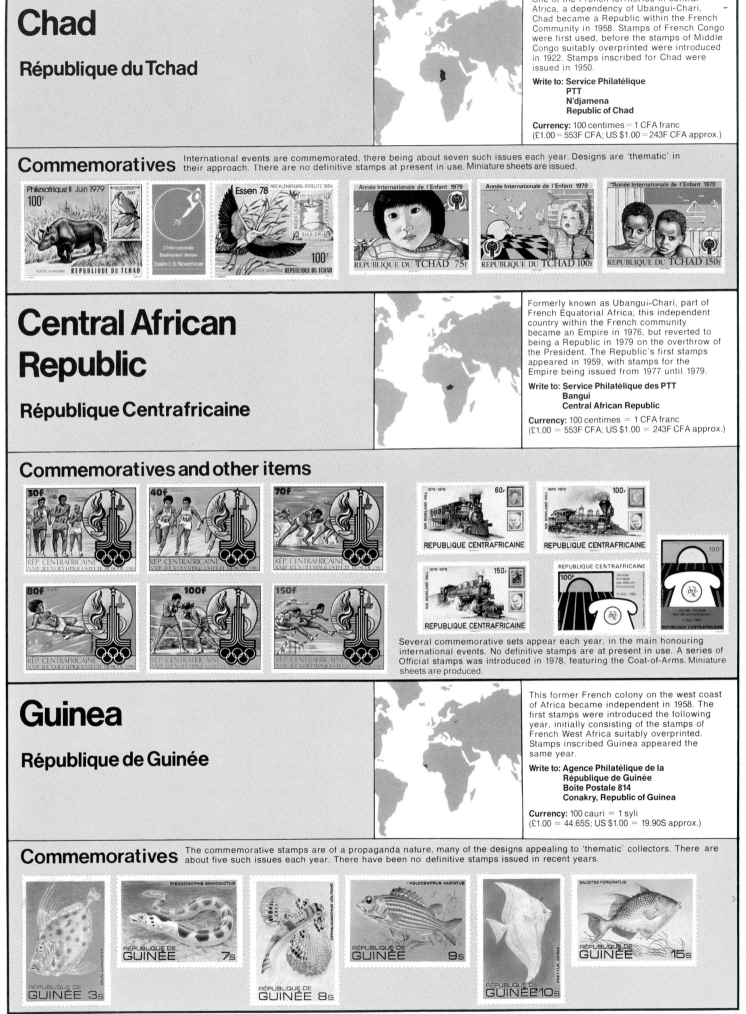

Nigeria

A Republic in West Africa, formerly consisting of the Royal Niger Company, the Niger Coast Protectorate and the Protectorate of Lagos. The first stamps inscribed Nigeria appeared in 1914, although there were previous issues for the Niger Coast Protectorate, Northern Nigeria and Southern Nigeria. During the Civil War in the late 1960s, stamps were produced for use in Biafra.

**Write to: Nigerian Philatelic Service
PMB, 12647, Tinubu Street
GPO, Lagos
Federal Republic of Nigeria**
Currency: 100 kobo = 1 naira
(£1.00 = 1.28n; US $1.00 = 0.54n approx.)

Definitives

The current definitive series is devoted to local industry.

Commemoratives

About six commemorative issues appear each year, normally consisting of only one or two denominations, of events of local interest. First day covers are usually prepared.

Postal stationery and postage dues

Postage due labels have been in use since 1959, the same basic design being used since that time. A stamped aerogramme, postcards and a registered envelope are available.

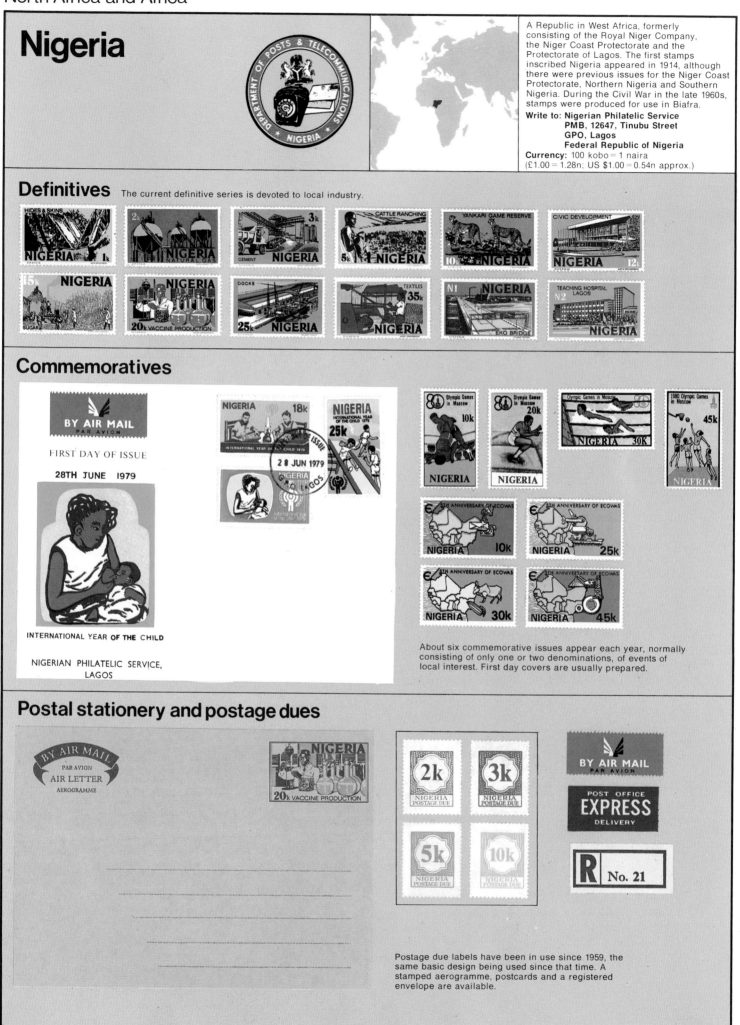

Benin

République Populaire du Benin

This country, which lies on the west coast of Africa, was incorporated into the French territory of Dahomey in 1894, but was once again re-named Benin when it became a People's Republic in 1975. Stamps under the present name appeared for the period of 1892 to 1899, and once again from 1976.

Write to: Service Philatélique
Office des Postes et
Télécommunications
Contonou
People's Republic of Benin

Currency: 100 centimes = 1 CFA franc
(£1.00 = 553F CFA; US $1.00 = 243F CFA approx.)

Definitives and commemoratives

Definitive stamps (not illustrated) were issued in 1976 comprising overprints on the stamps of Dahomey. There are about twenty commemorative sets each year, these tending to be connected with events of national interest, or aimed to appeal to 'thematic' collectors.

Togo

République Togolaise

This territory in West Africa was formerly a German colony. It was divided between France and Great Britain in 1919, gaining independence in 1960. German stamps were at first used, such stamps being specially overprinted in 1897. Stamps inscribed for Togo first made their appearance in 1924.

Write to: M. le Directeur des Postes
et Télécommunications
Bureau Philatélique
Lomé
Republic of Togo

Currency: 100 centimes = 1 CFA franc
(£1.00 = 553F CFA; US $1.00 = 243F CFA approx.)

Commemoratives

'Thematic' stamp collectors are catered for with about fifteen commemorative sets each year, most accompanied by a miniature sheet. There are no definitive stamps at present in use.

Ivory Coast

République de Côte d'Ivoire

Once a French colony in West Africa, the Ivory Coast became incorporated in French West Africa in 1944. In 1958 it became an autonomous Republic within the French community, achieving full independence in 1960. Stamps were issued from 1892 to 1944, when the stamps of French West Africa were used. Stamps for Ivory Coast again appeared in 1959.

Write to: Office des PTT
Direction des Services Postaux
Centre Philatélique d'Abidjan, Abidjan
Republic of the Ivory Coast

Currency: 100 centimes = 1 CFA franc
(£1.00 = 553F CFA; US $1.00 = 243F CFA approx.)

Definitives

The present definitive series shows a portrait of the President and the Coat-of-Arms. A stamp booklet is also available.

Commemoratives and other items

The commemorative issues relate to both national and international events. There are about fifteen such issues each year, which are often 'thematic' in their design. Postage due stamps are available. Pre-cancelled stamps are in use. Miniature sheets are produced.

Liberia

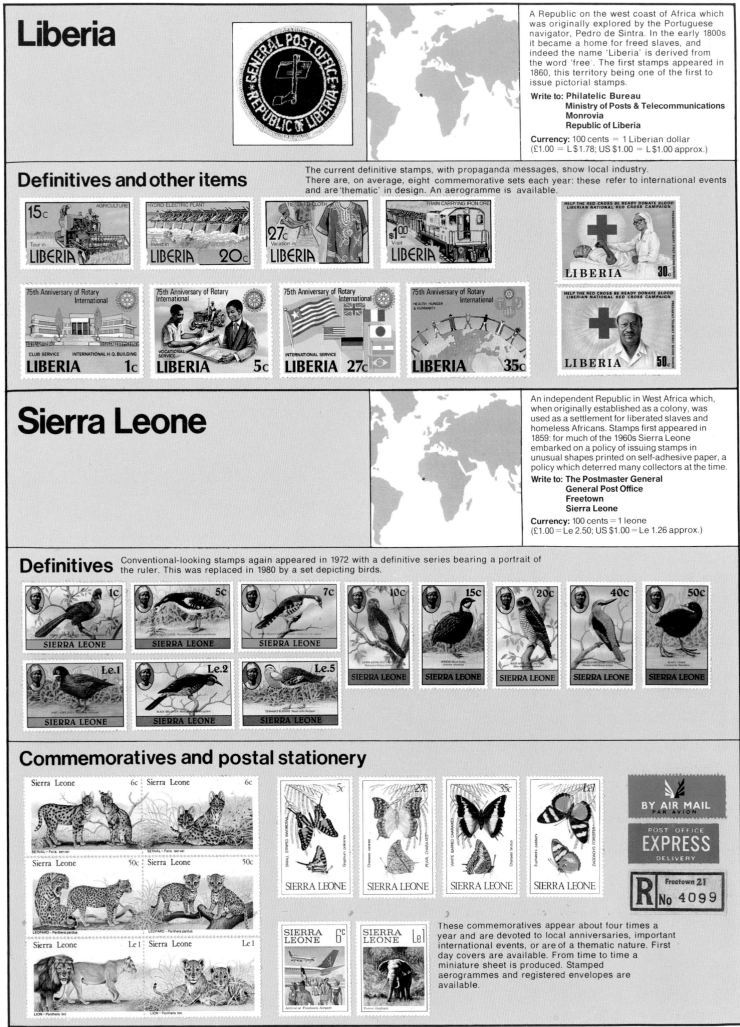

A Republic on the west coast of Africa which was originally explored by the Portuguese navigator, Pedro de Sintra. In the early 1800s it became a home for freed slaves, and indeed the name 'Liberia' is derived from the word 'free'. The first stamps appeared in 1860, this territory being one of the first to issue pictorial stamps.

Write to: Philatelic Bureau
Ministry of Posts & Telecommunications
Monrovia
Republic of Liberia

Currency: 100 cents = 1 Liberian dollar
(£1.00 = L $1.78; US $1.00 = L $1.00 approx.)

Definitives and other items

The current definitive stamps, with propaganda messages, show local industry.
There are, on average, eight commemorative sets each year: these refer to international events and are 'thematic' in design. An aerogramme is available.

Sierra Leone

An independent Republic in West Africa which, when originally established as a colony, was used as a settlement for liberated slaves and homeless Africans. Stamps first appeared in 1859: for much of the 1960s Sierra Leone embarked on a policy of issuing stamps in unusual shapes printed on self-adhesive paper, a policy which deterred many collectors at the time.

Write to: The Postmaster General
General Post Office
Freetown
Sierra Leone

Currency: 100 cents = 1 leone
(£1.00 = Le 2.50; US $1.00 = Le 1.26 approx.)

Definitives

Conventional-looking stamps again appeared in 1972 with a definitive series bearing a portrait of the ruler. This was replaced in 1980 by a set depicting birds.

Commemoratives and postal stationery

These commemoratives appear about four times a year and are devoted to local anniversaries, important international events, or are of a thematic nature. First day covers are available. From time to time a miniature sheet is produced. Stamped aerogrammes and registered envelopes are available.

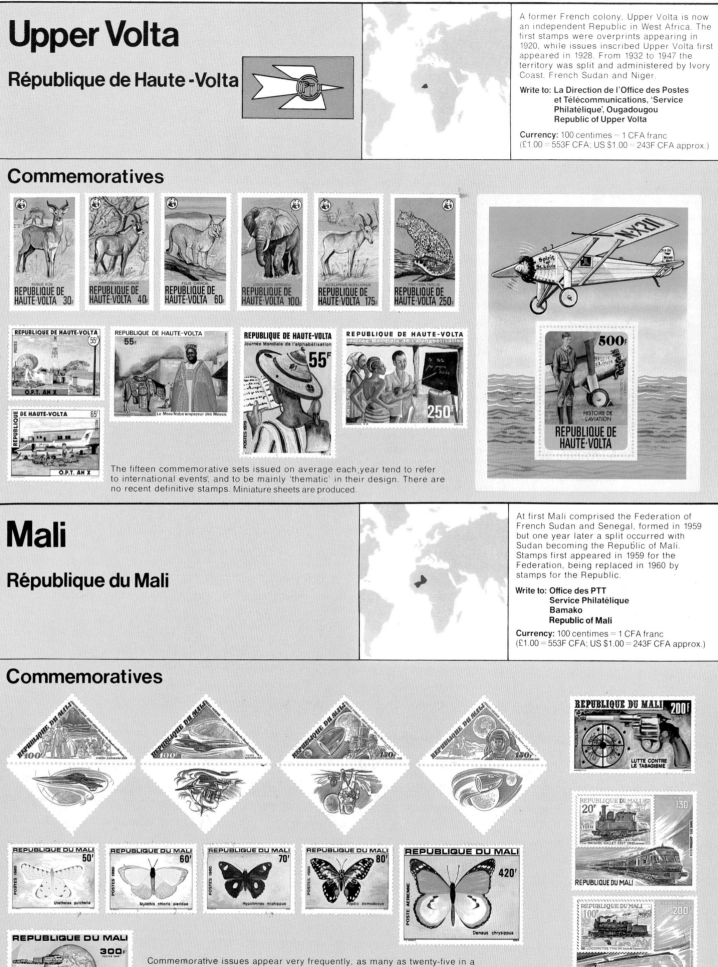

Upper Volta

République de Haute-Volta

A former French colony, Upper Volta is now an independent Republic in West Africa. The first stamps were overprints appearing in 1920, while issues inscribed Upper Volta first appeared in 1928. From 1932 to 1947 the territory was split and administered by Ivory Coast, French Sudan and Niger.

Write to: La Direction de l'Office des Postes et Télécommunications, 'Service Philatélique', Ougadougou Republic of Upper Volta

Currency: 100 centimes = 1 CFA franc (£1.00 = 553F CFA; US $1.00 = 243F CFA approx.)

Commemoratives

The fifteen commemorative sets issued on average each year tend to refer to international events, and to be mainly 'thematic' in their design. There are no recent definitive stamps. Miniature sheets are produced.

Mali

République du Mali

At first Mali comprised the Federation of French Sudan and Senegal, formed in 1959 but one year later a split occurred with Sudan becoming the Republic of Mali. Stamps first appeared in 1959 for the Federation, being replaced in 1960 by stamps for the Republic.

Write to: Office des PTT Service Philatélique Bamako Republic of Mali

Currency: 100 centimes = 1 CFA franc (£1.00 = 553F CFA; US $1.00 = 243F CFA approx.)

Commemoratives

Commemorative issues appear very frequently, as many as twenty-five in a year, with designs aimed at the 'thematic' collector. There are no definitives at present in use. Miniature sheets are produced.

The Gambia

An independent Republic in West Africa, which comprises a narrow stretch of land along the banks of the Gambia River. The river itself was discovered by the Portuguese in 1447. The first stamps appeared in 1869 and are known as the 'Cameos' having an embossed portrait of Queen Victoria.

Write to: Philatelic Bureau
GPO Banjul
Republic of The Gambia

Currency: 100 bututs = 1 dalasi
(£1.00 = D4.00; US $1.00 = D1.68 approx.)

Definitives

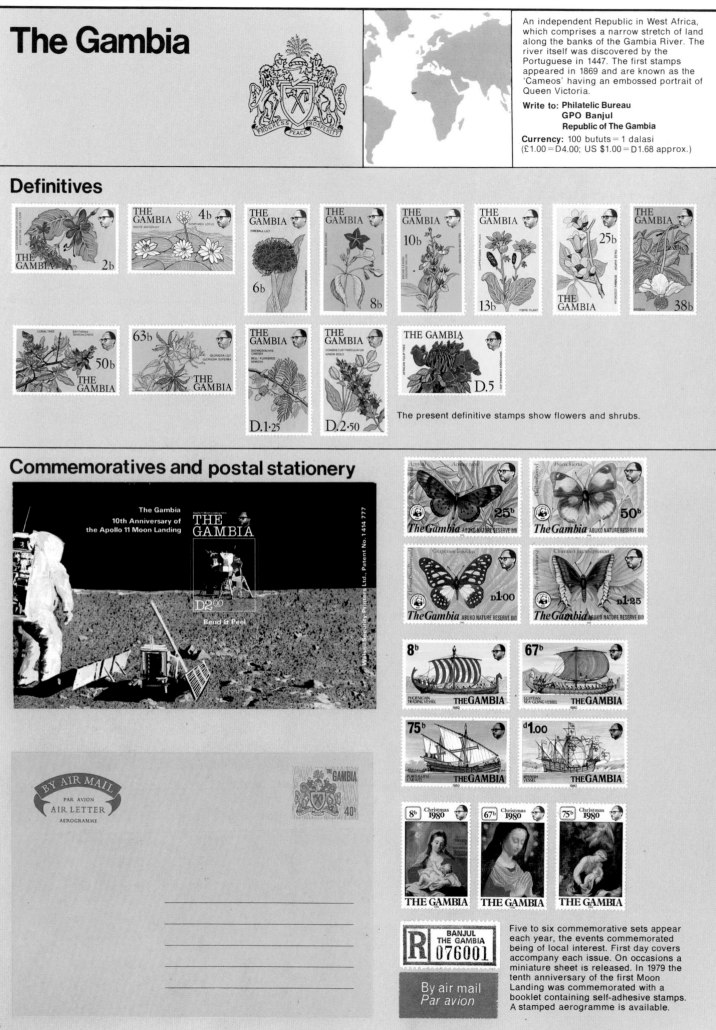

The present definitive stamps show flowers and shrubs.

Commemoratives and postal stationery

The Gambia
10th Anniversary of the Apollo 11 Moon Landing

THE GAMBIA
D2.00
Bend & Peel

Weisall Security Printers Ltd., Patent No. 1 414 777

BY AIR MAIL
PAR AVION
AIR LETTER
AEROGRAMME

THE GAMBIA 40b

BANJUL THE GAMBIA
R 076001

By air mail
Par avion

Five to six commemorative sets appear each year, the events commemorated being of local interest. First day covers accompany each issue. On occasions a miniature sheet is released. In 1979 the tenth anniversary of the first Moon Landing was commemorated with a booklet containing self-adhesive stamps. A stamped aerogramme is available.

Equatorial Guinea

República de Guinea Ecuatorial

Equatorial Guinea consists of the former Spanish provinces of Fernando Poo and Rio Muni, which were united and became a Republic in 1968. The first stamps appeared in the same year.

Write to: Dirección General de Correos
Seccion Filatélica
Malabo
Republic of Equatorial Guinea

Currency: 100 centimos = 1 eukele
(£1.00 = 381 E; US $1.00 = 167 E approx.)

Definitives

Commemoratives

There is an abundance of commemorative sets, all seemingly aimed at stamp collectors, rather than serving any local need.

Mauritania

République Islamique de Mauritanie

الجمهورية الاسلامية الموريتانية

Mauritania is an independent Islamic Republic in Africa, which extends inland to the Sahara. Once a French colony, it was incorporated into French West Africa in 1944. Stamps were issued from 1906 to 1944, with French West Africa stamps then being used until Mauritania's own stamps reappeared in 1960.

Write to: Agence Philatélique
Nouakchott
Republic of Mauritania

Currency: 5 khoum = 1 ouguiya
(£1.00 = 109.25UM; US $1.00 = 49.50UM approx.)

Commemoratives and other items

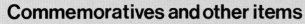

There are no definitive stamps at present in use. About ten commemorative sets appear each year, these being devoted to both national and international events. Both Official stamps and postage due labels are available. An aerogramme is also in use. Miniature sheets are produced.

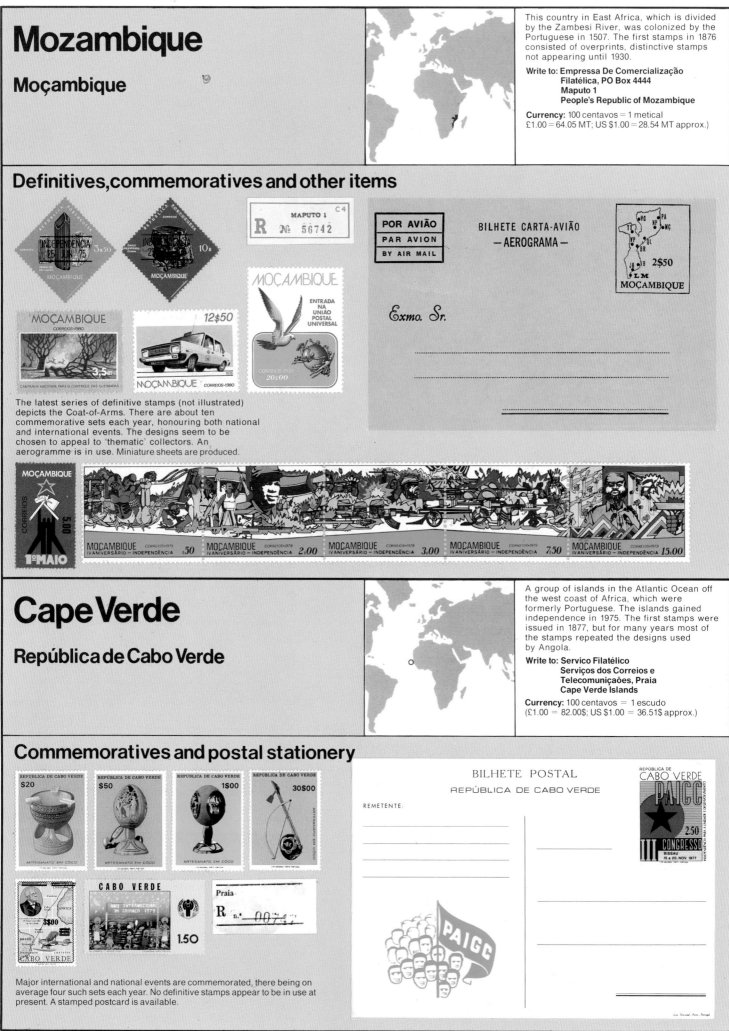

Mozambique

Moçambique

This country in East Africa, which is divided by the Zambesi River, was colonized by the Portuguese in 1507. The first stamps in 1876 consisted of overprints, distinctive stamps not appearing until 1930.

Write to: Empressa De Comercialização Filatélica, PO Box 4444 Maputo 1 People's Republic of Mozambique

Currency: 100 centavos = 1 metical
£1.00 = 64.05 MT; US $1.00 = 28.54 MT approx.

Definitives, commemoratives and other items

The latest series of definitive stamps (not illustrated) depicts the Coat-of-Arms. There are about ten commemorative sets each year, honouring both national and international events. The designs seem to be chosen to appeal to 'thematic' collectors. An aerogramme is in use. Miniature sheets are produced.

Cape Verde

República de Cabo Verde

A group of islands in the Atlantic Ocean off the west coast of Africa, which were formerly Portuguese. The islands gained independence in 1975. The first stamps were issued in 1877, but for many years most of the stamps repeated the designs used by Angola.

Write to: Servico Filatélico Serviços dos Correios e Telecomuniçaôes, Praia Cape Verde Islands

Currency: 100 centavos = 1 escudo
(£1.00 = 82.00$; US $1.00 = 36.51$ approx.)

Commemoratives and postal stationery

Major international and national events are commemorated, there being on average four such sets each year. No definitive stamps appear to be in use at present. A stamped postcard is available.

126

Guinea Bissau

República da Guiné-Bissau

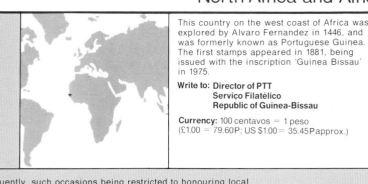

This country on the west coast of Africa was explored by Alvaro Fernandez in 1446, and was formerly known as Portuguese Guinea. The first stamps appeared in 1881, being issued with the inscription 'Guinea Bissau' in 1975.

Write to: Director of PTT
Serviço Filatélico
Republic of Guinea-Bissau

Currency: 100 centavos = 1 peso
(£1.00 = 79.60P; US $1.00 = 35.45P approx.)

Commemoratives

Commemorative stamps appear infrequently, such occasions being restricted to honouring local events. First day covers are available. No definitive stamps are at present in use.

Comoro Islands

République Fédérale Islamique des Comores

This group of islands lies in the Mozambique Channel between the east coast of Africa and the Malagasy Republic. It was a French colony from 1891, achieving independence in 1974. The first stamps to appear for the entire group were issued in 1914, although individual islands had issued stamps earlier.

Write to: Service des Postes
Service Philatélique
Moroni, Grand Comoro
Republic of Comoros

Currency: 100 centimes = 1 CFA franc
(£1.00 = 553F CFA; US $1.00 = 243F CFA approx.)

Commemoratives and other items

The commemorative issues are obviously aimed at an international market, with many designs of a 'thematic' nature. There are about ten such issues each year. No definitive stamps have been issued in recent years. A set of postage due labels depicting flowers is in use. Official stamps are also in use.

St. Thomas and Prince Islands

São Tomé e Principe

Two islands in the Gulf of Guinea, off the west coast of Africa, which were discovered by the Portuguese in 1470, and remained under Portuguese control until their independence in 1975. The first stamps were issued in 1870, although stamps for the Democratic Republic did not appear until 1976.

Write to: Direcção Geral dos Correios
São Tomé
St Thomas and Prince Islands
Democratic Republic of São Tomé & Principe

Currency: 100 centavos = 1 dobra
(£1.00 = Db 81.85, US $1.00 = Db 38.00 approx.)

Definitives, commemoratives and other items

Very few commemorative sets are released; these tend to refer to local events, although are sometimes accompanied by a miniature sheet. The last set of definitives, released in 1976 were overprints for the Democratic Republic. An aerogramme is available. Official stamps are issued.

Cameroon

République Unie du Cameroun

A Republic on the west coast of Africa, once forming the German colony of Kamerun, and later being divided between France and Great Britain. Stamps used have included German stamps overprinted 'Kamerun' in 1897, and French Occupation overprints on the stamps of Gabon in 1915. Stamps inscribed for use there first appeared in 1925.

Write to: Ministère des Postes et Télé-communications, Direction des Postes Bureau Philatélique, Yaoundé United Republic of Cameroon

Currency: 100 centimes = 1 CFA franc
(£1.00 = 553F CFA; US $1.00 = 243F CFA approx.)

Commemoratives

There are about four commemorative sets released each year, of local interest, each being available on first day cover. The last definitive series, released in 1962 depicted animals. Commemorative stamps are retained for definitive use. Postage due labels and Official stamps are also in use. Miniature sheets are produced.

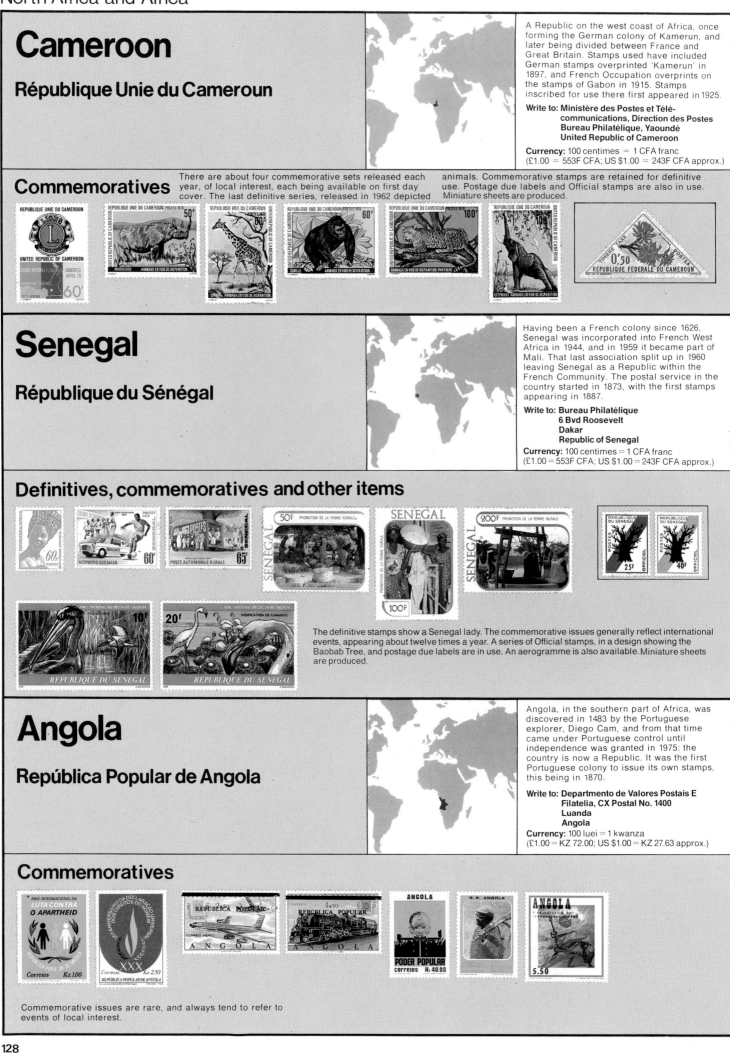

Senegal

République du Sénégal

Having been a French colony since 1626, Senegal was incorporated into French West Africa in 1944, and in 1959 it became part of Mali. That last association split up in 1960 leaving Senegal as a Republic within the French Community. The postal service in the country started in 1873, with the first stamps appearing in 1887.

Write to: Bureau Philatélique 6 Bvd Roosevelt Dakar Republic of Senegal

Currency: 100 centimes = 1 CFA franc
(£1.00 = 553F CFA; US $1.00 = 243F CFA approx.)

Definitives, commemoratives and other items

The definitive stamps show a Senegal lady. The commemorative issues generally reflect international events, appearing about twelve times a year. A series of Official stamps, in a design showing the Baobab Tree, and postage due labels are in use. An aerogramme is also available. Miniature sheets are produced.

Angola

República Popular de Angola

Angola, in the southern part of Africa, was discovered in 1483 by the Portuguese explorer, Diego Cam, and from that time came under Portuguese control until independence was granted in 1975: the country is now a Republic. It was the first Portuguese colony to issue its own stamps, this being in 1870.

Write to: Departmento de Valores Postais E Filatelia, CX Postal No. 1400 Luanda Angola

Currency: 100 luei = 1 kwanza
(£1.00 = KZ 72.00; US $1.00 = KZ 27.63 approx.)

Commemoratives

Commemorative issues are rare, and always tend to refer to events of local interest.

Tanzania

A Republic in East Africa which was created in 1964 by the uniting of Tanganyika and Zanzibar; stamps inscribed Tanzania first appeared in 1965. Stamps inscribed Tanganyika first appeared in 1922, the area having initially used German stamps. Indian stamps were first used in Zanzibar; stamps inscribed Zanzibar appeared in 1896.

Write to: Tanzania P & T Corporation
Stamp Bureau
PO Box 2988
Dar-es-Salaam, Tanzania

Currency: 100 cents = 1 Tanzania shilling
(£1.00 = 18.00s; US $1.00 = 8.10s approx.)

Definitives

The current definitives depict wildlife.

Commemoratives

Events commemorated are mainly local, there being about six new issues a year, each accompanied by a first day cover and many also issued as miniature sheets. For a period commemorative releases were shared with Kenya and Uganda.

Postal stationery and other items

The definitives are available in stamp booklets; stamps are also prepared for sale from vending machines. Use is made of stamps overprinted 'Official' for Government use. Unstamped stationery in the form of aerogrammes and registered envelopes is sold. Postage due labels are in use.

TANZANIA
POSTAGE STAMPS
This stamp booklet contains:—
8 Stamps at 10 cents
8 Stamps at 20 cents
4 Stamps at 40 cents
4 Stamps at 50 cents
6/-

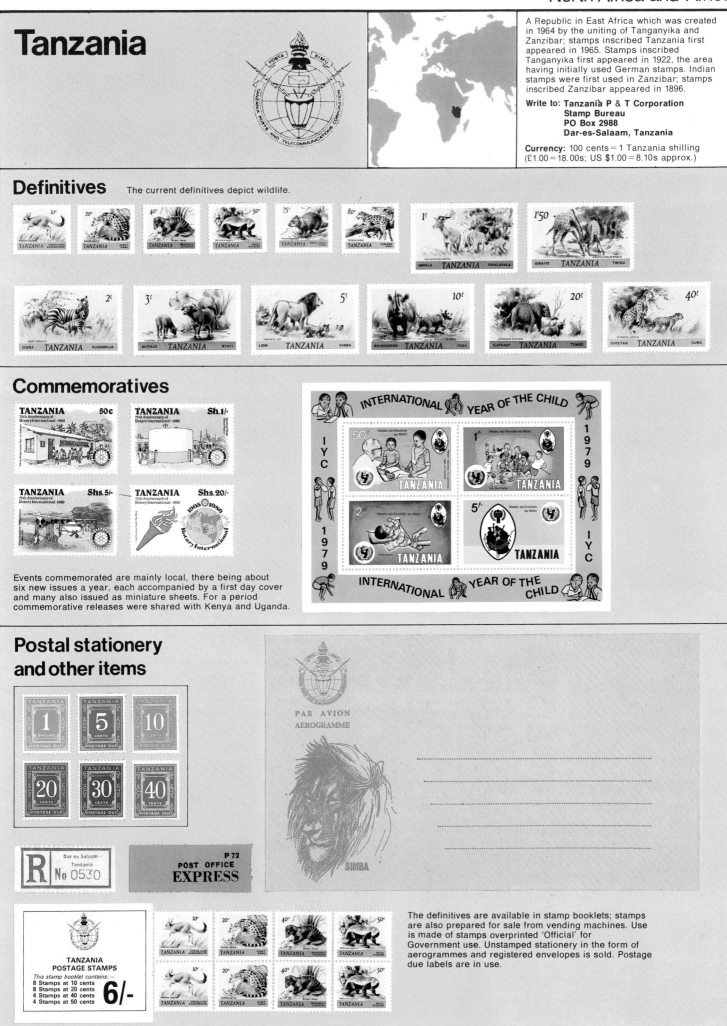

Malaŵi

This Republic in central Africa was formerly known as Nyasaland. On independence in 1964, stamps first appeared inscribed Malaŵi. Stamps incribed Nyasaland did not appear until 1908; previous stamps used in the territory had been those of the British Central Africa Protectorate, which initially comprised the stamps of Rhodesia overprinted 'B.C.A.

Write to: Malaŵi Post Office
Philatelic Bureau, PO Box 1000
Blantyre
Malaŵi
Currency: 100 tambalas = 1 kwacha
(£1.00 = K1.92; US $1.00 = K0.85 approx.)

Definitives
The present definitives of Malawi were introduced in 1979 and show orchids. Coil stamps are in use.

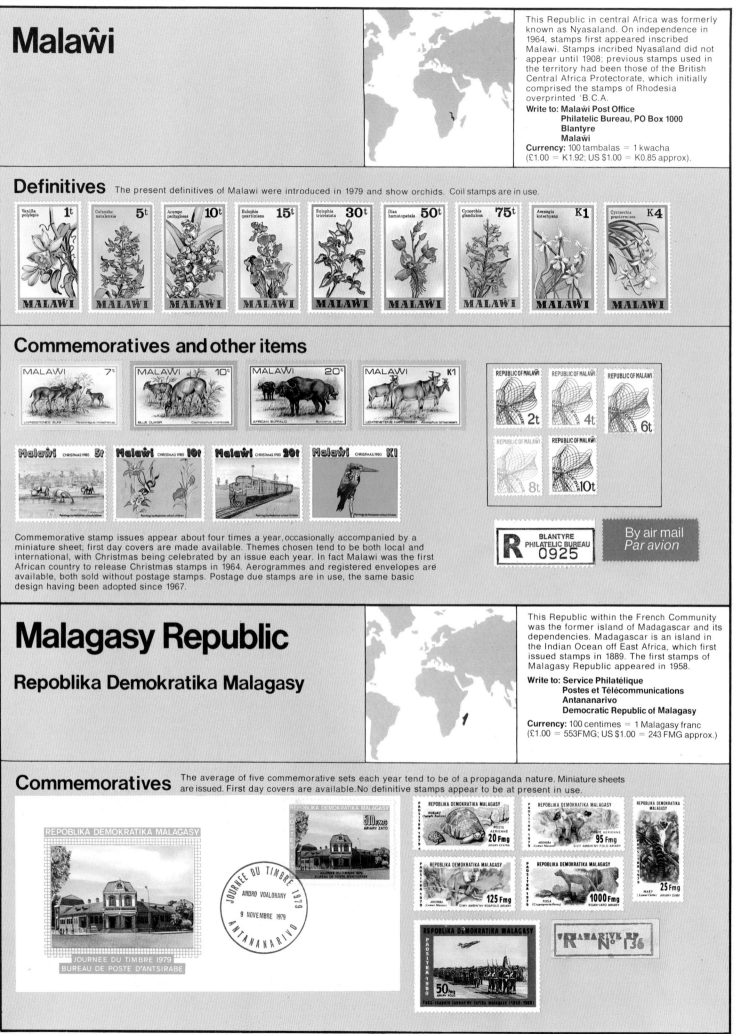

Commemoratives and other items

Commemorative stamp issues appear about four times a year, occasionally accompanied by a miniature sheet; first day covers are made available. Themes chosen tend to be both local and international, with Christmas being celebrated by an issue each year. In fact Malawi was the first African country to release Christmas stamps in 1964. Aerogrammes and registered envelopes are available, both sold without postage stamps. Postage due stamps are in use, the same basic design having been adopted since 1967.

Malagasy Republic

Repoblika Demokratika Malagasy

This Republic within the French Community was the former island of Madagascar and its dependencies. Madagascar is an island in the Indian Ocean off East Africa, which first issued stamps in 1889. The first stamps of Malagasy Republic appeared in 1958.

Write to: Service Philatélique
Postes et Télécommunications
Antananarivo
Democratic Republic of Malagasy

Currency: 100 centimes = 1 Malagasy franc
(£1.00 = 553FMG; US $1.00 = 243 FMG approx.)

Commemoratives
The average of five commemorative sets each year tend to be of a propaganda nature. Miniature sheets are issued. First day covers are available. No definitive stamps appear to be at present in use.

Zimbabwe

An independent state in central Africa, Zimbabwe was previously known as Rhodesia, and prior to that as Southern Rhodesia. The first stamps in use were those issued by the British South Africa Company in 1892, bearing the Company's Coat-of-Arms; these were overprinted 'Rhodesia' in 1909 and issued inscribed Rhodesia the following year.

Write to: Posts and Telecommunications Corporation
Philatelic Bureau, PO Box 4220
Salisbury, Zimbabwe

Currency: 100 cents = 1 Zimbabwe dollar
(£1.00 = Z $1.50; US $1.00 = Z $0.65 approx.)

Definitives

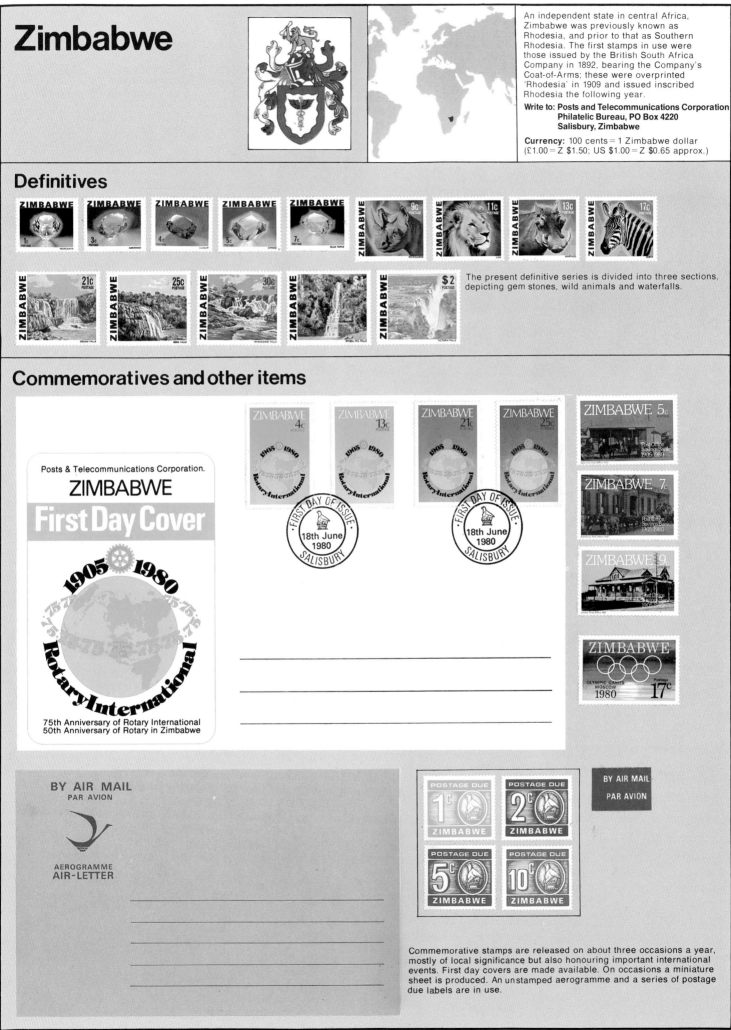

The present definitive series is divided into three sections, depicting gem stones, wild animals and waterfalls.

Commemoratives and other items

Posts & Telecommunications Corporation.
ZIMBABWE
First Day Cover
1905 1980
Rotary International
75th Anniversary of Rotary International
50th Anniversary of Rotary in Zimbabwe

FIRST DAY OF ISSUE
18th June 1980
SALISBURY

BY AIR MAIL
PAR AVION

AEROGRAMME
AIR-LETTER

BY AIR MAIL
PAR AVION

Commemorative stamps are released on about three occasions a year, mostly of local significance but also honouring important international events. First day covers are made available. On occasions a miniature sheet is produced. An unstamped aerogramme and a series of postage due labels are in use.

Botswana

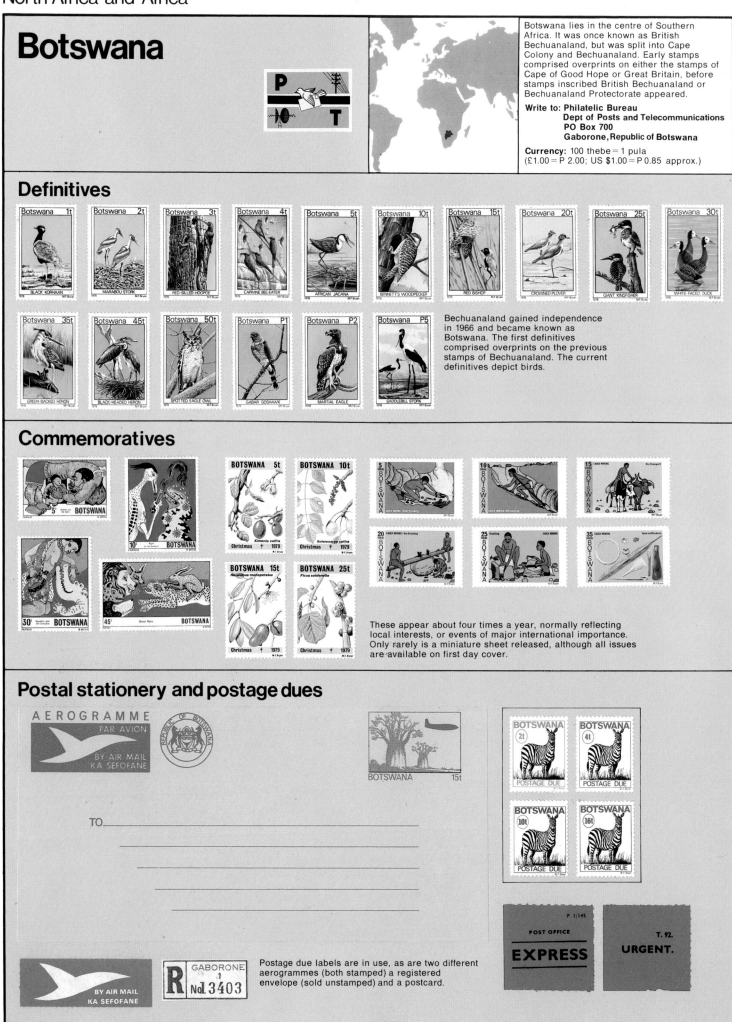

Botswana lies in the centre of Southern Africa. It was once known as British Bechuanaland, but was split into Cape Colony and Bechuanaland. Early stamps comprised overprints on either the stamps of Cape of Good Hope or Great Britain, before stamps inscribed British Bechuanaland or Bechuanaland Protectorate appeared.

Write to: Philatelic Bureau
Dept of Posts and Telecommunications
PO Box 700
Gaborone, Republic of Botswana

Currency: 100 thebe = 1 pula
(£1.00 = P 2.00; US $1.00 = P 0.85 approx.)

Definitives

Bechuanaland gained independence in 1966 and became known as Botswana. The first definitives comprised overprints on the previous stamps of Bechuanaland. The current definitives depict birds.

Commemoratives

These appear about four times a year, normally reflecting local interests, or events of major international importance. Only rarely is a miniature sheet released, although all issues are available on first day cover.

Postal stationery and postage dues

Postage due labels are in use, as are two different aerogrammes (both stamped) a registered envelope (sold unstamped) and a postcard.

Swaziland

Swaziland is an independent Kingdom in Southern Africa which was settled by the Dutch and British in the late nineteenth century. Stamps of the South African Republic, overprinted 'Swaziland', were in use between 1889 and 1894. From 1894 to 1933 the stamps of Transvaal and South Africa were in use until stamps inscribed Swaziland were introduced in 1933.

Write to: Swaziland Stamp Bureau, Dept of Posts & Telecommunications PO Box 555 Mbabane, Swaziland

Currency: 100 cents = 1 emalangeni (£1.00 = E1.80; US $1.00 = E0.75 approx.)

Definitives

The current definitive series was introduced in 1980.

Commemoratives

About four special issues are released each year, mainly of local significance. First day covers are prepared. Miniature sheets are occasionally issued.

Postal stationery and postage dues

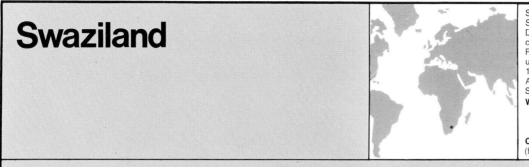

Postage due labels have been in existence since 1933, the current design being introduced in 1971. Unstamped aerogrammes and registered envelopes are on sale. A postcard is available.

Mauritius

An island in the Indian Ocean which has been independent since 1968, having the distinction of being the first British colony to issue postage stamps. Its first stamps were the famous 1d and 2d of 1847 which were inscribed 'Post Office' instead of 'Post Paid'. A post office was established in 1811 and British stamps were initially used.

Write to: Mauritius Philatelic Bureau
General Post Office
Port Louis
Mauritius

Currency: 100 cents = 1 Mauritius rupee
(£1.00 = R18.10; US $1.00 = R8.06 approx.)

Definitives

The current definitives trace the history of Mauritius. They have been made available in a presentation booklet which gives additional background information to the designs.

Commemoratives and other items

About four commemorative sets appear each year, celebrating both local and international events. First day covers are made available, and from time to time a miniature sheet is issued. In 1979 a booklet was released to commemorate the tenth anniversary of the first Moon landing: the stamps in this booklet were self-adhesive. An aerogramme bearing a printed stamp in the design of the R1 definitive is available. Postage due labels are in use.

Djibouti

République de Djibouti

Djibouti lies in the Gulf of Aden, off the east coast of Africa. It was once the French Territory of the Afars and Issas and before that was known as the French Somali Coast. Stamps overprinted for use there appeared in 1891. Stamps for French Somali Coast appeared in 1902; for the Afars and Issas in 1967 and for Djibouti in 1977.

Write to: Office des Postes et
Télécommunications
Service Philatélique, Djibouti
Republic of Djibouti

Currency: 100 centimes = 1 Djibouti franc
(£1.00 = 375FD; US $1.00 = 167FD approx.)

Commemoratives

The commemorative issues tend to be of a 'thematic' nature, appearing about twelve times a year. Definitive stamps were issued in 1977, being overprints on the former Afars and Issas stamps, but are no longer in use.

Lesotho

LESOTHO PHILATELIC BUREAU

A country in South Africa which has issued stamps inscribed Lesotho since independence in 1966. Previously known as Basutoland, it at times used the stamps of the Cape of Good Hope and South Africa, until stamps inscribed 'Basutoland' were first issued in 1933. In 1959 and 1965 stamps were issued inscribed both Basutoland and Lesotho.

Write to: Lesotho Philatelic Bureau
Private Bag No. 1
Maseru, Lesotho

Currency: 100 lisente = 1 maloti
(£1.00 = M1.80; US $1.00 = M0.75 approx.)

Definitives

The first definitives were the stamps of Basutoland overprinted 'Lesotho'. The current series comprises various designs with a local flavour, including a map, the Lesotho Bank, and pottery. These are being overprinted with the new national currency units, lisente (s) and maloti (M), prior to the introduction of new definitives in mid-1981.

Commemoratives

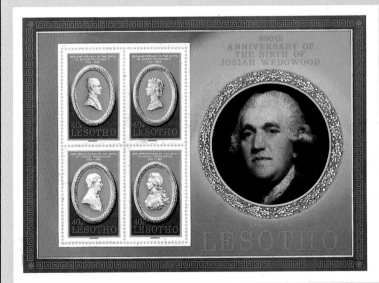

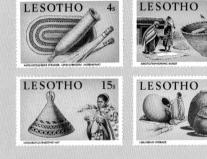

Commemorative stamps appear about six times a year, frequently showing the local flora and fauna, but also celebrating local and international events. First day covers are made available for each issue. Occasionally miniature sheets are also released.

Postal stationery and postage dues

Aerogramme
Ka Sefofane
Par Avion

An aerogramme with a printed 10c stamp showing a dove carrying an envelope is available. Also in use is an envelope for registered mail, but this does not bear a postage stamp. Postage due stamps are in use. A postcard is also available.

Zambia

A Republic in central Africa formerly known as Northern Rhodesia. Stamps inscribed Northern Rhodesia first appeared in 1925, to be replaced by stamps for Zambia in 1964. Prior to 1925 the stamps of Rhodesia were used, although a provisional ½d stamp, produced in 1917 at Livingstone, belonged to Northern Rhodesia alone.

**Write to: P & T Corporation
Philatelic Bureau
PO Box 1857, Ndola
Zambia**

Currency: 100 ngwee = 1 kwacha
(£1.00 = K 1.90; US $1.00 = K 0.80 approx.)

Definitives

The current definitives feature aspects of local life. The design of the definitives is to be changed during 1981.

Commemoratives and other items

Four to five commemorative sets are issued each year, mostly of purely local significance. First day covers are available. On occasions a miniature sheet is issued. Aerogrammes and registered envelopes – both without stamps – are in use. Booklets containing the previous definitive stamps are available.

Seychelles

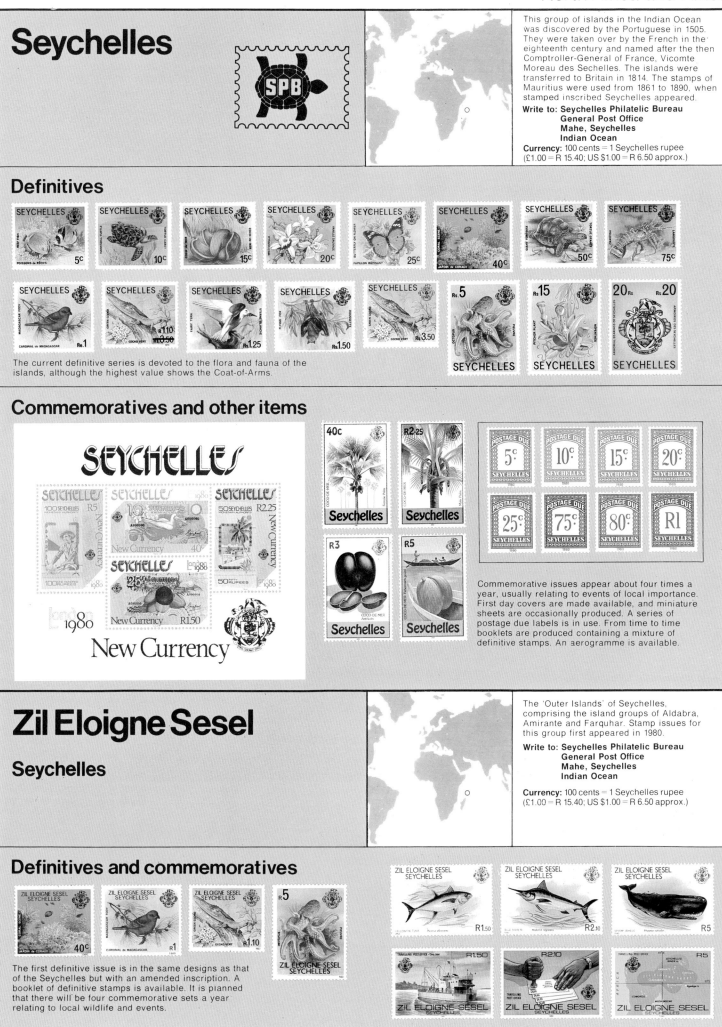

This group of islands in the Indian Ocean was discovered by the Portuguese in 1505. They were taken over by the French in the eighteenth century and named after the then Comptroller-General of France, Vicomte Moreau des Sechelles. The islands were transferred to Britain in 1814. The stamps of Mauritius were used from 1861 to 1890, when stamped inscribed Seychelles appeared.

Write to: Seychelles Philatelic Bureau
General Post Office
Mahe, Seychelles
Indian Ocean
Currency: 100 cents = 1 Seychelles rupee
(£1.00 = R 15.40; US $1.00 = R 6.50 approx.)

Definitives

The current definitive series is devoted to the flora and fauna of the islands, although the highest value shows the Coat-of-Arms.

Commemoratives and other items

Commemorative issues appear about four times a year, usually relating to events of local importance. First day covers are made available, and miniature sheets are occasionally produced. A series of postage due labels is in use. From time to time booklets are produced containing a mixture of definitive stamps. An aerogramme is available.

Zil Eloigne Sesel

Seychelles

The 'Outer Islands' of Seychelles, comprising the island groups of Aldabra, Amirante and Farquhar. Stamp issues for this group first appeared in 1980.

Write to: Seychelles Philatelic Bureau
General Post Office
Mahe, Seychelles
Indian Ocean

Currency: 100 cents = 1 Seychelles rupee
(£1.00 = R 15.40; US $1.00 = R 6.50 approx.)

Definitives and commemoratives

The first definitive issue is in the same designs as that of the Seychelles but with an amended inscription. A booklet of definitive stamps is available. It is planned that there will be four commemorative sets a year relating to local wildlife and events.

South Africa
RSA

An independent Republic, South Africa was first settled by the Dutch and English. Its early postal system was rather romantic: letters would be left under large stones and collected by captains visiting Cape Town. At first stamps appeared for the Cape of Good Hope, Natal, Transvaal and Orange River Colony individually, until the formation of the Union of South Africa in 1910.

Write to: Philatelic Services and Intersapa
Private Bag X505, Pretoria
0001 Republic of South Africa

Currency: 100 cents = 1 South African rand
(£1.00 = R1.78; US $1.00 = R0.79 approx.)

Definitives

The present definitives feature the attractive protea found throughout South Africa. In addition to stamps sold from sheets, stamps in rolls are dispensed from vending machines. Folders containing sets of postmarked stamps are produced.

Commemoratives

About eight commemorative stamp issues appear each year related to South African people and events: often these consist of just one or two denominations. First day covers are available. On rare occasions miniature sheets are produced.

Postal stationery

A stamped aerogramme is available, as well as a series of stamped postcards and a registered envelope.

Bophuthatswana
Transkei
Venda

Certain areas in South Africa have been designated as 'homelands', being self-administering and being permitted to conduct their own postal services and issue their own stamps. It seems likely that further such 'homelands' will be created in future.

**Write to: Philatelic Services and Intersapa
Private Bag X505, Pretoria
0001 Republic of South Africa**

Currency: 100 cents = 1 South African rand
(£1.00 = R1.78; US $1.00 = R0.79 approx.)

Definitives
Each area has its own definitive series. For Bophuthatswana the theme is wildlife; for Transkei they depict scenes of life in the land; for Venda the definitives feature flowers.

Commemoratives
Each of the areas releases about four commemorative sets a year on topics of local interest. First day covers are available.

Postal stationery
For each area stamped aerogrammes and stamped postcards are available, as are folders containing sets of postmarked stamps. Registered envelopes are also in use.

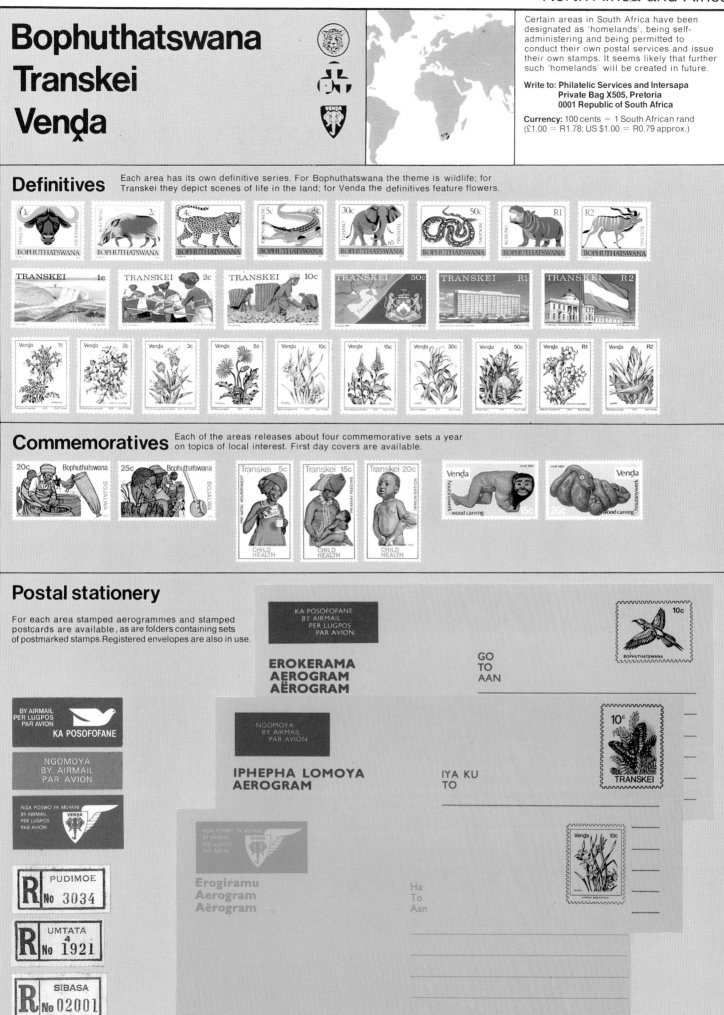

South West Africa

SWA

Mandated territory in southern Africa, which was formerly a German colony. It is also known as Namibia. German stamps overprinted were used from 1897; Union of South Africa stamps were employed from 1915; South African stamps suitably overprinted were introduced in 1923; stamps actually inscribed South West Africa first appeared in 1931.

Write to: SWA, Philatelic Services and Intersapa, Private Bag X505 Pretoria 0001 Republic of South Africa

Currency: as for South Africa

Definitives

The present definitive series was introduced in 1980 and depicts wildlife. In addition to the stamps sold from normal sheets, stamps are also sold from vending machines in rolls. Souvenir folders are produced, containing the definitives, cancelled on the first day of issue.

Commemoratives

About four commemorative stamp issues appear each year, being of local importance. First day covers are prepared. Occasionally a miniature sheet is issued.

Postal stationery

A stamped aerogramme and stamped postcards are available, as well as a registered envelope.

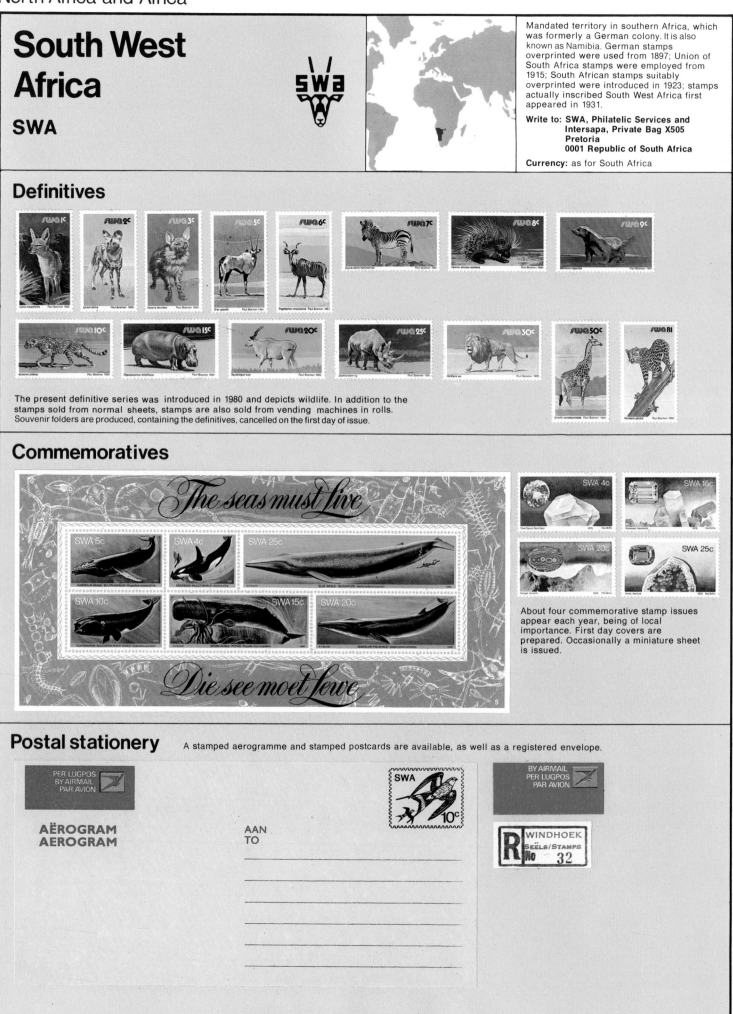

St. Helena

An island in the South Atlantic which was discovered by the Portuguese navigator, Joao de Nova Castella, in 1502. It was not until 1667 that the population really grew, thanks to settlers made homeless by the Great Fire of London. The imprisonment of Napoleon on the island brought about an increase in correspondence.

Write to: The Postmaster
Post Office Jamestown
St Helena Island
South Atlantic

Currency: 100 pence = 1 pound sterling
(US $1.00 = £0.45 approx.)

Definitives

The first stamps appeared in January 1856. The current definitives feature lithoprints of St Helena, mainly as seen in the nineteenth century.

Commemoratives

Only about two or three commemorative issues are produced each year, although first day covers are available for each. On rare occasions miniature sheets are produced.

Tristan da Cunha

An island in the Atlantic Ocean, named after the Portuguese admiral, Tristao da Cunha, which became a British possession in 1816. The first stamps, in 1952, were overprints on St Helena, stamps actually inscribed Tristan da Cunha appearing in 1953. In 1922 some British stamps were overprinted 'Tristan da Cunha' to mark Shackleton's expedition but these were not issued.

Write to: The Postmaster
Tristan da Cunha (via Cape Town RSA)
South Atlantic

Currency: 100 pence = 1 pound sterling
(US $1.00 = £0.45 approx.)

Definitives

The present definitive series features birds.

Commemoratives and other items

Events commemorated by stamps are of local significance, there being about four or five such issues a year. First day covers are made available. Occasionally a miniature sheet is produced. A stamped aerogramme and postage due labels are in use. Pictorial postcards and maximum cards are in use.

Ascension Island

A volcanic island in the South Atlantic, discovered by the Portuguese navigator, Joao da Nova, on Ascension Day, 1501. It was occupied by the British some 300 years later, and British stamps were used from 1866. It became a dependency of St Helena in 1922, and used St Helena stamps overprinted 'Ascension', replaced by stamps inscribed Ascension in 1924

Write to: The Postmaster
         Ascension Island
         Atlantic Ocean

Currency: 100 pence = 1 pound sterling (US $1.00 = £0.45 approx.)

Definitives

The definitive series is replaced approximately every five years. The 1981 series depicts flowers.

Commemoratives and stamp booklets

About four commemorative stamp issues are produced each year, mostly with a local flavour. Miniature sheets are occasionally produced, while first day covers accompany most issues. Stamp booklets are made available from time to time.

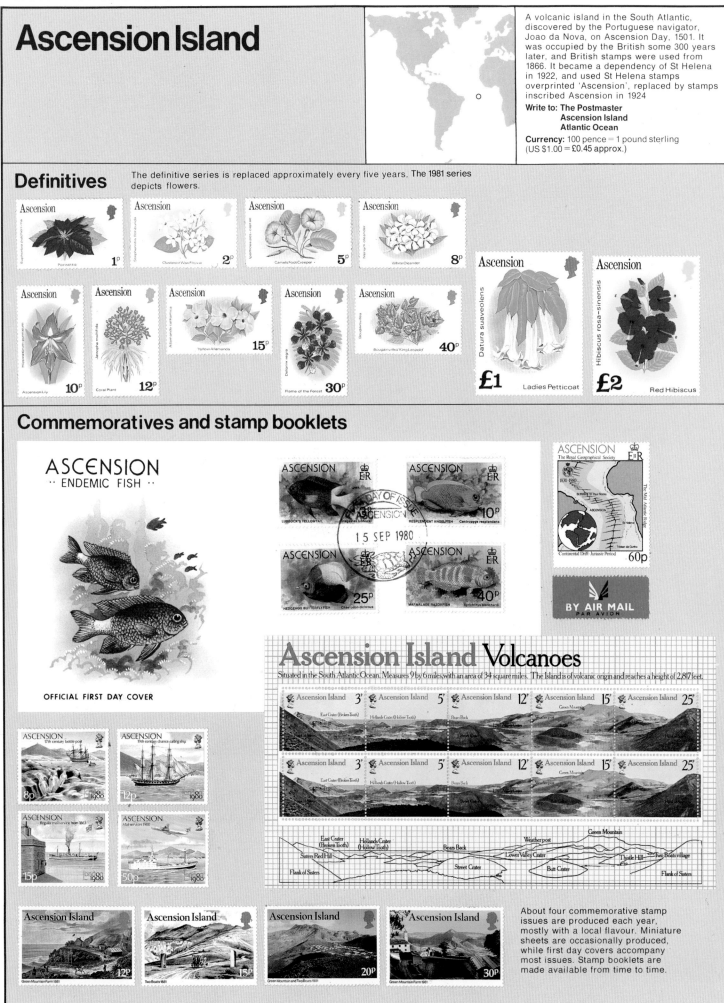

Australasia - Pacific Islands

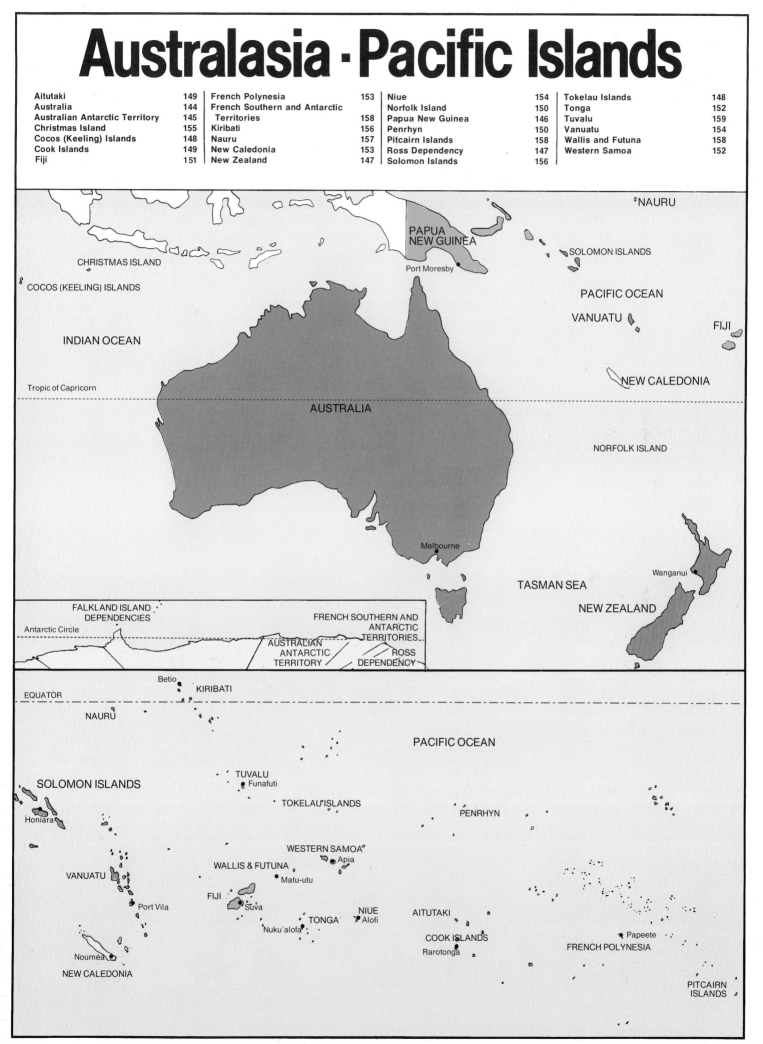

NAURU

PAPUA NEW GUINEA

SOLOMON ISLANDS

Port Moresby

CHRISTMAS ISLAND

COCOS (KEELING) ISLANDS

PACIFIC OCEAN

VANUATU

FIJI

INDIAN OCEAN

NEW CALEDONIA

Tropic of Capricorn

AUSTRALIA

NORFOLK ISLAND

Melbourne

Wanganui

TASMAN SEA

NEW ZEALAND

FALKLAND ISLAND DEPENDENCIES

Antarctic Circle

FRENCH SOUTHERN AND ANTARCTIC TERRITORIES

AUSTRALIAN ANTARCTIC TERRITORY

ROSS DEPENDENCY

Betio

KIRIBATI

EQUATOR

NAURU

PACIFIC OCEAN

TUVALU
Funafuti

SOLOMON ISLANDS

TOKELAU ISLANDS

PENRHYN

Honiara

WESTERN SAMOA
Apia

WALLIS & FUTUNA

VANUATU

Matu-utu

FIJI

Port Vila

Suva

TONGA

NIUE
Alofi

AITUTAKI

Nuku'alofa

Papeete

COOK ISLANDS
Rarotonga

FRENCH POLYNESIA

Nouméa

NEW CALEDONIA

PITCAIRN ISLANDS

143

Australia

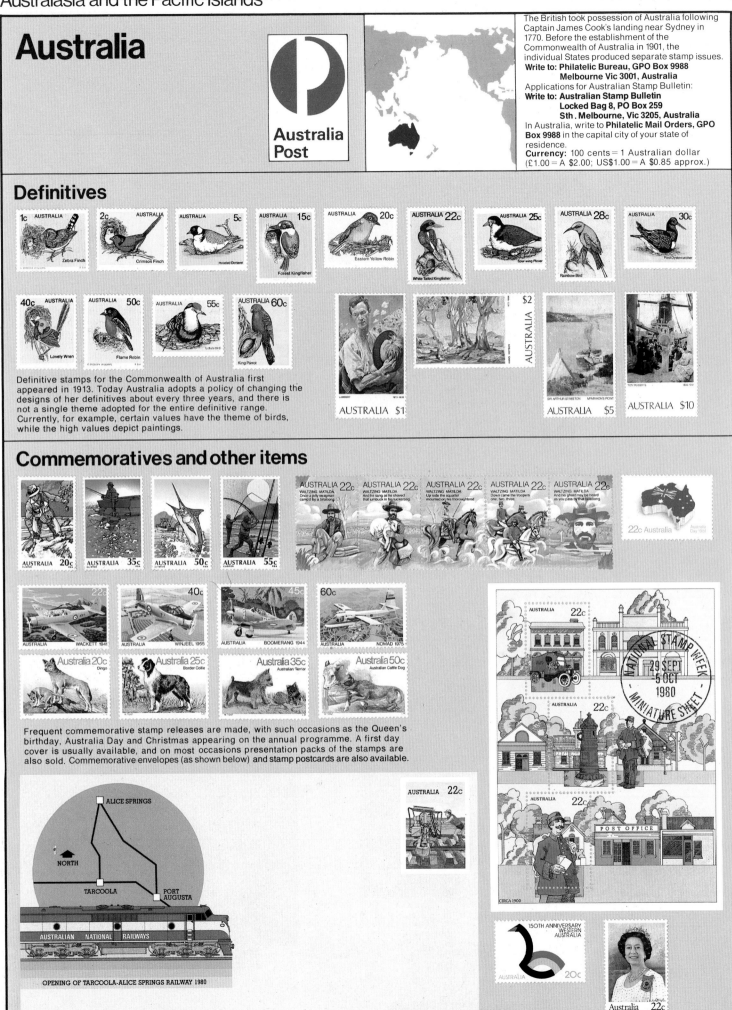

Australia Post

The British took possession of Australia following Captain James Cook's landing near Sydney in 1770. Before the establishment of the Commonwealth of Australia in 1901, the individual States produced separate stamp issues.
Write to: Philatelic Bureau, GPO Box 9988
Melbourne Vic 3001, Australia
Applications for Australian Stamp Bulletin:
Write to: Australian Stamp Bulletin
Locked Bag 8, PO Box 259
Sth . Melbourne, Vic 3205, Australia
In Australia, write to **Philatelic Mail Orders, GPO Box 9988** in the capital city of your state of residence.
Currency: 100 cents = 1 Australian dollar
(£1.00 = A $2.00; US$1.00 = A $0.85 approx.)

Definitives

Definitive stamps for the Commonwealth of Australia first appeared in 1913. Today Australia adopts a policy of changing the designs of her definitives about every three years, and there is not a single theme adopted for the entire definitive range. Currently, for example, certain values have the theme of birds, while the high values depict paintings.

Commemoratives and other items

Frequent commemorative stamp releases are made, with such occasions as the Queen's birthday, Australia Day and Christmas appearing on the annual programme. A first day cover is usually available, and on most occasions presentation packs of the stamps are also sold. Commemorative envelopes (as shown below) and stamp postcards are also available.

OPENING OF TARCOOLA-ALICE SPRINGS RAILWAY 1980

AEROGRAMME
BY AIRMAIL · PAR AVION

30c AUSTRALIA

COUNTRY OF DESTINATION _____

BY AIR MAIL · PAR AVION

AEROGRAMME

COUNTRY OF DESTINATION

Australia Post
stamp folder
four 20c stamps
80c

20c AUSTRALIA 20c AUSTRALIA 20c AUSTRALIA
Little Grebe Little Grebe Little Grebe

Australia Post
stamp folder
three 20c stamps
60c

R.6 NORTH TAMBORINE QUEENSLAND
R N° 0993

EXPRÈS OVERSEAS EXPRESS DELIVERY EXPRÈS

AIR MAIL PAR AVION

MESSENGER DELIVERY

SAL
Surface Air Lifted   From Australia
Australian Post Office   Qantas

PRIORITY PAID ///

POSTPAK

Aerogrammes are issued, including a special version each year for use during the Christmas period. Envelopes and postcards are also produced bearing special 'stamp' designs, frequently of a commemorative nature. Stamp booklets, for a time withdrawn from use, have recently reappeared on an experimental basis. Miniature sheets are occasionally produced.

Australian Antarctic Territory

The area of Antarctica claimed by Australia in 1933 which, while having no permanent population, does house a number of research stations. Stamps were provided for the scientists working there, the first stamp appearing in 1957.

Write to: Philatelic Bureau, GPO Box 9988 Melbourne Vic 3001, Australia

Currency: as for Australia

Definitives and commemoratives

AUSTRALIAN ANTARCTIC TERRITORY 1c R.Y. AURORA
AUSTRALIAN ANTARCTIC TERRITORY 5c M.S. THALA DAN
AUSTRALIAN ANTARCTIC TERRITORY 15c A.E. KISTA DAN
AUSTRALIAN ANTARCTIC TERRITORY 20c H.M.S. DISCOVERY II
AUSTRALIAN ANTARCTIC TERRITORY 22c R.Y.S. TERRA NOVA
AUSTRALIAN ANTARCTIC TERRITORY 25c S.S. ENDURANCE
AUSTRALIAN ANTARCTIC TERRITORY 20c
AUSTRALIAN ANTARCTIC TERRITORY 55c

AUSTRALIAN ANTARCTIC TERRITORY 30c S.S. FRAM
AUSTRALIAN ANTARCTIC TERRITORY 35c M.S. NELLA DAN
AUSTRALIAN ANTARCTIC TERRITORY 55c S.Y. DISCOVERY
AUSTRALIAN ANTARCTIC TERRITORY $1 H.M.S. RESOLUTION

The present definitive set, issued in sections, features ships. Commemorative stamps appear very infrequently, as and when a suitable commemoration arises.

Papua New Guinea

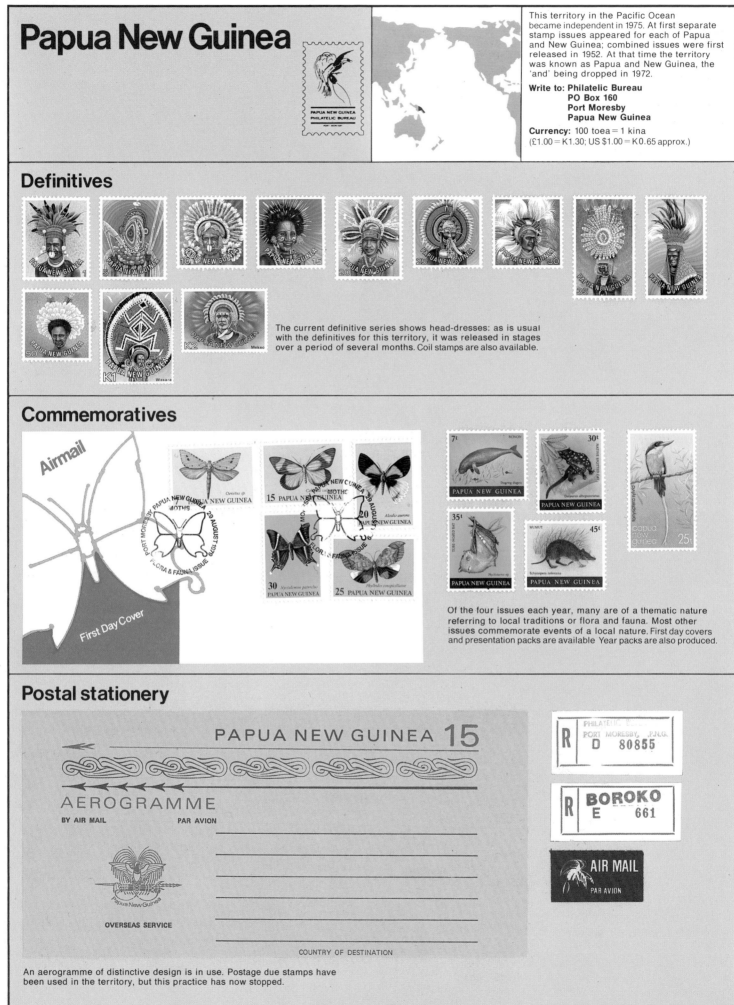

This territory in the Pacific Ocean became independent in 1975. At first separate stamp issues appeared for each of Papua and New Guinea; combined issues were first released in 1952. At that time the territory was known as Papua and New Guinea, the 'and' being dropped in 1972.

Write to: Philatelic Bureau
 PO Box 160
 Port Moresby
 Papua New Guinea

Currency: 100 toea = 1 kina
(£1.00 = K1.30; US $1.00 = K0.65 approx.)

Definitives

The current definitive series shows head-dresses: as is usual with the definitives for this territory, it was released in stages over a period of several months. Coil stamps are also available.

Commemoratives

Of the four issues each year, many are of a thematic nature referring to local traditions or flora and fauna. Most other issues commemorate events of a local nature. First day covers and presentation packs are available. Year packs are also produced.

Postal stationery

An aerogramme of distinctive design is in use. Postage due stamps have been used in the territory, but this practice has now stopped.

New Zealand

A Dominion of the British Commonwealth in the Pacific Ocean, New Zealand comprises two islands, North and South. It was originally inhabited by the Maoris from Polynesia. The first recorded sighting was made in 1642 by Tasman, a Dutch explorer, and Captain Cook rediscovered the islands in 1769. The first stamps for New Zealand appeared in 1855.

Write to: Philatelic Bureau
Private Bag
Wanganui, New Zealand

Currency: 100 cents = 1 New Zealand dollar (£1.00 = NZ $2.50; US $1.00 = NZ $1.05 approx.)

Definitives

The current definitives have been released in several stages and have a range of designs including roses, Maori artefacts and seashells, while the portrait of the Queen appears on one value. Likewise the Royal portrait is used on the coil stamps sold from vending machines.

Commemoratives

New Zealand Post Office
First Day Cover
Christmas 1979

About five issues appear each year, mostly of local significance: one set appears for Christmas. Stamps are also produced to raise money for health camps: 'Health' stamps are sold at a premium which is donated to the work of the camps. These stamps are normally also made available in small sheets, so that they can be sold on a 'door to door' basis. First day covers accompany each issue, while once a year a presentation pack is sold containing the commemorative stamps of the past twelve months.

Postal stationery and other items

Postal stationery includes postcards, lettercards, registered envelopes, unstamped aerogrammes, air letter envelopes and newspaper wrappers. Stamp booklets containing definitives are sold, as are a range of presentation packs containing such items as stationery, first day covers, and so on. Separate stamps are used by the Government Life Insurance Department.

Ross Dependency

This dependency of New Zealand is situated in the Antarctic, lying in the Ross Sea.
Address & currency as New Zealand

Definitives

It has only ever issued definitive stamps, the first appearing in 1957. The current series shows scenes of Ross Dependency.

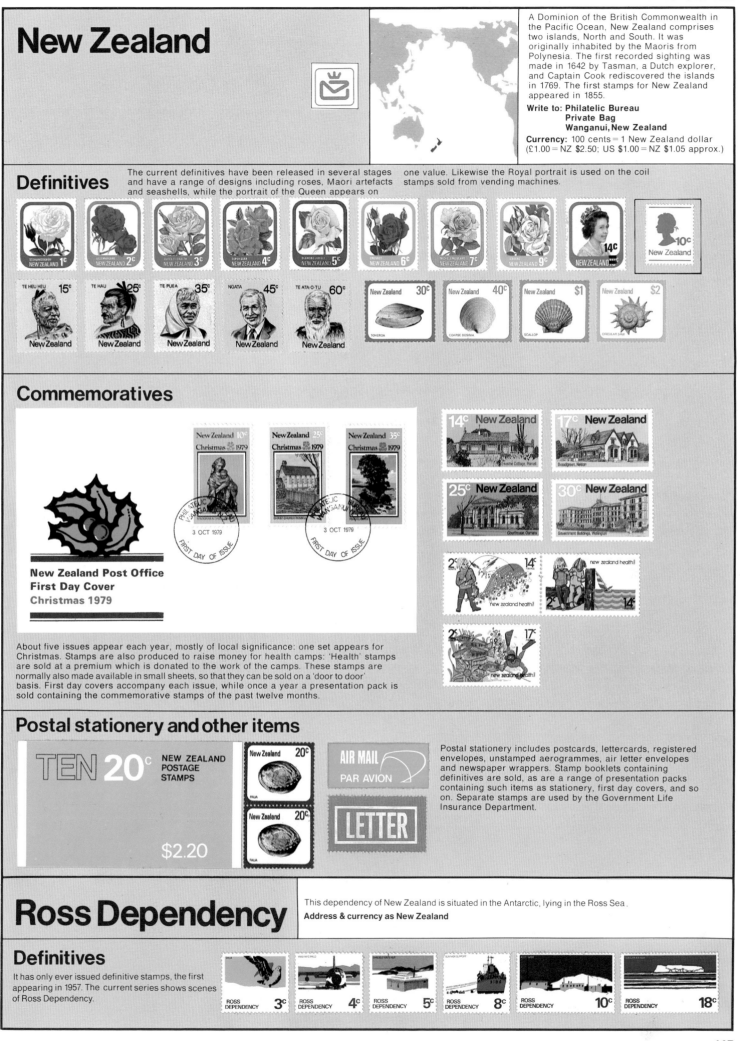

Cocos (Keeling) Islands

A group of twenty-seven islands in the Indian Ocean discovered by Captain Keeling in 1609. Their administration has been under the control of Ceylon, Singapore and finally Australia from 1955. Stamps were issued from 1963 to 1966, after which Australian stamps were used until 1969, when the territory again began issuing its own stamps.

Write to: Philatelic Officer
Philatelic Bureau
Cocos (Keeling) Islands
Indian Ocean 6799

Currency: 100 cents = 1 Australian dollar
(£1.00 = A $2.00; US $1.00 = A $0.85 approx.)

Definitives The present definitive series depicts fish.

Commemoratives

There are only about three or four commemorative sets each year which are of particular relevance to the territory. Presentation packs and first day covers are available.

Tokelau Islands

Three islands in the Pacific Ocean to the north of Samoa which became British in 1893, being known as the Union Islands and administered as part of the Gilbert and Ellice Islands group. In 1949 they became part of New Zealand, distinctive stamps having been issued in the previous year.

Write to: Post Office Philatelic Bureau
Private Bag
Wanganui
New Zealand

Currency: 100 cents = 1 New Zealand dollar
(£1.00 = NZ $2.50; US $1.00 = NZ $1.05 approx.)

Definitives

The present definitive series features a range of local activities, including canoe making and washing day.

Commemoratives

There are only about two or three commemorative sets each year, important international events being the main subject of such issues. First day covers are available.

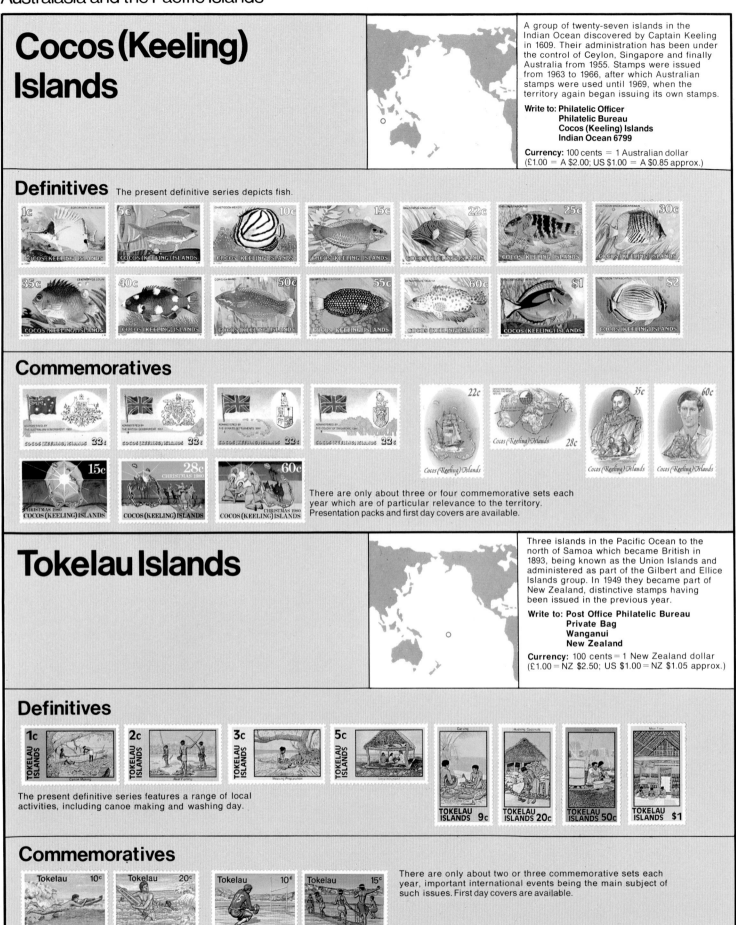

Cook Islands

Group of islands in the South West Pacific which, not surprisingly, were discovered by Captain Cook, in 1773. They have come under the protection of Great Britain and have also been part of the Dominion of New Zealand. The first stamps, in 1892, were inscribed Cook Islands Federation. Various islands have at times issued their own stamps, namely Aitutaki, Niue and Penrhyn.

Write to: Philatelic Bureau
General Post Office
Rarotonga, Cook Islands
South Pacific

Currency: 100 cents = 1 New Zealand dollar (£1.00 = NZ $2.50; US $1.00 = NZ $1.05 approx.)

Definitives

Definitives featuring shells were in use, but these have now been replaced by a new series showing coral. These stamps exist overprinted 'O.H.M.S.' for use by Government Departments.

Commemoratives

Among the events recorded by commemorative stamps each year are Easter and Christmas. Many recent issues have been in honour of Captain Cook. Most issues are accompanied by a miniature sheet. First day covers are usually available. Stamps with a premium for charitable use are released for Christmas and Easter issues.

Aitutaki

Cook Islands

Part of the Cook Islands group, but discovered by Captain William Bligh in 1789. The stamps of the Cook Islands were used from 1892, but between 1903 and 1932 stamps of New Zealand suitably overprinted were employed. Cook Islands stamps were again used until 1972, when stamps inscribed Aitutaki (initially overprints on Cook Islands) reappeared.

Write to: The Postmaster
General Post Office, Aitutaki
Cook Islands, South Pacific

Currency: 100 cents = 1 New Zealand dollar (£1.00 = NZ $2.50; US $1.00 = NZ $1.05 approx.)

Definitives

The current definitives depict shells. Stamps for use by Government Departments (primarily the Philatelic Bureau) comprising various stamps overprinted 'O.H.M.S.' are also produced.

Commemoratives

National and international events are commemorated, plus annual issues for Easter and Christmas. Frequently sets are accompanied by miniature sheets. First day covers are available. Stamps with a premium for charitable use are available.

Norfolk Island

An island in the South-West Pacific which comes under Australian administration. It was discovered by Captain Cook in 1774, and became a penal settlement in the 1780s, before being populated with the islanders from Pitcairn in 1856. The post office dates back to the 1830s, having variously used the stamps of Tasmania, New South Wales and Australia before distinctive issues arrived.

Write to: Senior Philatelic Officer
Norfolk Island
South Pacific 2899

Currency: 100 cents = 1 Australian dollar
(£1.00 = A $2.00; US $1.00 = A $0.85 approx.)

Definitives

The first distinctive stamps inscribed Norfolk Island appeared in 1947. The current definitives show aircraft. The previous definitives showed butterflies.

Other items

While important international events are commemorated, most issues are of more local interest. Several sets in recent years have paid tribute to Captain Cook.

First day covers and, occasionally, miniature sheets are produced. Stamped envelopes and aerogrammes are available.

Penrhyn

Northern Cook Islands

The main island in the North Cook Islands Group, Penrhyn was discovered in 1788. A post office was first opened in 1901, the stamps of the Cook Islands being initially used until New Zealand stamps overprinted 'Penrhyn' were introduced from 1902 to 1930. Cook Islands stamps were again used until 1973, when individual stamps for Penrhyn reappeared

Write to: Post Office, Penrhyn
Northern Cook Islands
South Pacific

Currency: 100 cents = 1 New Zealand dollar
(£1.00 = NZ $2.50; US $1.00 = NZ $1.05 approx.)

Definitives

A new definitive series, showing sailing ships of the Pacific, was released in February 1981. The previous definitives showed fish (low values) and a map of Penrhyn (high values). These stamps also exist overprinted 'O.H.M.S.' for official Government use.

Commemoratives

These appear about six times a year, usually also issued in the form of miniature sheets and available on first day covers. Events commemorated include Easter and Christmas and major international occasions. Stamps with a premium are produced for charitable purposes.

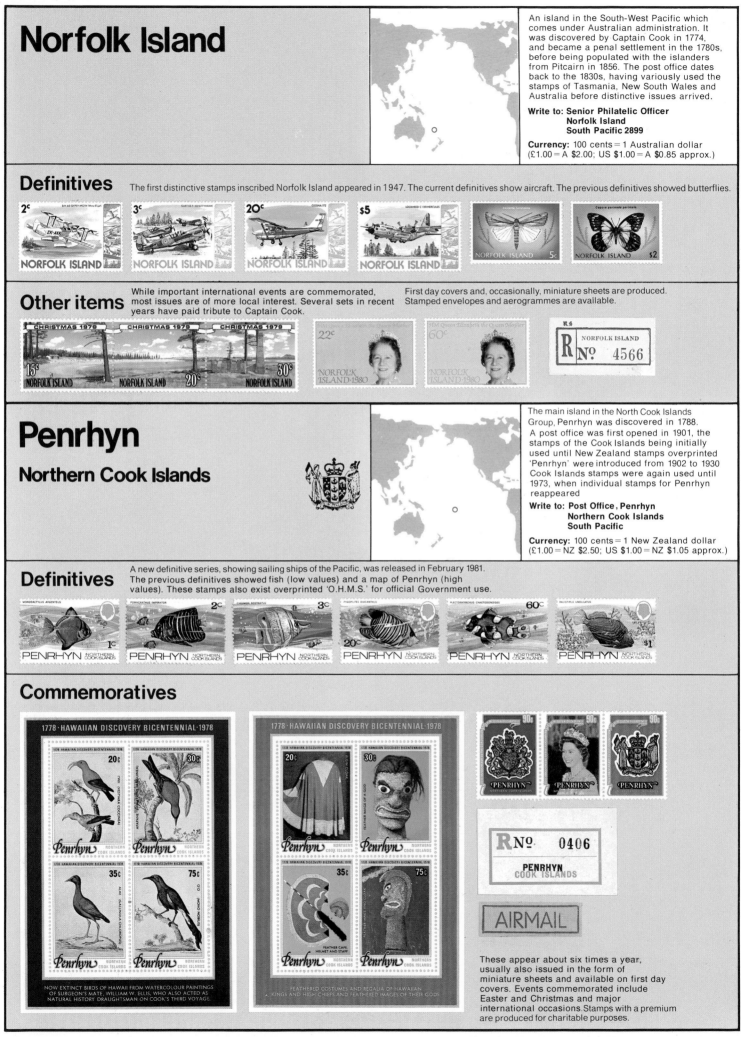

Fiji

P&T
FIJI

The group of islands in the South Western Pacific known as Fiji were sighted by the Dutchman, Tasman. They became a British colony in 1874. The first stamps appeared in 1870, being produced by the local newspaper, *The Fiji Times*. The first 'proper' stamps appeared in 1871, these being overprinted 'V.R.' in 1874 when the islands were ceded to Great Britain.

Write to: Philatelic Bureau
G.P.O. Box 40
Suva, Fiji

Currency: 100 cents = 1 Fijian dollar
(£1.00 = F $1.90; US $1.00 = F $0.80 approx.)

Definitives

The current definitives show famous buildings on the islands, the set being released in stages starting in late 1979.

Commemoratives

Commemorative stamps appear about four times a year, commemorating both local and international events. They are usually accompanied by first day covers.

Postal stationery

Aerogrammes, envelopes and registered letter envelopes are all available, being printed with specially designed 'stamps'.

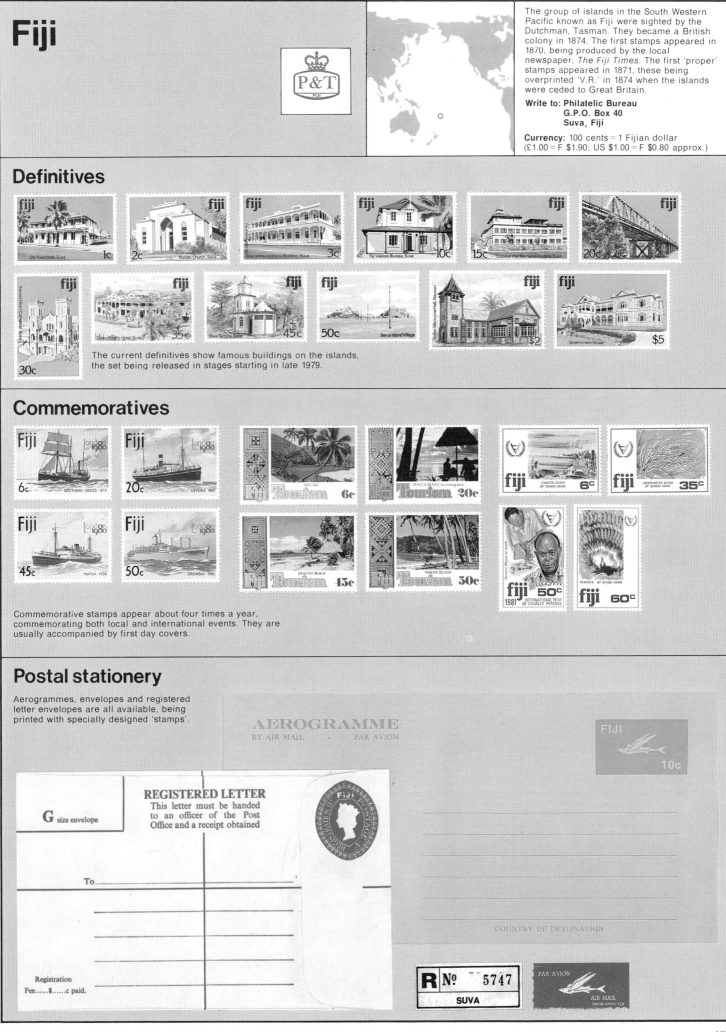

Tonga

A group of islands in the Pacific Ocean constituting an independent Polynesian Kingdom, which were once under British protection and became part of the Commonwealth in 1970. The largest island in the group, Tongatapu, by discovered by Tasman, but it was Captain Cook who gave them their alternative title of The Friendly Islands. Stamps were first issued in 1886.

Write to: The Stamp Section
Treasury Building, Nuku'alofa
Tonga, South West Pacific

Currency: 100 senti = 1 pa'anga
(£1.00 = T$1.92; US $1.00 = T$0.85 approx.)

Definitives, commemoratives and other items

In recent times Tonga has been distinguished by its release of stamps produced on self-adhesive paper, and in various shapes and sizes. The definitives, split into normal definitives, airmail, and Official airmail, depict bananas, birds and aircraft.

The commemorative sets, which also appear in odd shapes, are issued fairly frequently and often with rather high face values. Their designs are normally related to international events. A stamped aerogramme is in use.

Western Samoa

Samoa I Sisifo

A group of islands in the Pacific Ocean: Western Samoa gained independence in 1962; Eastern Samoa is administered by the United States of America. The first stamps were of a local nature, the first postal service having been established in 1877 by the *Samoa Times*, and stamps for the service being issued in 1880.

Write to: Philatelic Bureau
GPO Apia
Western Samoa

Currency: 100 sene = 1 tala
(£1.00 = WS $2.18; US $1.00 = WS $0.97 approx.)

Definitives, commemoratives and other items

The first proper definitives for Western Samoa appeared in 1886 and showed palm trees. The current definitives depict shells.

Five commemorative stamp issues are released each year, occasionally with a miniature sheet. Events tend to be of local interest, although Western Samoa's participation in overseas stamp exhibitions also warrants a special issue. First day covers are available. Two aerogrammes are available, each with a 'printed' stamp in a design appropriate to the current definitives.

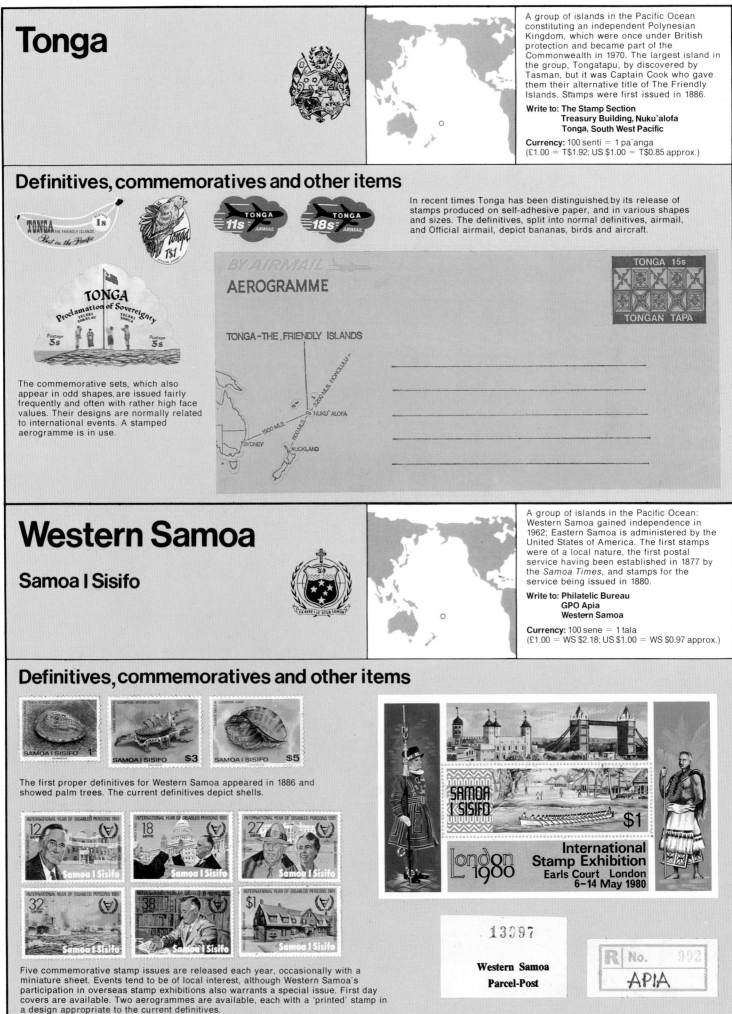

French Polynesia

Polynésie Française

A group of islands in the south-west Pacific which became French possessions in 1768, when they were claimed for Louis XV by Bougainville. They were previously called the Oceanic Settlements. The first stamps for French Polynesia appeared in 1958.

Write to: Centre Philatélique
Papeete
Tahiti
French Polynesia

Currency: 100 centimes = 1 CFP franc
(£1.00 = 190.00F; US $1.00 = 83.60F approx.)

Commemoratives and other items

The commemorative issues have an international flavour, being 'thematic' in their design; about twelve issues appear each year. No definitive stamps have been issued in recent times. Official stamps and postage due labels are in use. An aerogramme is also available. Maximum cards are produced.

New Caledonia

Nouvelle · Calédonie et Dépendances

Islands in the Central Pacific, discovered and named by Captain Cook in 1774, and settled by the French from 1793. The first stamp appeared in 1860, being a single 10c value depicting Emperor Napoleon III. From 1862 to 1881 the French 'colonial' series was used, and then various overprints. Stamps for New Caledonia reappeared in 1905.

Write to: Service Philatélique
Noumea RP
New Caledonia

Currency: 100 centimes = 1 CFP franc
(£1.00 = 190.00F; US $1.00 = 83.60F approx.)

Commemoratives and other items

About twelve commemorative sets appear each year, although in fact most are of just a single value. Topics are of local importance and the stamps are available on first day cover. The last definitive series in use depicts seashells. A stamped aerogramme is also available. Postage due labels, stamp booklets and Official stamps are in use.

Vanuatu

A group of islands which prior to independence in 1980 were known as the New Hebrides. They were discovered by Pedro Fernandez de Quiros, but were named by Captain Cook. Up to independence they were jointly administered by Great Britain and France and, from the first stamp in 1908 up to 1980, each issue had been released both in English and French.

Write to: The Philatelic Bureau
Post Office
Port Vila, Vanuatu, South Pacific

Currency: vatu (replaced New Hebrides franc)
(£1.00 = 170 vatu; US $1.00 = 78.65 vatu approx.)

Definitives, commemoratives and other items

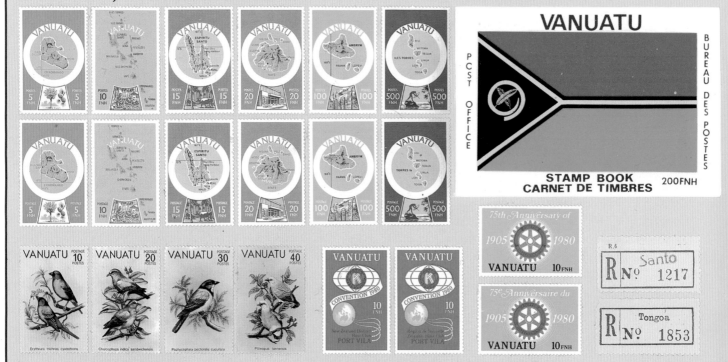

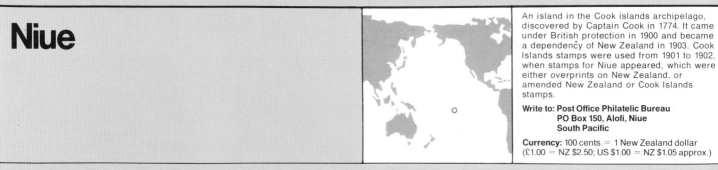

The present definitive stamps depict maps of the islands in the group. There are about four commemorative sets each year, mainly relating to the territory, although 'thematic' sets are also produced. A stamped aerogramme is in use, while booklets containing the definitive stamps have been made available.

Niue

An island in the Cook islands archipelago, discovered by Captain Cook in 1774. It came under British protection in 1900 and became a dependency of New Zealand in 1903. Cook Islands stamps were used from 1901 to 1902, when stamps for Niue appeared, which were either overprints on New Zealand, or amended New Zealand or Cook Islands stamps.

Write to: Post Office Philatelic Bureau
PO Box 150, Alofi, Niue
South Pacific

Currency: 100 cents = 1 New Zealand dollar
(£1.00 = NZ $2.50; US $1.00 = NZ $1.05 approx.)

Definitives, commemoratives and other items

The current definitives depict local activities such as reef fishing and planting taro. Values also exist inscribed 'Airmail' for use on letters being sent by air. In recent years Niue has issued about six commemorative sets a year, including stamps for Easter and Christmas, and major international events. All issues tend to be accompanied by miniature sheets and are available on first day covers. The new definitive series, to be issued in 1981, shows flowers of the South Pacific. Stamps are sold at a premium for charitable purposes.

Christmas Island

Indian Ocean

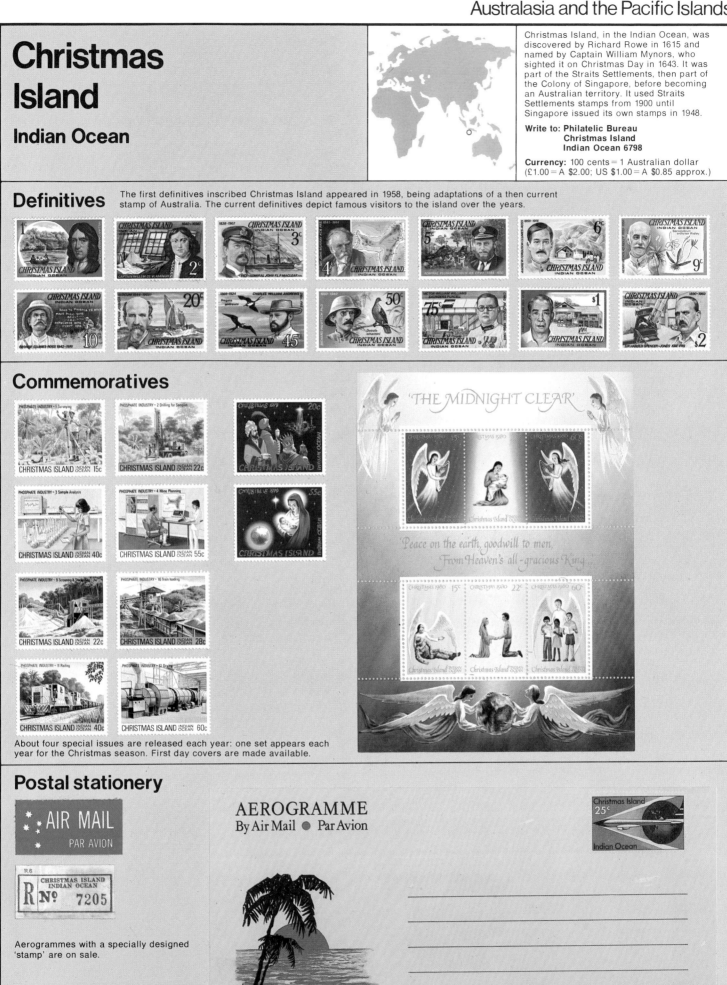

Christmas Island, in the Indian Ocean, was discovered by Richard Rowe in 1615 and named by Captain William Mynors, who sighted it on Christmas Day in 1643. It was part of the Straits Settlements, then part of the Colony of Singapore, before becoming an Australian territory. It used Straits Settlements stamps from 1900 until Singapore issued its own stamps in 1948.

Write to: Philatelic Bureau
Christmas Island
Indian Ocean 6798

Currency: 100 cents = 1 Australian dollar
(£1.00 = A $2.00; US $1.00 = A $0.85 approx.)

Definitives

The first definitives inscribed Christmas Island appeared in 1958, being adaptations of a then current stamp of Australia. The current definitives depict famous visitors to the island over the years.

Commemoratives

'THE MIDNIGHT CLEAR'

Peace on the earth, goodwill to men,
From Heaven's all-gracious King

About four special issues are released each year: one set appears each year for the Christmas season. First day covers are made available.

Postal stationery

AIR MAIL
PAR AVION

R6
R CHRISTMAS ISLAND
INDIAN OCEAN
Nº 7205

Aerogrammes with a specially designed 'stamp' are on sale.

AEROGRAMME
By Air Mail ● Par Avion

Christmas Island
25c
Indian Ocean

Kiribati

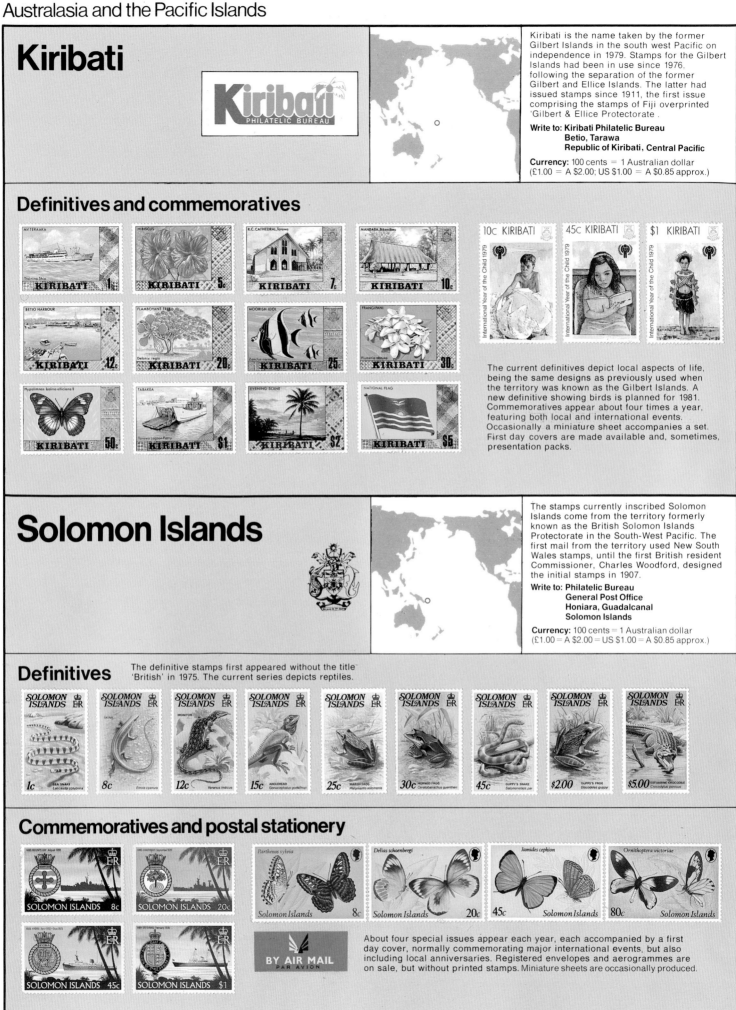

Kiribati is the name taken by the former Gilbert Islands in the south west Pacific on independence in 1979. Stamps for the Gilbert Islands had been in use since 1976, following the separation of the former Gilbert and Ellice Islands. The latter had issued stamps since 1911, the first issue comprising the stamps of Fiji overprinted 'Gilbert & Ellice Protectorate'.

Write to: Kiribati Philatelic Bureau
Betio, Tarawa
Republic of Kiribati, Central Pacific

Currency: 100 cents = 1 Australian dollar
(£1.00 = A $2.00; US $1.00 = A $0.85 approx.)

Definitives and commemoratives

The current definitives depict local aspects of life, being the same designs as previously used when the territory was known as the Gilbert Islands. A new definitive showing birds is planned for 1981. Commemoratives appear about four times a year, featuring both local and international events. Occasionally a miniature sheet accompanies a set. First day covers are made available and, sometimes, presentation packs.

Solomon Islands

The stamps currently inscribed Solomon Islands come from the territory formerly known as the British Solomon Islands Protectorate in the South-West Pacific. The first mail from the territory used New South Wales stamps, until the first British resident Commissioner, Charles Woodford, designed the initial stamps in 1907.

Write to: Philatelic Bureau
General Post Office
Honiara, Guadalcanal
Solomon Islands

Currency: 100 cents = 1 Australian dollar
(£1.00 = A $2.00 = US $1.00 = A $0.85 approx.)

Definitives

The definitive stamps first appeared without the title 'British' in 1975. The current series depicts reptiles.

Commemoratives and postal stationery

About four special issues appear each year, each accompanied by a first day cover, normally commemorating major international events, but also including local anniversaries. Registered envelopes and aerogrammes are on sale, but without printed stamps. Miniature sheets are occasionally produced.

Nauru

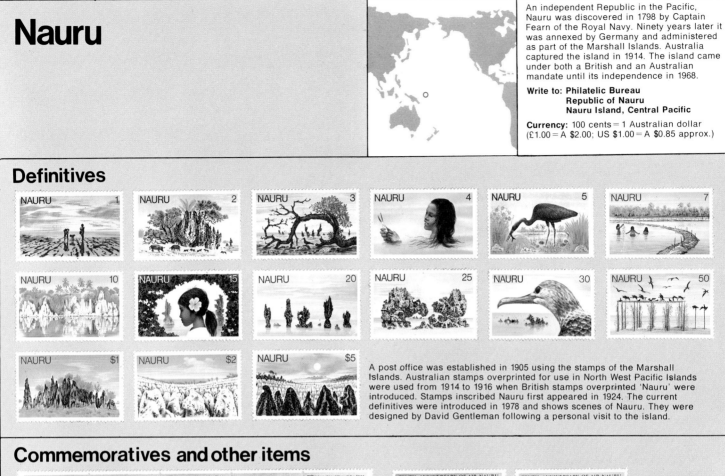

An independent Republic in the Pacific, Nauru was discovered in 1798 by Captain Fearn of the Royal Navy. Ninety years later it was annexed by Germany and administered as part of the Marshall Islands. Australia captured the island in 1914. The island came under both a British and an Australian mandate until its independence in 1968.

Write to: Philatelic Bureau
Republic of Nauru
Nauru Island, Central Pacific

Currency: 100 cents = 1 Australian dollar
(£1.00 = A $2.00; US $1.00 = A $0.85 approx.)

Definitives

A post office was established in 1905 using the stamps of the Marshall Islands. Australian stamps overprinted for use in North West Pacific Islands were used from 1914 to 1916 when British stamps overprinted 'Nauru' were introduced. Stamps inscribed Nauru first appeared in 1924. The current definitives were introduced in 1978 and shows scenes of Nauru. They were designed by David Gentleman following a personal visit to the island.

Commemoratives and other items

The annual programme includes stamps for Christmas, plus major local and international events, there being about four issues each year. Each set is accompanied by a first day cover and presentation pack and occasionally miniature sheets are produced.

FIRST DAY OF ISSUE

Nauru occasionally produces 'Maximum cards', which are postcards reproducing stamp designs. So far the cards have reproduced designs from the current definitive series. Aerogrammes are available in two forms: with a printed stamp design and without.

Pitcairn Islands

An island group in the South Pacific named after Robert Pitcairn, a midshipman on board *HMS Swallow*, which sighted the islands in 1767. The population is mainly derived from the mutineers from the *Bounty* who arrived on Pitcairn in 1790. Stamps of New Zealand were used from 1927 until Pitcairn's own stamps appeared in 1940.

Write to: **Philatelic Bureau**
(Pitcairn Islands)
c/o Fiji Post Office
GPO Box 40, Suva, Fiji

Currency: 100 cents = 1 New Zealand dollar
(£1.00 = NZ $2.50; US $1.00 = NZ $1.05 approx.)

Definitives

The current definitives depict scenes of life on Pitcairn, with the highest value showing a portrait of Queen Elizabeth II.

Commemoratives

About four new issues are released each year (each accompanied by a first day cover) of local interest and significance. Miniature sheets are sometimes produced.

Wallis and Futuna Islands

Wallis et Futuna

This group of islands in the Pacific Ocean are the smallest of the French overseas territories, and are a dependency of New Caledonia. Futuna was discovered in 1616, while Wallis was discovered by an Englishman, Samuel Wallis, in 1767. The first stamps appeared in 1920, being overprints on New Caledonia.

Write to: **Bureau des Postes**
Service Philatélique
Matu-utu
Wallis and Futuna Islands
South Pacific

Currency: 100 centimes = 1 CFP franc
(£1.00 = 190.00F; US $1.00 = 83.60F approx.)

Commemoratives

There are on average ten commemorative sets each year, which relate mainly to international events, and are aimed to appeal to 'thematic' collectors. There are no definitive stamps at present in use.

French Southern and Antarctic Territories

Terres Australes et Antarctiques Françaises

These territories have been administered as a group since 1955 and consist of the French settlements in the southern Indian Ocean and the Antarctic area. Although they cover a large area, they support a small population, mainly of researchers. The first stamp, issued in 1955, was an overprint on a stamp of Madagascar.

Write to: **Agence TAAF**
85 Avenue de la Bourdonnaïs
F-75007 Paris
France

Currency: 100 centimes = 1 French franc
(£1.00 = 11.06F; US $1.00 = 4.87F approx.)

Definitives and commemoratives

Definitive stamps are in use.
About five commemorative sets appear each year, showing subjects of local interest.

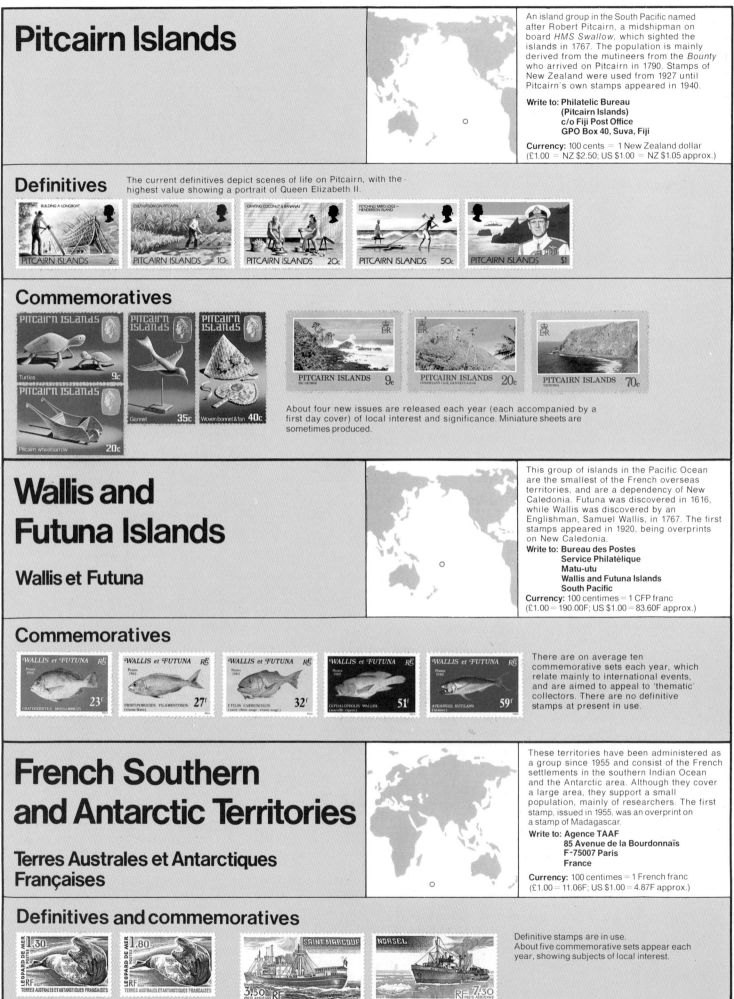

Tuvalu

TUVALU PHILATELIC BUREAU

The name now given to the former Ellice Islands, which were separated from the Gilbert Islands on January 1, 1976. The group consists of 9 islands, with a total area of 10 square miles (26 sq. km.) scattered over half a million square miles (1.3 million sq. km.). The first stamps were the former issues of Gilbert and Ellice Islands overprinted 'Tuvalu

Write to: Tuvalu Philatelic Bureau
GPO Funafuti
Tuvalu
Central Pacific

Currency: 100 cents = 1 Australian dollar
(£1.00 = A $2.00; US $1.00 = A $0.85 approx.)

Definitives

The current definitives feature fish, and are available in presentation pack form.

Commemoratives and other items

About four commemorative sets appear each year, of local, international and thematic interest. First day covers and presentation packs are made available. About one issue each year is accompanied by a miniature sheet. A booklet of definitives also exists containing denominations for which there is greatest postal use. Postage due labels are in use.

Country Index